THE WORST OF SPORTS

Jesse
LAMOVSKY

Matthew
ROSETTI

Charlie
DeMARCO

THE WORST OF SPORTS

Chumps, Cheats, and Chokers from the Games We Love

BALLANTINE BOOKS NEW YORK

A Ballantine Books Trade Paperback Original

Published in the United States by Ballantine Books, an imprint of The Random House Publishing Group, a division of Random House, Inc., New York.

BALLANTINE and colophon are registered trademarks of Random House, Inc.

LIBRARY OF CONGRESS CATALOGING-IN-PUBLICATION DATA

Lamovsky, Jesse.
    The worst of sports : chumps, cheats, and chokers from the games we love / Jesse Lamovsky, Matthew Rosetti, and Charlie DeMarco.
      p. cm.
    ISBN 978-0-345-49891-5 (pbk.)
    1. Sports—Anecdotes. 2. Sportsmanship—Humor. 3. Sports—Moral and ethical aspects. I. Rosetti, Matt. II. DeMarco, Charlie. III. Title.
    GV707.L36 2007
    796.0207—dc22   2007015015

Printed in the United States of America

www.ballantinebooks.com

9 8 7 6 5 4 3 2 1

Book design by Casey Hampton

CONTENTS

Acknowledgments　　　　　　　　ix
Introduction　　　　　　　　　　xiii

PART 1: DON'T BELIEVE THE HYPE　　　1

Dan and Dave: To Be Settled in . . . New Orleans?　　3
Overrated!　　8
The Heisman Trophy　　21
The Worst of Heisman Pro Busts　　30

PART 2: BAD MANAGEMENT　　　33

The 1950s Kansas City A's　　35
The Worst Trades　　44
Corporate Naming Rights Gone Bust　　59
The Old Boys' Coaching Network　　62
The All-Bad Free-Agent Pitching Staff　　77

PART 3: CHOKERY　　　83

Self-destruction!　　85
Great Individual Meltdowns of the '90s　　91

Three Bad Calls   98
Demolished at the Gates   102
And One Very, Very *Fortunate* Collapse   112

PART 4: TEAM ISSUES   115

When the All-Time Best was the All-Time Worst   117
The Worst Teams   126
The Curse of Jeffrey Maier   136
The Worst Franchise-Killing Losses   145
The Baltimore Colts, 1975–83   149

PART 5: LOOK AWAY   159

Evolution versus Devolution   161
The All-Rotund Pitching Staff   166
"Blood in the Water"   174
The Worst of Grotesque Injuries   178
Uniform Violations   183
The Native American Conundrum   189
The Minnesota Massacre   193

PART 6: FAN FOIBLES   197

Ten-Cent Beer Night   199
Five Fan-FUBARed Forfeits   204
When Fans Attack   207
The Worst of Youth Sports   217
The Malice at the Palace   220

PART 7: WHAT WERE THEY THINKING?   229

"Fifth Down"   231
After the Glory   235
The Worst of Criminal Acts by an Athlete   246
The Worst Mistakes Leading to a Lifetime of Ridicule   262

PART 8: BY ANY MEANS NECESSARY   273

The 1890s Baltimore Orioles   275
Olympic Fraudulence   281
Cheating as a Way of Life   290
The 1998 Home Run Chase   297

PART 9: WRONG NUMBERS   303

ACKNOWLEDGMENTS

To the Phamily, Kent and Kent-ifornia, old and new; to our agent, Byrd Leavell, who believed in us and in the project; to our editor, Mark Tavani, who kept things clean and cured me of my addiction to semicolons; to my family: Saul, who's a mentor and doesn't know it; Shaina, Eli, Jeremy, and Greg; and to my mom and dad. Much love all around.

An enterprise this vast and all-encompassing couldn't have been undertaken without proper sources. Acknowledgments go to a number of websites: Pro Football Reference, Baseball Reference, and Basketball Reference; Database Basketball; the College Football Data Warehouse; the Internet Hockey Database; Retrosheet; Drafthistory.com; and the NCAA's storehouse of records, which are available gratis in PDF form. A special nod goes out to YouTube, as well as the invaluable (whisper) Wikipedia.

I also couldn't have done it without my dead-tree sources: *Total Baseball*, *The Official NFL Encyclopedia*, and Jim Savage's *The Encyclopedia of the NCAA Basketball Tournament*.

—J.L.

Only a true sports fan knows the pain that walks hand in hand with passionate devotion to a team of men who know not of your existence. To get back in the saddle and reengage, season after season, when the overwhelming likelihood is resulting disappointment, is either insane or beautiful. Or both. This book is, first and foremost, for you.

I'd like to thank my mother, father, and the Brothers Rosetti for their giddy encouragement throughout. My family supports one another's endeavors to the point of absurdity, and I want to acknowledge my appreciation and wonderment of that rare and special thing. I also want to thank my extended family and friends, particularly the men of Greenridge, who share a fraternal bond that borders on the surreal. (All right, Swinnick and North Scranton, too, but *just* this time.)

This book wouldn't have been possible without, ahem, the Internet. Specific sources that were extremely helpful include baseball-reference.com, baseballlibrary.com, basketball-reference.com, pro-football-reference.com, *The New York Times*, *Sports Illustrated*, *Time*, NPR, and the Olympic Games section of The University of Pennsylvania Museum's website. Andrew Postman and Larry Stone's book *The Ultimate Book of Sports Lists* was a nice go-to, and Jill Geer, the director of communications for USA Track & Field, was gracious in providing some pertinent details for the Dan and Dave piece.

I'd especially like to thank those intimately involved with the creation of this book because they were the ones who took it to another level: our editor, Mark Tavani, whose future is so bright in this industry it makes my eyes hurt; our agent, Byrd Leavell with the Waxman Agency, who offered up pearls of wisdom on the occasions when we lost our way; Charlie DeMarco—this was his brainchild—whose guidance, direction, and graphic design talents were invaluable; my coauthor, Jesse Lamovsky, whose knowledge of sports is so vast it made me feel inadequate on a daily basis. I'm a better writer and even a better sports fan from having worked with you all. And to Kara Cesare, whose pro bono assistance throughout was beyond the call of duty, and revealed, once again, how selfless an individual she truly is.

Godspeed.

—M.R.

To my dad, who taught me everything I know about sports, and most of the other things as well. To my wife, who will watch football with me, and just goes in the other room during basketball and baseball. To Jesse and Matt, who wrote the vast majority of this book and allowed me to tag along.

—C.D.

INTRODUCTION

Anyone who was breathing oxygen in the days of olive-colored linoleum, rotary phones, and console TVs most likely remembers the opening montage to ABC's *Wide World of Sports*. The actual contents of the show—from bowling to horse racing to gigantic South African men dragging Renaults—are now a blur, but the stirring music and the distinct voice of Jim McKay: *"The thrill of victory, and the agony of defeat!"* were anything but forgettable. And while the smiling faces and raised arms of those lucky enough to represent the "thrill of victory" might have slipped our minds, the images that accompanied "the agony of defeat" still glow as brightly as ever in our memories.

The defining piece of opening footage from *Wide World of Sports* is the out-of-control ski jumper, Vinko Bogataj of the country formerly known as Yugoslavia, tumbling headlong off the ramp into a cloud of limbs, skis, and snow in a wipeout for the ages. Success just doesn't linger in the mind or the stomach like failure.

Vinko Bogataj *is the Worst of Sports.* Yet this book is so much more. It's the chronicling of the most egregious mistakes and defeats, the most awful teams and regimes on record, and an opinionated take on some of the most controversial events from the history of the games we all love. By no means is this book all-inclusive—an all-inclusive *Worst of Sports* would require a forklift for carrying around—but the breadth of topics covered is as wide and varying as the opinions professed by passionate sports fans everywhere.

In taking our shots, we did so from the heart—not sardonically or derisively. Satirically? Absolutely! The goal is not to offend, but to stir things up and, in a weird way, to celebrate. The beauty of sports and the fans who love them is that no matter how clear or judicial the outcome, it will not be accepted as such. Emotion, subjectivity, and disputation aren't just welcome, they're wholeheartedly encouraged. So pull up a chair and get involved.

Dan O'Brien fails Reebok and himself as he is unable to clear the pole vault bar at the 1992 U.S. Olympic Trials. *AFP/Thom Scott*

DON'T BELIEVE THE HYPE

Want to sic the repoman on Gino Torretta's Heisman? Ever wonder about Joe Namath's career aside from Super Bowl III? Want to inquire of Reebok what was actually settled in Barcelona? Yeah, we do, too.

* ★ DAN AND DAVE: TO BE SETTLED IN . . . NEW ORLEANS?
* ★ OVERRATED!
* ★ THE HEISMAN TROPHY
* ★ THE WORST OF HEISMAN PRO BUSTS

DAN AND DAVE:
TO BE SETTLED IN . . .
NEW ORLEANS?

A Shakespearean Tragedy About
a Dreamy and Dynamic Decathlon Duo[*]

THE BACKDROP

It was the summer of 1988 in Seoul, Korea, just thirty klicks south of
the DMZ, and the U.S. Olympic decathletes were struggling as
mightily as the North Korean economy on the other side of the
Thirty-eighth Parallel. A nation that produced decathlon greats such
as Jim Thorpe, Bob Mathias, Rafer Johnson, and Bruce Jenner was
unable to place a single competitor on the medal stand in Seoul. It
was an embarrassing low point for the proud American decathlete.

Meanwhile, Jane Fonda and her overwhelmingly popular work-
out videos were continuing to motivate housewives across the country into ill-fitting leotards for thirty to sixty minutes of squat thrusts
and leg kicks. These women couldn't do their aerobics in heels—
they needed proper footwear, and Reebok filled the vacuum, becoming the first company to exploit the female athletic-shoe market.

With more than $1 billion in sales and a healthy slice of the
overall athletic-shoe industry, business was good for Reebok. Particularly good considering the fact that they were stealing market

[*]Sponsored by Reebok

share from Nike, the Greek goddess of (shareholder) victory. Things got even better when they released the exorbitantly priced Pump basketball shoe in 1989. And because every kid wanted to elevate above the rim, Reebok sold about 20 million pairs of those big-ticket items over the next few years.

So it can be said that in the period following the Seoul Olympics, on the proverbial teeter-totter of sports, the American decathlete was the class chubbo while Reebok was flying high, squealing, legs kicking and arms raised in the air.

Their fortunes would soon reverse, then intertwine.

THE PLAYERS

Dan O'Brien was an American decathlete. So was Dave Johnson. In the late '80s, while O'Brien was a relative newcomer, Johnson was the veteran leading the American decathlon resurgence that developed in the wake of Seoul. And this resurgence happened very quickly. In 1989, Johnson topped the decathlon world leaders list, setting an American record in the process. The following year, Johnson and O'Brien finished first and second in the Seattle installment of the Goodwill Games—Ted Turner's ill-fated, apolitical, and money-hemorrhaging rival to the Olympics.

Sensing a U.S. decathlon turnaround—and, thus, a possible marketing opportunity—Visa (the nice credit card company that offers money to anyone with a mailbox) opened its coffers to USA Track & Field, in the form of a generous sponsorship, as opposed to a loan with a double-digit APR attached to it. Starting in 1990, the Visa-funded U.S. decathlon program helped enable American [athletes'] return to prominence. A year later, in 1991, O'Brien trounced the competition in Tokyo, winning gold at the World Championships. The Americans were back, baby!

THE SCENE

It was 1992. Nike had managed to recover from the negative press related to its overseas labor practices and once again find its stride.

In doing so, the Swoosh had begun to absolutely clobber Reebok in the sneaker war. Unable to compete in "cool factor" (translation: Air Jordan trumps all), Reebok's U.S. market share fell from nearly 25 percent in 1991 to just over 10 percent in 1992. Correspondingly, during the same period, *Nike*'s market share rose from slightly under 25 percent to 45 percent. In an attempt to cut costs, Reebok announced plans to lay off one-tenth of its workforce worldwide.

Meanwhile, O'Brien and Johnson were rounding into form and emerging as the overwhelming favorites to take the gold and silver medals in the upcoming Barcelona Games. Heading into an Olympic year, the pair appeared evenly matched; Johnson held a three-to-two lead over O'Brien in direct competition, but O'Brien's résumé showed a higher personal best in the event. Johnson posted a world-leading mark in 1990 en route to winning the U.S. Track & Field Championships. And O'Brien followed suit in '91, winning the U.S. national title and posting a very impressive world-best point total of his own. It appeared that the stiffest competition each of these gents would face in the Olympic decathlon would be the other.

As it turned out, Visa wasn't the only corporate bloodhound sniffing out a marketing opportunity. O'Brien and Johnson were hot, and while they still toiled in relative obscurity as far as the general viewing public was concerned, things were about to change.

THE ACT

Life is short. Play hard. Reebok had been passing that advice along to the masses since the summer of 1991. But during the Super Bowl broadcast in 1992, it unveiled what would become the overwhelmingly popular "Dan and Dave" campaign. This series of commercials was obviously meant to create greater brand awareness of Reebok by publicizing their intriguing U.S. decathlon rivalry in the eight-month run-up to the Olympic Games.

They succeeded, and then some. The ads were a huge hit. The viewing public didn't care any more for track and field than it had previously, but it did care about Dan and Dave. Of course, the success of Reebok's campaign was dependent upon the ultimate success of the two, but these were the two best decathletes on the planet. What could go wrong?

THE TRAGEDY

It was late June 1992, and the U.S. Olympic Track & Field trials were being held at Tad Gormley Stadium in New Orleans. This was the first opportunity for those aside from track fans to witness Dan and Dave in action. And thanks to the Reebok-generated hype, they were especially excited to do so.

As is customary, the U.S. team would be sending three decathletes to the Games, so the trials seemed simply a formality—a sparring session for the two heavyweights in advance of the main event. As the commercials stated, it was all "to be settled in Barcelona." The only question left unanswered—and, frankly, it wasn't being asked all that frequently—was who would be the *third* decathlete to qualify and earn the privilege of carrying Dan's and Dave's jocks to the Olympic Games?

The decathlon is a two-day event. After the first day of competition in New Orleans, Dan was on world-record pace. His score of 4,698 points was the second-best Day One tally in the history of the event. Dave was in fifth, but his best events were yet to come. It was unfolding just as Reebok had promised everyone it would.

On Day Two, after seven events, Dan was still cruising. The pole vault loomed. Dan chose to pass on the lower heights. The strategy was a bit presumptuous, but not altogether unusual, particularly in an event as grueling as the decathlon, where any bit of energy saved is an advantage over your competitors. Besides, his chosen height— 15'9"—was more than manageable, especially for the best decathlete in the world.

Yet Dan failed in his first two attempts. Only one remained. The spectators in the stadium and those watching on television inched forward in their seats as they became acutely aware that a third failure would mean the end of O'Brien's Olympic chances. The tension thickened the already steamy air as O'Brien lined up for his last attempt. He had to make it. How could "Dan and Dave" work without Dan?

He didn't make it. Whether it was the pressure of the moment, or whether it was simply a failure in his mechanics, the result was the same. O'Brien went up, wobbled . . . and fell far short, giving him a disastrous zero points for the event. When the dust settled, Dan O'Brien was out of Olympic qualification, Reebok's lovingly constructed marketing campaign was in shambles, and the Olympics were still a month and a half away.

Dave went on to win the trials that day, with a couple of guys named Aric Long and Rob Muzzio earning the second and third spots on the U.S. Olympic decathlon team. For the purposes of Reebok's campaign, Dave might as well have been eliminated along with Dan. Battling injuries, Johnson scrambled honorably to a bronze medal in the Barcelona games.

O'Brien was also in Barcelona, where he wore not spandex but a blue blazer with a multicolored peacock on the breast, and held not a medal but a microphone. The hype of Dan and Dave had produced one skin-of-the-teeth bronze medal and nothing else. It was, to be gentle, a somewhat anticlimactic denouement.

To his credit, Dan O'Brien rebounded nicely from the embarrassment of 1992. He made sure to qualify for the '96 Games in Atlanta, and once there he dominated as he had been expected to in Barcelona, taking home the gold medal in the decathlon. The University of Idaho, Dan's alma mater, named its track and field complex after him—a nice honor usually reserved for deceased people. Dave Johnson retired with his bronze medal and became a Christian inspirational speaker—a higher level of hype altogether. "Dan and Dave" was Reebok's one last gambit at athletic-shoe dominance. The company now quietly makes the bulk of its bucks catering to women and the elderly. It leaves the hype to Nike.

OVERRATED!

Challenging Conventional Wisdom
and Bursting the Bubble of Myth

L egendary players, legendary plays, and legendary moments are the finest things that sports create:

> Kirk Gibson's storybook walk-off
> Nadia Comaneci's seven perfect 10s
> Christian Laettner's last-second, turnaround jumper to beat
>   Kentucky
> Lake Placid's "Miracle on Ice"
> Lou Gehrig's "Luckiest Man" Farewell
> Roger Bannister's breaking of the tape—and, more important,
>   the four-minute mile

These comprise only a tiny sampling of the most renowned and celebrated moments in sports history. They are memories that will be forever recounted and cherished, over and over and over again, for their unique and unparalleled greatness. And deservedly so.

There are numerous other "great" moments, athletes, coaches, and programs in sports, and these, too, are remembered fondly. But for whatever reason, some of the more memorable have taken on a life of their own—misconstruing facts and distorting the truth until the telling of them bears only minimal resemblance to the actual reality of what took place. In these cases, we call, "Bullshit!" and pull back the curtain so as to expose them as the overrated behemoths of hype that they've grown to be.

JOE NAMATH

Yes, Broadway Joe directed the Jets' Super Bowl III upset. Yes, this was a game of vast historical significance. And yes, Namath's performance in it was flawless. But did you know that Namath played eight more seasons after Super Bowl III, and *beat only two teams with winning records*? Or that he threw 220 interceptions in his career, versus 173 touchdowns? Or that he's in the Hall of Fame essentially because of one game, and for the balance of his career, he was an erratic, injury-prone quarterback playing for a lousy team? Namath's best body of work was probably done in the shadows of Manhattan's bars and clubs as a hard-partying bachelor in mink.

BILL BUCKNER'S ERROR IN GAME SIX OF THE '86 WORLD SERIES

The game was already tied. The Red Sox had already blown their two-run lead. Momentum was now wearing a Mets uniform, and for all intents and purposes the game was over. Billy Buck's error was simply the coup de grâce; the Red Sox had already been mortally wounded.

Though it's the *only* thing for which he's remembered, this error wasn't even Buckner's worst mistake in a Fall Classic. In the deciding Game Five of the 1974 Series, with the Dodgers trailing the A's 3–2, Buckner was thrown out trying to stretch a double into a triple to open the seventh inning—a strategic error considered one of baseball's cardinal sins. L.A. didn't score, and the A's clinched the Series two innings later. Errors happen, but Billy Buck's base-running gaffe in '74 was a mental mistake—and therefore far less forgivable.

(Note: The season following the '86 Series, Buckner even got a standing ovation at Fenway Park on Opening Day. But ultimately, Sox fans turned on him, as they were in need of a definitive scapegoat. And for some reason, unlike how they crucified Grady Little

years later, they chose to lay the blame on Buckner, as opposed to John McNamara.)

KELLEN WINSLOW GETTING HELPED OFF THE FIELD AFTER THE '81 CHARGERS–DOLPHINS PLAYOFF GAME

You've probably seen the clip: Winslow, utterly spent from his thirteen catches and game-saving field-goal block, getting assisted off the field by Charger teammates Eric Sievers and Billy Shields following the San Diego–Miami playoff classic. How heroic. And diva-ish! No doubt Kellen played his brilliant, Hall of Fame best that hot evening in Miami, but about fifty other guys from each team also laid it on the line, and you didn't see them being carried off the field. Maybe, just maybe, Winslow was laying it on a little (extra) thick for the NFL Films camera.

MICHAEL JORDAN GETTING "CUT" FROM HIS HIGH SCHOOL BASKETBALL TEAM

He didn't get cut altogether. Rather, he got bumped down to junior varsity as a sophomore. Not a big deal. People seem to think he got, you know, *cut*—like, watched Emsley Laney High School's 1978–79 basketball season from the bleachers—and he didn't. However, the notion that M.J. was found wanting, possibly unfairly, fit quite nicely into His Airness's patented "everybody worships the ground I walk on, but I still have to conjure up ways to feel disrespected at all times" manner of self-motivation.

JESSE OWENS "SHOWING UP" THE NAZIS AT THE 1936 OLYMPICS

No disrespect to the late, great Mr. Owens, but the sociopolitical importance of his four-gold-medal performance at Berlin has been way overblown. Where African Americans ranked on the Nazis' "Ethnic Groups We Detest and Wish to See Eradicated" list is unknown, but they certainly weren't high in the pecking order—

maybe number seventeen or so. Owens won his fourth gold medal only because he and fellow African American Ralph Metcalfe were inserted onto the 4 × 100 team in place of Sam Stoller and Marty Glickman, Jewish runners who were pulled so as to not offend the Nazis. Some statement.

Plus, when Owens got back to the States, he was still forced to race against horses for a living, and once the Nazis wiped the Olympic egg off their faces, they went right ahead with their nefarious plans to remake Europe anyway.

THE UNITED STATES GETTING SCREWED IN THE 1972 OLYMPIC GOLD-MEDAL BASKETBALL GAME

The Soviets may have gotten at least one too many cracks at an inbounds play, but the game was poorly managed by the Americans. Even after their first and second chances, the cold Teutonic voice over the PA, and all the assorted Sturm und Drang, the Soviets still had to go the length of the court in three seconds to win. That's something they shouldn't have been permitted to do, no matter the circumstances. Yet they did, and rather easily at that. The players on the U.S. team, embittered over how the last seconds went down in Munich, refused to accept their silver medals in 1972, and still haven't to this day. While they were poorly served by officialdom, the U.S. players and their coaches still lost their composure, failed to defend the USSR's final, winning play, and, consequently should be made to shoulder the ultimate culpability for their defeat.

THE 1969 CHICAGO CUBS COLLAPSE

On August 13, 1969, the Cubs were in first place in the National League East, nine games *ahead* of the Mets. By the end of the season they were in second place, eight games *behind* New York. The Cubs went 8–18 after September 1. That didn't help their cause, but the Mets won thirty-eight of their last forty-nine games, including twenty-four of thirty-two after September 1. New York was so white-hot that the Cubs could have gone 15–11 in September and October—a .577 winning percentage—and still not have beaten out the Mets for the division title. Few teams in the history of the game got as hot and stayed as hot, all the way through October, as the '69 Mets. The Cubs didn't lose; they were simply in the way, and got plowed over.

CAL RIPKEN'S CONSECUTIVE-GAMES STREAK

Showing up to work for 2,632 straight days is admirable, but it's hardly an athletic accomplishment of renown, simply because the record has no relation to performance. Yet an awfully big deal is made out of Ripken winning what is, in essence, baseball's version of the Perfect Attendance Award. As for Ripken's own place in the cosmos, well, he's got impressive numbers, but it's tough not to wonder about the all-time great status of a player whose only memorable career highlights consist of a consecutive-games-played streak and several home runs in All-Star Games.

(Dissension in the ranks: Overrated my ass! I'd seriously entertain an argument that Brett Favre's record streak of consecutive games started is more impressive, but attempting to discredit Ripken's consecutive-games-played streak is strange, misdirected hate-itude, and, frankly, conduct unbecoming of an American. If Cal was a designated hitter, I'd somewhat sympathize with such ignorance, but the man was both a shortstop and a guardian of the hot corner, turning double plays and anchoring the Orioles defense for years. He was an All-Star for sixteen straight seasons, earned two Gold Gloves, two AL MVP awards, and a World Series ring. He clobbered the Iron Horse by more than five hundred games and eclipsed Japan's Sachio Kinugasa's record, if you want to get Japanese about it, by more than four hundred games. Granted, he was the benefactor of a lot of guardian angel assistance over those years, but there's a reason the nearest active player to his record is well over one thousand games from breaking it. For those with only an abacus handy, that's more than six full seasons.)

BUSTER DOUGLAS KNOCKING OUT MIKE TYSON

When it happened in January 1990, it was considered the greatest upset in boxing history. But as it turned out, Iron Mike's conditioning for the fight in Tokyo was abysmal, and during the fight itself he was cursed with some of the most incompetent corner work ever seen in a heavyweight title bout. In retrospect, it's clear that Tyson's career decline had begun well before this fateful fight in Japan. Somebody was going to put the train wreck that Tyson had become on the canvas sooner rather than later, and James "Buster" Douglas just happened to be the fortunate first to have a crack at doing so.

Buster's "career" after his knockout of Tyson bolsters this argument: in what almost seemed to be a tribute to Iron Mike, Douglas did minimal training in the months following the fight and eventually ate himself into a diabetic coma. Before that feat of chow, he feebly attempted to defend his title against Evander Holyfield in 1991, but was knocked out in the third round. He would eventually retire from boxing in 1997, following a short-lived comeback attempt.

THE 1958 NFL CHAMPIONSHIP GAME

The importance of Baltimore's overtime win over the Giants, in terms of visibility for the NFL as a televised phenomenon (and for it being the first overtime game in NFL history), cannot be overstated. Artistically, though, it fails to live up to its retrospective billing. Even players involved admit that for the most part it was a sloppy, wholly unmemorable game, one that didn't become particularly compelling until late in the fourth quarter, when Johnny Unitas cranked up Baltimore's two-minute offense and led the Colts to victory.

NOTRE DAME FOOTBALL

No National Championships since 1988. No legitimate National Championship contention since 1993. A nine-game bowl losing streak—seven of the defeats by two touchdowns or more. Despite its very own TV contract and the loving attentions of the sporting media, Notre Dame just isn't an elite football program anymore.

(Note: The school's famed green jersey phenomenon has run its course as well. This once-proud tradition and motivational tactic was employed successfully in heroic victories over Navy in the Rockne era and was said to have contributed to multiple green-clad triumphs over hated rival USC in the '70s and '80s, among others. But the Irish have gone to the proverbial well all too often.

Wearing green, ND lost to Colorado in the '95 Fiesta Bowl, lost to Georgia Tech in the '99 Gator Bowl, lost to Boston College in the 2002 Catholic Bowl, and in 2005 lost to top-ranked USC. So what did they do during the 2006 season to further taint this tradition? Following pregame warm-ups in blue, they burst from the tunnel wearing the green jerseys for their final home game against . . . Army. The fans groaned, the Irish won the game, no one cared, and a once-cool tradition went by the wayside. What a shame.)

THE ARMY–NAVY GAME

Certainly no disrespect is intended to the men and women in uniform, and this rivalry boasts as much history and tradition as *any* in college football, but let's face it: in terms of the national college football landscape, the Army–Navy game hasn't actually meant anything since about the time JFK was elected. By far the most intriguing aspect of it is the throngs of cadets and midshipmen going bananas in the stands. And when the cannon goes kaboom, of course.

THE NBA DUNK CONTEST

The year 1988 was the last time Michael Jordan and Dominique Wilkins appeared in the Dunk Contest together. The following year, with the two mega-dunkers retired from the competition, Knick benchwarmer Kenny "Sky" Walker won it. It's been downhill ever since.

LYNN SWANN

He didn't play particularly long (nine years) and never caught more than sixty-one passes in a season for more than 880 yards, yet he's in the Pro Football Hall of Fame. And his being passed over in earlier voting rounds caused howls of anguish from Steelers backers who simply weren't satisfied with the roughly thirty-two members of their '70s teams already inducted. (We expect they'll be sculpting a bust of Roy Gerela at some point.) But in terms of endurance and production, the fact is that Swann wasn't even the best receiver on his own team—John Stallworth was.

RAIDERS FANS

If the act of painting one's face or body in support of a team is the height of silliness, then Raiders fans take the absurdity screaming into the stratosphere. Every home game in Oakland could be confused for an S and M convention. There's no crying in baseball, so there certainly shouldn't be gimps in football. And when the Raiders are particularly horrible, the whole "men in black" thing isn't really intimidating. Rather, it's just kind of sad, especially when you consider the way they've been jerked around by Al Davis for two decades.

U.S.A. WORLD CUP SOCCER

One can excuse the U.S. Soccer Federation for egregiously promoting the men's national team's hopes in advance of the 2006 World Cup in Germany. After all, it's their job to promote the sport, both in the United States and abroad. And following the United States' surprising success in Korea four years earlier, it wasn't completely unjustified. But let's be realistic: despite the talent gap closing somewhat in the past couple decades, American footballers still possess nowhere near the ball-handling skills of the Brazilians, nor the passing skills of even the most mediocre European squads. And one can't help being curious as to how the United States rose all the way to number five in the FIFA World Rankings prior to the '06 World Cup. While FIFA has proven to be about as clairvoyant as college football's Bowl Championship Series, it was still a gross overestimation of the United States' abilities on the pitch relative to those of the rest of the world. Our best chance in the near future would likely be *first* to practice replicating the infernal "diving" theatrics employed by some of the best squads—which defile the beautiful game, by the way—*then* work on the fundamentals.

THE WORLD SERIES OF POKER

It's a matter of time before someone pulls a gun at one of these tournaments. The irritating sunglasses, the aggravating website sponsorships, and now headphones? Poker has reigned supreme for decades as the married man's number-one excuse to get out of the house and hang with his boys for a couple of hours. However, the so-called stars of the poker movement are, in actuality, simply gambling addicts. These "professionals" are shadier than the dead-broke AARP members you try to pretend not to see at the casino staring mindlessly into the void as they feed their favorite slot machine. We imagine that ESPN's viewers look back fondly on the day when curling and lumberjacks occupied a much larger percentage of the programming schedule.

CHAMPIONSHIP TEAMS VISITING THE WHITE HOUSE

In July 2005, members of Northwestern University's national champion women's lacrosse team showed up at the White House in flip-flops. This should've been the *aha!* moment for some overeducated staffer: these types of ceremonies had run their course. National championship volleyball, soccer, and even ski teams are getting time with the president of the United States. Enough. Especially since these visits generally occur fifteen months after anyone stopped caring about the victory anyway.

THE HISTORICAL SIGNIFICANCE OF DOUG FLUTIE'S
HAIL MARY PASS THAT STUNNED MIAMI

The legend of this wonderful moment in sports history continues to grow like the weeds in your crazy neighbor's yard. Whenever appropriate, and even when not, that now-famous footage of Flutie's heave into the stormy Miami night and Gerard Phelan's end-zone cradle catch is replayed over and over. Sure, Flutie's lovable, the catch was amazing, and the win over Miami was great, but is it *that* big a deal?

Hell, Kordell Stewart's seventy-four-yard, last-second bomb to Michael Westbrook to lead Colorado past Michigan was a more impressive play (seventy-four yards in the air!). Is it because Colorado was *supposed* to beat Michigan that this catch is basically ignored year in and year out by the media? Or is it Doug Flutie's diminutive stature that appeals to the David and Goliath gene in each of us? Or that Miami has long been the easiest college football program in the country to dislike? Whatever the reason, the only historical significance to the catch was that it put Boston College on the map, even spiking school applications in the following years. Yet to this day BC's program toils in mediocrity—albeit in a different conference, as they abandoned the Big East for the "better" ACC.

(Dissension in the ranks: Where to begin? First of all, the comparison in the games is no contest. The 1994 Colorado–Michigan game was a decent game made memorable by one play. The 1984 BC–Miami game, with almost thirteen hundred total yards and four lead changes in the fourth quarter alone, would have been a classic with or without the Hail Mary. Played on the day after Thanksgiving, BC–Miami was the highest-rated TV game of the college football season, and proved to be that rarity in sports—the talked-up matchup that actually delivers on the hype. There were two great quarterbacks on the field—Flutie and Miami's Bernie

Kosar—and both of them were sensational. Only a trivia buff or a Michigan fan can name Kordell Stewart's quarterbacking opposite in 1994. (I'm the former—it was Todd Collins.) Plus Flutie-to-Phelan also happens to be the single greatest event in the history of Boston College athletics, period. There's your significance right there.)

THE WINTER OLYMPICS

Generally speaking, the Olympics have gotten out of hand. The horrifying coverage by the broadcast networks notwithstanding, the International Olympic Committee's belief that the addition of numerous events to the card will elicit genuine interest from a broader segment of the public has not panned out whatsoever. Canoeing/kayaking? Trampoline gymnastics? The skeleton? Stop the insanity.

But the Winter Olympics, specifically, require an extreme makeover. Ignoring that they commence and conclude with a bizarre, Cirque de Soleil-esque spectacle, much of the three or so weeks of competition suffers from a lack of relevance and historical significance—never mind the numerous scandals that have repeatedly tarnished the Games' image. It's quite clear that the flagging television ratings represent more than just the public's burnout on being subjected to silly, melodramatic documentaries prior to every event. The majority of us just don't care.

THE REST OF THE OVERRATED BEST

Duke hoops—Maybe it's the fact that Dick Vitale is on their payroll, or maybe it's that the six white dudes who appear at the end of their bench every year are cloned in Coach K's laboratory of evil, but whatever the reason, this gem of a program has lost its luster.

Throwing back a visiting team's home run ball—Peer pressure and a chance to harken back to the glory days and show off the old arm. Those are the only imaginable (but by no means acceptable) reasons for doing this outside of Wrigley Field. It's a great souvenir! Give it to your kid! Or someone else's kid!

Sound effects at live sporting events—It's an overt admission by the host organization that your fans are not entertained enough by the events unfolding on the field of play. And random synthesized beats injected into slow moments are a stark reminder to those in the seats that they are, in fact, bored as hell. *NBA say what?*

Fantasy sports—*Everyone* plays them. It's grown into a multibillion-dollar industry and is a portal into the most cherished of male demographics. But fantasy sports turn many fans into turncoat jackasses and have spawned a new breed of superdork—the type of fan who arrives at a bar with his lineup and a highlighter.

Yankee Stadium—By virtue of the sheer breadth of history that's taken place within its confines, the House that Ruth Built is an icon. But there exist multiple reasons for Steinbrenner's choosing to build a new one. To begin with, it pales in comparison to other "chapels" such as Wrigley or Fenway; to continue, it simply doesn't provide the game-watching experience offered by new parks such as Pac Bell and Camden Yards.

Monday Night Football—It's over for this former American institution, either because it comes on too late for most on the East Coast to even consider watching the second half, or because stuffing three men in the booth results in one continuously trying to prove his usefulness by forcing inane commentary.

da na na NA NA-NA! . . . CHARGE!—'Nuff said.

Sideline reporters—Nowadays, these on-field talking heads can't even get teams to give them insider nuggets on recently occurred injuries. They serve no purpose and rarely contribute anything interesting or particularly intelligent. When Namath leaned in for his drunken attempt at a smooch on Suzy Kolber, it should've marked the end of the breed.

Three hundred wins—It's considered automatic for Baseball Hall of Fame status among pitchers, but really, you don't have to be great to win 300. You just have to be "pretty good" for a long, long time. Remember Don Sutton, who won 324? His '70s white-guy 'fro was far more memorable than his stuff.

NFL sack records—Any record derived from a statistic that didn't exist until 1979, and that has been held by Mark Gastineau for any period of time, doesn't have real value in the pantheon of achievement. Or at least it shouldn't.

Danica Patrick—We've seen this movie before. You're attractive? That's nice, honey. Now quit posing in pleather astride your car, get *in* it, and win something. Thanks.

THE HEISMAN TROPHY

*College Football's Annual Beauty Pageant
Where the Best Often Get Stiff-Armed*

The Heisman Trophy is without question the most prestigious individual award in college sports. Maybe in *all* of sports. The nationally televised presentation of the famed twenty-five-pound bronze stiff-armer is unique in that it's the only individual athletic award given that level of exposure. (No, not even the vaunted ESPYs hold a candle.) Schools around the country put together lavish and creative campaigns to showcase their own candidates. While presidents are elected to a new term once every four years, college football America elects its own head of state every single fall.

Since 1935, the Heisman Memorial Trophy has been awarded to the nation's "most outstanding college football player." The subjectivity in the award's description is the primary reason that the Heisman, in its seventy-plus-year history, has rarely been presented to the *best* college football player. Too often, the voting process resembles a junior high class presidential election rather than a serious, sober means of determining the best college football player in America. And it's no wonder: out of the thousands of kids who pad up to do battle on an NCAA gridiron each autumn, how on earth can it be possible to anoint just one the "best"? It's not. Hence, the "most outstanding" is anointed instead.

It's a daunting task for the 870 media members, the 50+ and counting former Heisman winners, and the (irrelevant) single fan vote—all of whom, together, comprise the electoral syndicate. But over the years, the 220 members of the Downtown Athletic Club have simplified things for themselves: they've chosen a handful of criteria that they feel qualify candidates for nomination. Certainly, at times, the process works. Barry Sanders, a man among boys in his days at Oklahoma State, comes to mind as someone who truly deserved the honor. But since the process is not designed to actually locate and select the *best* player, and since talent like Barry Sanders comes around about as frequently as Halley's Comet, that perfect storm of player and Trophy just doesn't materialize that often.

Usually, the winners aren't actually the best. Occasionally, they're not even close.

CRITERIA: WHO'S NUMBER ONE, AND WHO'S THEIR QUARTERBACK?

When there's nary a dominant player in the country, the Heisman often defaults to the quarterback of whichever team is at or near the top of the polls. Case in point: 1964, when Notre Dame signal-caller John Huarte won the Trophy for the 9–1 Fighting Irish, resurgent under new coach Ara Parsegian. Huarte's numbers were hardly overwhelming. He threw for sixteen touchdown passes, eleven interceptions, and a yawn-inducing 55 percent completion rate. What mattered, though, was that Notre Dame was number one, and he was the guy crouched under the center's ass. Not only was Huarte *not* the *best* player in the country, he wasn't even the best on his own offense. His favorite target, split end Jack Snow (father of baseball's J. T. Snow), caught sixty passes for 1,114 yards, finishing fifth in the voting himself. And while the Heisman should certainly not be an award given to whoever's predicted to be the best pro (although at many times it appears that that's exactly the case), Snow went on to an outstanding career in the NFL, whereas Huarte was a big bust as a pro.

Who was the best player in the country in 1964? Well, he didn't even finish in the top ten of the balloting, but there's a strong possibility that the best player was a running back out of the University of Kansas. A guy named Sayers. You may have heard of him.

In similar fashion, the 1992 Heisman went to Gino Torretta, quarterback of the undefeated and number one–ranked Miami Hurricanes. Everyone knew Torretta wasn't really the best player in college football—San Diego State's Marshall Faulk had more than a few backers for that distinction—but the statuette was bestowed on the prematurely balding Californian, more by virtue of his team's potential back-to-back national championships and twenty-nine-game winning streak than for anything Torretta actually did during the '92 season. There are two glaringly obvious problems with that occurrence: the Heisman Trophy is not some kind of lifetime achievement award (à la Clint Eastwood's Oscars), and four weeks after the presentation Torretta was abused by Alabama's defense in a 34–13 Crimson Tide Sugar Bowl rout that put a violent end to both Miami's and Torretta's winning streak.

CRITERIA: STATS! STATS! STATS!

Statistics don't lie. They shouldn't, anyway. And they didn't in the case of Barry Sanders's 2,628 rushing yards and thirty-nine touchdowns in 1988, for example. But sometimes they do fib. Exhibit A of the flawed, statistics-based approach to Heisman Trophy voting is Andre Ware, quarterback for the University of Houston and winner of the award in 1989. Jack Pardee's Cougars were among the first teams to use the Run 'n' Shoot offense, and Ware spent the '89 season doing what Run 'n' Shoot quarterbacks do: throwing the ball, and throwing it, and throwing it, and throwing it some more. Ware threw to the tune of 4,699 yards and forty-six touchdowns.

Houston was a master craftsman in the art of running up the score for the purposes of stat-padding; the Cougars scored forty or more points eight times; fifty or more five times; sixty or more four times; and on October 21, 1989, beat a feeble SMU team fresh off the death penalty by the cartoonish score of 95–21. That Ware was a product of a system designed to pile up numbers against woefully overmatched competitors didn't matter to Heisman voters. They may have thought differently about their decision when (a) David Klingler took over the Houston offense in 1990 and put up even better numbers than his predecessor, and (b) Ware turned out to be an unmitigated bust as a pro.

Five years later, in 1994, Colorado's Rashaan Salaam won the Heisman, becoming the fourth Division I running back to gain more than two thousand yards in a season. The previous three to top the two-thousand-yard mark—Marcus Allen (1981), Mike Rozier (1983), and Barry Sanders (1988)—all won the Heisman, making the yardage tally a virtual slam dunk for winning the award to that point. Whether or not Salaam was really the best player in the country was up for question; Penn State running back Ki-Jana Carter and Alcorn State quarterback Steve McNair presented strong cases for themselves. Still, two thousand yards was two thousand yards, and those yards got Salaam to the podium in New York.

Two years later, Iowa State's Troy Davis surpassed the 2,000-yard mark, but he finished second in the balloting to Florida quarterback Danny Wuerffel . . . the quarterback for the top-ranked team, of course. By then, Salaam was busy packing his NFL career into a pipe, lighting it, and sucking it into his lungs. And in 2002, the voters eschewed yet another 2,000-yard rusher in favor of a quarterback from a top-ranked school. That year, a seemingly possessed Larry Johnson ran roughshod over defenses, averaging an NCAA regular season record of 8.02 yards per carry. But L.J.'s best performances occurred mainly in the second half of the season, and he finished a very distant third in the vote tally behind USC's Carson Palmer and Iowa quarterback Brad Banks.

CRITERIA: SENIORS (*CLAP-CLAP*)! SENIORS (*CLAP-CLAP*)!

Quarterback Gary Beban of UCLA won the Heisman in 1967, beating out O. J. Simpson of archrival USC and Purdue's great two-way player Leroy Keyes. Beban's numbers were pedestrian—he threw as many interceptions as touchdown passes (eight)—but he had one thing going for him: he was a senior, while Simpson and Keyes were both juniors. Like the toupee-less Torretta's, Beban's Heisman was a career award, given as much for the sum of his achievements while at UCLA (especially directing an upset of top-ranked Michigan State in the 1966 Rose Bowl) as for what he did in his final season.

Beban's team didn't even win the Pac Eight title; Simpson's USC team did. Simpson outplayed Beban in the Trojans' 21–20 win over UCLA in November of that year. And casting further doubt on Beban's worthiness as a Heisman winner was the fact that he bombed as both a quarterback and a halfback in the NFL.

The "senior bias" became the "outgoing junior bias" in 1982, when Herschel Walker of Georgia won the Heisman. Walker was a great college back and a worthy winner; however, his best season came as a freshman in 1980, when he powered the Bulldogs to the National Championship. But the committee recoiled from giving the award to a first-year player, even when the freshman in question was the *best* player on the best team in college football. Instead, they awarded the Heisman to a senior, South Carolina's George Rogers.

The following season, then-sophomore Walker was beaten out by USC senior Marcus Allen. When Walker, who everyone knew would forgo his senior year for the pros, finally won the Heisman as a junior in 1982, he did so despite not having had the kind of season he'd had as a freshman. But after finishing third and second in the balloting the previous two years, there was no way he would be denied in his last season as a collegiate, despite the presence of other worthy candidates such as SMU's Eric Dickerson.

CRITERIA: DEFENSE? WHAT DEFENSE?

The year 1980 highlighted (some might say exposed) two cherished traditions in the Heisman voting: the game of "Screw the Freshman" and the ritual of pretending that defensive players are inherently unworthy of winning the award. More than a few observers thought the best player in the country that year was Hugh Green, the quarterback-hunting defensive end from the University of Pittsburgh. But when the votes were tallied, the winner was George Rogers, despite the fact that Green's Panthers were one of the country's best teams while Rogers's South Carolina Gamecocks were unranked. As a matter of fact, Rogers had head-to-head matchups with both Herschel Walker's team and Hugh Green's, and lost both. Georgia edged South Carolina 13–10 in the regular season, and in the Gator Bowl Pitt destroyed the Gamecocks 37–9.

But Hugh Green is only the tip of the iceberg. Defenders aren't just shunned from the ceremony, they're generally treated as if they don't exist. That same year, 1980, North Carolina linebacker Lawrence Taylor didn't even sniff the vote's top ten, which is clearly insanity of the highest order. It's just not true that there were ten more outstanding players in college football than L.T. But it is the sad truth that the biggest, baddest men on the football field might as well be long snappers.

CRITERIA: THE NOTRE DAME FACTOR

When it comes to winning the Heisman, playing for the Fighting Irish certainly doesn't hurt one's chances. Notre Dame's publicity machine cranks up like America's post–World War II economy every time it has a candidate. Its most famous PR stunt came in 1970, when an Irish flack changed the pronunciation of Joe Theisman's name (it was originally pronounced *Theez-man,* which, problematically, didn't rhyme with "Heisman") to better resonate with voters. But never did Notre Dame's amen corner pull off a greater coup than in 1956, when Irish quarterback Paul Hornung took home the bronzed action figure. Hornung was a terrific player—he could pass, run, and kick, and had a Hall of Fame career in the NFL—but he won the Trophy despite the Irish going a dismal 2–8 in 1956, one of the worst seasons in school history. Can the *best* player in college football really be the quarterback for a terrible team? Possibly, but the "most outstanding" player most *certainly* can! And as good as the Golden Boy was, was he really better than the man who finished fifth in the voting—Jim Brown,* who averaged 6.2 yards per carry, scored fourteen touchdowns, kicked, punted, and even intercepted three passes for a powerful Syracuse team?

In 1987, the Notre Dame Factor again reared its gold-helmeted head when receiver/return man Tim Brown won the Heisman. Brown was an exciting all-around player, but he didn't touch the ball all that much (only thirty-nine receptions in '87), and the Irish weren't that great, going just 8–4 and getting trounced in the Cotton Bowl by Texas A&M, 35–10. On a play-by-play basis, quarterback Don McPherson of Syracuse and a pair of running backs—Thurman Thomas of Oklahoma State and Craig "Ironhead" Hayward of Pitt—were much more important to their team's successes than was Brown to his. But all three finished as bridesmaids to the Domer in the voting. To his credit, Tim Brown did add some luster to his dubious Heisman with a brilliant career in the NFL. Of course, there was also another outstanding player garnering some votes for the 1987 award. His plight, however, is more befitting a discussion of another criteria on.

CRITERIA: THE SMALL-SCHOOL BIAS

In 1987 Heisman voting, Gordie Lockbaum of Division I-AA Holy Cross finished third behind the aforementioned Brown and McPherson. Getting an invite to New York was no small feat considering that Lockbaum played in the Patriot League: an *academics-first, athletics-distant-second* conference that models itself after the Ivy League. Going out on a limb, we assume the Cross's Sports Information Department's "Heisman Promo Blitz" budget wasn't exactly robust.

Most notable about Lockbaum was that he was a "sixty-minute man," playing every down of the game as a defensive back, tailback, flanker, and special teams terror. In his offensive career, Lock-

---

* Also making stronger cases than Hornung for the Heisman Trophy in '56 were Tennessee quarterback Johnny Majors (runner-up) and Oklahoma halfback Tommy Macdonald, the best player on the best team in college football that year.

baum scored forty-four touchdowns, all of which came during his junior and senior seasons. On the defensive side of the ball, he made 146 tackles, recorded four sacks, and intercepted five passes while playing in purple. Opposing defenses focused solely on stopping him, and offenses, in turn, completely avoided throwing to his side of the field. He was a dominant force for one of the better I-AA teams of all time. In the era of leather aviator helmets and wool jerseys, going both ways was commonplace. But in the '80s, when the age of specialization was in full swing, Lockbaum was one of the last of a dying breed.

In 2000, middle-aged Chris Weinke and Josh Huepel, quarterbacks for Florida State and Oklahoma, respectively, finished 1–2 in the Heisman voting. Not coincidentally, the Seminoles and Sooners were the top-ranked teams in the country as well. The best player in college football was neither of these two. It was LaDainian Tomlinson, running back from Texas Christian University. Tomlinson ran for 2,158 yards that season—the second straight year he led the nation in rushing—hung 406 yards on Texas El Paso, and powered the Horned Frogs to their first national ranking since 1959. Carrying a Western Athletic Conference team on his back every week, Tomlinson was game-planned for in a way Weinke and Huepel never were, yet not once was L.T. Jr. held under 100 yards. The only place in which Tomlinson was stopped, in fact, was the Downtown Athletic Club, where he finished a distant fourth in the voting, behind Weinke, Huepel, and future teammate Drew Brees, who, by the way, took Purdue to the Rose Bowl and was a better candidate himself than either of the top two QBs.

In 1984, hands down the best player in college football was Jerry Rice, a wide receiver from tiny Mississippi Valley State University. Rice was unstoppable—catching 112 passes for 1,845 yards and twenty-seven touchdowns in a no-huddle offense that scored 628 points. He broke nearly every NCAA receiving record known to man and, despite lacking a high-powered PR team, attracted enough national media attention to finish ninth in the Heisman balloting. But alas, Google Maps wasn't around yet, and neither the CBS nor the ABC cameras had any intention of seeking out Itta

Bena, Mississippi. They did go to Miami's Orange Bowl, though, and it was there that Doug Flutie threw his Hail Mary to Gerard Phelan in a day-after-Thanksgiving, nationally televised shootout. The votes were reported to have already been in and tabulated at that point, but it was a metaphorical Heisman moment.

Flutie was a great college quarterback; he revived Boston College's program and actually got people in Massachusetts to care about college football. The little man with the bionic arm was a worthy candidate and, apparently, the most outstanding player that season. But Jerry Rice was clearly the *best*.

And of course, who could forget 1971, when Auburn quarterback Pat Sullivan beat out Cornell's do-everything halfback Ed Marinaro, the first player in NCAA history to rush for four thousand career yards? In Marinaro's case, he definitely got the last laugh. Not only was he more productive as a pro than Sullivan, becoming a solid pass-catching back for the mighty Vikings while Sullivan's career petered out in Atlanta, he also achieved heartthrob status as Officer Joe Coffey on *Hill Street Blues*.

And who will be the next Jerry Rice? The next Gordie Lockbaum? We won't have to wait long to find out.

THE WORST OF
HEISMAN PRO BUSTS

To truly be a draft "bust," a player has to be picked high. Through the selection of Reggie Bush with 2006's second overall pick, all but fifteen of seventy-one Heisman winners have been chosen in round number one. And for every Barry Sanders, Earl Campbell, and Marcus Allen, you get, well, one of these guys:

5. BILLY VESSELS, HB: FIRST ROUND, SECOND PICK, 1953 (COLTS)

The 1952 Heisman winner out of Oklahoma spurned his selection by the expansion Colts and chose to play for the CFL's Edmonton Eskimos instead. Three years later (after finding success in Canada) he finally reported to Baltimore, but his time had come and gone—the Colts by now had Alan Ameche and Lenny Moore in the backfield. A recurring injury drove Vessels from football after just one NFL season.

4. DESMOND HOWARD, WR: FIRST ROUND, FOURTH PICK, 1992 (REDSKINS)

Howard returned only one kick for a touchdown in three less-than-stellar seasons in Washington. His Super Bowl MVP with the Packers hardly justified his draft selection . . . or the large contract given him by Raiders owner Al Davis in 1997. In eleven pro seasons, the former Michigan Heisman winner scored a not-exactly-Rice-like fifteen touchdowns.

3. ANDRE WARE, QB: FIRST ROUND, SEVENTH PICK, 1989 (LIONS)

Ware, the '89 Heisman winner from Houston, spent his college career running up loud statistics in a gimmicky offense against less-than-stringent competition. But his act never took in Detroit. Ware never took over the starting quarterback job for the Lions, and threw only five touchdown passes, against eight interceptions, in his short career.

2. TERRY BAKER, QB: FIRST ROUND, FIRST PICK, 1963 (RAMS)

Baker, the '62 Heisman winner from Oregon State, wasn't really a pro-caliber quarterback (think Eric Crouch in a single-bar helmet). The Rams, sadly, found this out *after* the '63 Draft. Attempts to move him to halfback and flanker fizzled, and Baker was out of the League by 1966. He's the answer to a trivia question: Who is the only man to win a Heisman and play in the Final Four? Terry Baker, a guard on OSU's 1963 West Regional champ.

1. JAY BERWANGER, HB: FIRST ROUND, FIRST PICK, 1936 (EAGLES)

Berwanger, the Heisman winner from the University of Chicago, was the first pick of the first round of the very first NFL Draft—a brainstorm of Eagles owner Bert Bell. Unfortunately for Mr. Bell, Berwanger never showed up in Philadelphia. After Bell didn't meet his contract demands, he said to heck with football and went into the foam-rubber business instead.

Owner Ted Turner in his only game as Braves manager before Commissioner Bowie Kuhn ordered him back to the owner's box—1977.
AP Images

BAD
MANAGEMENT

In sports, the powerful people entrusted with key decisions often lack the acumen to chair a high school prom committee.

- ★ THE 1950s KANSAS CITY A'S
- ★ THE WORST TRADES
- ★ CORPORATE NAMING RIGHTS GONE BUST
- ★ THE OLD BOYS' COACHING NETWORK
- ★ THE ALL-BAD FREE-AGENT PITCHING STAFF

THE 1950s KANSAS CITY A'S

A Major League Baseball Franchise
Does Its Best Farm Team Impersonation

When the Philadelphia Athletics announced that they'd be pulling up stakes and moving to Kansas City following the 1954 season, there was widespread rejoicing along the banks of the Missour-uh River. Baseball's westernmost outpost, Kansas City looked like the perfect destination for the sport's third franchise relocation in as many years.

Up to that point, Kansas City had had a long and honorable tradition as a baseball town. It was the hometown of Casey Stengel, among other notables; it had ball clubs in both the old Union and American Association leagues, as well as the National League during the late nineteenth century; it had a franchise in the Federal League, an eventually doomed circuit that attempted to challenge the AL–NL monopoly during World War I; it had the Monarchs, maybe the most celebrated of all the Negro League teams; and for the first half of the twentieth century it was home to the Kansas City Blues, a top New York Yankees farm team.

On April 12, 1955, the Athletics opened their season in Kansas City's Municipal Stadium against Detroit. There was a parade, and ex-president and former Kansas City machine politician Harry Truman even threw out the first pitch. It was the first honest-to-goodness Major League baseball played in the city since 1889. Things went swell. The hometown team won 6–2, and the city's residents celebrated late into the evening.

The hangover lasted for the next thirteen seasons.

To put it nicely, the Kansas City Athletics were wretched. From 1955 to 1967, the thirteen years the A's were in town, the team never finished a season with a winning record. In that time, they went 829–1,222, and did so under the stewardship of *ten* managers. They lost one hundred or more games in four of those years and either finished alone in last place or shared cellar-dweller honors on six other occasions. According to statistical guru Bill James, a suffering A's fan as a Kansas youth, the team had a losing record in sixty-nine of the seventy-eight months it called K.C. home.

The reason for the wretchedness was simple: despite their ostensible Major League status, the Kansas City Athletics were still very much a farm team. Not in the way people nowadays speak of "Major League farm teams"—the small-market clubs that basically serve as feeders for the moneyed elites of the game. No, these A's were a farm team, as in, players were developed and stored in Kansas City for the specific purpose of being sent to one particular club.

Fans who thought they were getting a bona fide Major League product in the A's weren't long in realizing that this new team was simply a gussied-up version of the old Kansas City Blues: the actual Yankees farm team that had left town in 1954. And here is what really stuck in the craw of the city: the team that operated as the "big club" for the Kansas City A's was none other than . . . the New York Yankees.

THE TRADES

Between 1955 and 1961, the New York and Kansas City baseball organizations made a total of fifteen trades, far more than the Yankees or A's made with any other club during this same period. To put it lightly, most of the trades wound up with New York on the much better end. On the few occasions that Kansas City appeared to have pulled a fast one on the Yanks, the player in question would usually end up back in New York before A's fans got the chance to warm up to him.

New York traded with Kansas City for a variety of reasons: to give undeveloped youngsters a chance to mature in a situation where they'd get big-league experience; to acquire key veterans for a stretch drive; and, on at least one occasion, to exile a player whose conduct was unbecoming of the Yankees organization. In almost every instance, the trades were made with the benefit of only one team in mind. And that team was not the Kansas City Athletics.

The two organizations wasted no time commencing their symbiotic relationship. On May 11, 1955, in the first major deal between the two clubs, the Yankees sent veteran outfielder Enos "Country" Slaughter, who was off to a cold start with the bat, to the A's along with pitcher Johnny Sain for a nondescript hurler named Sonny Dixon. Slaughter proceeded to hit .322 for the A's, while Dixon pitched in a total of three games for New York. Kansas City fans might have smiled smugly, thinking their team had pulled a fast one on the pin-striped behemoth from Gotham. If so, they had those smirks wiped away on August 25, 1956, when the Athletics waived Slaughter back to the Yankees. The Yanks needed outfield depth for the stretch run and the World Series, and they got it in Slaughter, who excelled as a platoon player for several of Casey Stengel's championship teams before ending his Hall of Fame career.

The two trades involving Country Slaughter reeked of a team sending down a player when they didn't need him, then recalling him on demand when they did—a facsimile of the relationship between a Major League club and its triple-A affiliate.

Much the same happened in the case of Bob Cerv, a power-hitting outfielder who couldn't find a place on the Yankees roster. In 1956, New York sent Cerv (pronounced "serve") to Kansas City for cash. All Cerv needed was playing time; he blossomed in his four seasons with the Athletics, hitting 85 home runs and making the All-Star Team in 1958, when he belted 38 dingers and knocked in 104 runs. By 1960, the Yankees reevaluated and decided that maybe Cerv could fit on their roster after all. On May 19 of that year, New York "pried" Cerv away from the A's for third baseman Andy Carey, better known for his wife, actress Lucy Marlow, than for his game at the hot corner. Cerv was a reliable off-the-bench bat for the pennant-winning 1960 Yankees. Carey hit .233 for the A's.

New York could afford to part with a third baseman because of a deal they had made with the Athletics three years earlier. On February 19, 1957, the A's sent three players—pitchers Art Ditmar and Bobby Schantz and third baseman Clete Boyer—to the Yankees for five in return, none of whom are worth the keystrokes involved in mentioning them here. Ditmar and Schantz provided invaluable service to the Yankees, mostly out of the bullpen, but Boyer was the point man in what might have been the shadiest of all the Yankees–A's deals.

Clete Boyer was a "bonus baby," the term given to rookie players of the day who were signed to big-dollar contracts. Most bonus babies were highly rated prospects, and the slick-fielding Boyer was no exception. But the catch was that bonus babies were prohibited from starting out in the minors; these prized purchases were required to spend their first two contract years on a big-league roster. Reluctant to carry such a green prospect, the Yankees found a way around the clause. They simply shipped Boyer off to Kansas City for seasoning. Exactly four days after the requisite two years expired, the A's included him as the "player to be named later" in the Ditmar–Schantz deal.

After two more seasons spent learning the trade in New York's crack farm system, the kid was ready to start at third for the Yankees. It was at the hot corner where Boyer became one of the game's great gloves for the fence-busting New York teams of the 1960s. All the (triple) A's got out of Clete Boyer was 208 at-bats, a .226 batting average, one home run, and some Eisenhower-era Web Gems as a substitute fielder for their terrible team.

Shortstop Billy Martin was a fiery clutch player for the Yankees, but the team's management considered him a bad influence on stars Mickey Mantle and Whitey Ford. On the night of June 14, 1957, the three players were involved in a brawl at the Copacabana, the famed New York nightspot and subject of the Barry Manilow song. The following day, the Yankees sent Martin, young pitcher Ralph Terry, shortstop Woodie Held, and another player to the A's for outfielder Harry "Suitcase" Simpson and pitcher Ryne Duren. Billy Martin, understandably, wept when he received word of the trade.

The parties involved:

✗ "Suitcase" Simpson (so called because he was frequently traded) had led the league in triples and made the All-Star team for the A's in 1956. This meant that the Yankees had to have him.

✗ Ryne Duren, a raging alcoholic who wore Coke-bottle glasses and terrified batters by being drunk, half-blind, wild, and in possession of a hundred-mile-per-hour fastball (à la Rick ["give 'em the heater, Ricky"] Vaughn), became one of the League's best relievers in pinstripes.

✗ Ralph Terry was twenty-one years old and simply needed some time with the Major League farm club out in Missouri. After a couple of years of maturation, he was sent back to New York along with Hector Lopez, Kansas City's regular second baseman, for infielder Jerry Lumpe and a couple of washed-up pitchers. Terry went 76–56 with the Yankees, including a twenty-three-win season in 1962, and pitched a 1–0 shutout in Game Seven of the '62 World Series. Oh yeah, he also gave up Bill Mazeroski's Series-winning home run in 1960.

✗ Woodie Held spent about a season in Kansas City before he and first baseman Vic Power were sent to Cleveland for a gifted young outfielder named Roger Maris. Held and Power proved to be solid players but Maris was something special, a player with a cannon arm in right field and a smooth, left-handed uppercut swing that seemed almost designed for the

short porch in Yankee Stadium. The Tribe had to have
known that Maris was destined to end up in New York
at some point. But they made the trade anyway.

Sure enough, on December 11, 1959, Kansas City did their best
Three Wise Men impersonation and sent Maris, starting shortstop
Joe DeMaestri, and another player to the Yankees for Norm
Siebern, Hank Bauer, "Marvelous" Marv Throneberry, and Don
Larsen. The three players sent to New York were effectively gold,
frankincense, and myrrh, and those the A's received in return were
a who's who of Christmas refuse.

Bauer was thirty-eight and effectively done as a player. He
would also serve an unproductive stint as Kansas City's manager in
the early '60s. Siebern had played himself out of New York with a
woeful performance in Yankee Stadium's "sun field" in left during
the '58 World Series. Throneberry was a prospect-turned-suspect
whose eccentricities and poor performance later made him the per-
sonification of the awful expansion New York Mets. And Larsen,
the only man to pitch a perfect game in the World Series, had
wrapped his car around one too many telephone poles at four a.m.
during spring training.

None of the players the A's acquired made an impact, unless the
negative impact of Larsen's 1–10 record in 1960 is counted. Roger
Maris went on to win back-to-back American League MVP awards,
including one for 1961, the season in which he broke Babe Ruth's
single-season home run record. Of all the one-sided Yankees–A's
deals of the '50s, this was easily the worst. The irony is that Maris,
a shy North Dakota native who was uneasy in the spotlight, is one
player who probably would have rather played in Kansas City than
in New York.

The fifteenth and final trade between the two teams took place
on June 14, 1961, when the Athletics sent pitcher Bud Daley to the
Yanks for pitcher Art Ditmar. This was actually a pretty even deal
on paper—Daley had won sixteen games in 1960, Ditmar fifteen—
but by then A's fans had had their fill of the little "relationship" be-

tween their team and New York's. As a result of much public out-cry, the Athletics' owner publicly pledged not to make any more trades with the Yankees, unless, of course, New York called offer-ing, say, Mickey Mantle.

Ten former Athletics played key roles for the 1961 Yankees, a team that won 109 games, destroyed the Reds in the World Series, and is generally considered one of the top ten clubs ever to play the game. The 1961 A's went 61–100 and finished tied with the expan-sion Washington Senators for last place in the American League.

IMPROPRIETIES ABOUND

By 1961 the A's had a new owner, Charles O. Finley. The *previous* owner, a Chicago vending-machine tycoon named Arnold Johnson, is at the heart of this odd tale of impropriety. Prior to Johnson buy-ing the Athletics in October 1954, when they were still a Philadel-phia organization, the controlling interest in the team was held by the legendary Connie Mack's eldest sons. To gain control, Roy and Earle Mack bought out their stepmother; their stepbrother, Connie Mack Jr.; and other minority stockholders. Like a materialistic housewife with an itchy trigger finger and a Sears charge card in her holster, they leveraged themselves to the hilt. Financial instability combined with the team's poor on-field performance and flagging attendance figures led to dissension among management. American League owners voted to approve the team's sale to Arnold Johnson, so that he could move the team to Kansas City for the 1955 season.

The six seasons that Johnson owned the Athletics would prove to be by far the franchise's worst. Johnson's motivations were not at all in the interest of Kansas City's baseball fans. Due to an escape clause in the lease signed with Municipal Stadium—he could opt out if the team failed to draw one million per season—most sus-pected that Kansas City was simply a temporary home until John-son had the chance to move the team elsewhere.

So where did Arnold Johnson's allegiance truly lie? Well, in light of the horrifying trades and his close business and personal relationship with Yankees owners Dan Topping and Del Webb, one need not solicit the help of Scotland Yard. Johnson even owned Yankee Stadium.*

Say what? Johnson was a vice chairman of Automatic Canteen Co. of America. Dan Topping also happened to be a director with Automatic Canteen. This vending-machine company would go on to rake in approximately $200 million in annual sales by the mid-'60's. That's a lot of Clark bars.

Although the American League owners forced him to sell the property rights before acquiring the Athletics, the relationship with Topping and Webb still stank of malfeasance. The coziness between the two ownership groups proved so inappropriate, in fact, that it caught the attention of federal antitrust investigators. On July 18, 1957, in what was later revealed as false testimony, Arnold Johnson denied before the Celler Committee that he had any ties to the Yankees ownership or favored them in any trades. His nose was reputed to have grown during the proceedings.

Arnold Johnson dropped dead in 1960 when his shriveled heart exploded. Charles O. Finley, who had lost out to Johnson in his bid to acquire the Athletics in 1954, offered $2 million to Johnson's widow for her 52 percent stake in the Athletics. Despite the fact that baseball owners were appalled by the thought of a disreputable character like Finley becoming a member of the club, the deal went through and he bought out the minority stakeholders a year later. During one of his initial publicity stunts, Finley purchased a bus, pointed it in the direction of New York City, and had it burned, to symbolize the end of the "special relationship" with the Yankees. He told the fans, "My intentions are to keep the A's permanently in Kansas City and build a winning ballclub. I have no intention of ever moving the franchise."

On October 18, 1967, after attempts to relocate to Dallas–Fort

---

* In December 1953, the New York Yankees structured a real-estate deal that was peculiar at best. Owners Dan Topping and Del Webb sold Yankee Stadium, but not the team, for $3.6 million in cash, and took back a $2.9 million mortgage and a long-term lease. The buyer was a syndicate headed by none other than Chicago investor Arnold Johnson.

Worth and Louisville were rebuffed, AL owners finally gave Finley permission to move the Athletics to Oakland. This prompted Senator Stuart Symington of Missouri to blast Finley on the floor of the Senate, calling him "one of the most disreputable characters ever to enter the American sports scene," and referred to Oakland as "the luckiest city since Hiroshima," an unfortunate analogy, considering who had thrown out the first ball at Kansas City's first home opener, twelve years before.

THE WORST TRADES

In Sports Deal Making, What Appears Logical Often Later Seems Profoundly Stupid

A trade at any level and in any sport, from the widely noted superstar swap to the back-page Minor League deal, is an inherently high-risk, high-reward venture. It's a little bit like a stock market gambit and a little bit like asking for a hot girl's number at the bar while her boyfriend's in the bathroom. If it works out, the trade not only brings tangible benefits, but it also provides a psychological lift for any team—the satisfaction that can come only from pulling a fast one and profiting from it. However, if it doesn't work out, it can become a wound that festers for years and even decades. A rain forest's worth of timber has been logged and pulped to provide paper for the uncountable sportswriters' columns about the players who got away.

Well-intentioned men have seen their livelihoods and reputations founder on the rocks of a bad trade. And well-intentioned they are. Nobody is out there looking to get snookered. Every trade is entertained and subsequently made with the intent of improving the organization, whether for the short term or the long term. The reasons behind every move can be broken down into several basic categories, none of which include "Doing something galactically stupid so I can cripple my team, earn the ire of the fans, lose my job, and have my name live in infamy for the next eight decades." Sometimes, it just turns out that way.

TALENT FOR "TALENT"

It's all about team chemistry when two players of the same position are exchanged. For whatever reason, it just isn't working out, the next level hasn't been reached, and a change of scenery for both guys is in order. Each side sincerely hopes this is one of those "trades of equal value." But let's be serious. The vast majority of trades are zero-sum: one team benefits, the other gets screwed.

Chicago Blackhawks Trade Goalie Dominik Hasek to Buffalo Sabres for Goalie Stephane Beauregard and a Fourth-Round Draft Choice—August 7, 1992

Chicago selected Hasek in the tenth round (207th overall) of the 1983 draft. Rather than hop the barbed-wire fence in the middle of the night, Hasek chose to play in his native Czechoslovakia until after the Wall came down. On the heels of Gorbachev's glasnost, the Dominator joined the Blackhawks for the 1990–91 season as a backup goalie to Eddie "the Eagle" Belfour. As with most platoons, the arrangement was a contentious one at best. So the Blackhawks shipped him off to Buffalo for a less ambitious backup goalie by the name of Beauregard—not the Confederate general, the other guy—and a fourth-round draft choice who ended up being left-winger Eric Daze.

Daze went on to a long but injury-riddled career with the Blackhawks. As for Beauregard, he was traded to the Winnipeg Jets three days later and his last professional performance between the pipes was with Schwennigen Wild in die Bonner Republik, a.k.a. West Germany.

As for Hasek, well, an injury to the Sabres starting goaltender, Grant Fuhr, gave him just the opportunity he needed. He won the first of his six Vezina Trophies (awarded to the NHL's top goaltender) that first season in Buffalo and became the first European-trained goalie to lead the NHL in goals-against average. Hasek went on to win two MVP awards and a Stanley Cup, and is considered one of the greatest netminders in NHL history.

Philadelphia Eagles Trade Sonny Jurgenson to Washington Redskins for Norm Snead—February 27, 1964

Philadelphia's Sonny Jurgenson was the best pure passer of his day, but he was often injured and he alienated Eagles management by holding out prior to the 1963 season. When the opportunity arose to swap the disgruntled passer, straight up, for Redskins quarterback Norm Snead, who was five years younger than Jurgenson and thought to have more upside, the Eagles flew at it. Six years later, the wildly inconsistent Snead was booed out of Philly, whereas at the same time Jurgenson was still busy adding bullet points to his Hall of Fame résumé in Washington. Ironically, a good portion of that work came against the Eagles secondary.

San Diego Padres Trade Ozzie Smith to St. Louis Cardinals for Garry Templeton—December 10, 1981

After losing Dave Winfield to free agency a couple of years earlier, the San Diego Padres were looking to upgrade their popgun attack. They figured a good place to start was with their shortstop, Ozzie Smith, who was sensational defensively but had hit a meager .222 the prior season. On December 10, 1981, the Padres sent Ozzie to the Cardinals for a player to be named later and shortstop Garry Templeton, a multiple .300 hitter whose glove was as icy as his bat was hot. Smith blossomed into a pretty decent hitter while wielding the same spectacular glove in St. Louis. Templeton's bat soon cooled off (he never hit above .282 in San Diego) and his defense remained poor. In 1987, the Wizard of Oz hit .303 with seventy-five RBI and won the Gold Glove. Templeton, appropriately enough, hit .222.

St. Louis Hawks Trade Bill Russell to Boston Celtics for Ed Macauley and Cliff Hagen—Summer 1956

The St. Louis Hawks needed a veteran post presence to complement star forward Bob Pettit, and figured Boston center Ed Macauley, a six-time All-Star and St. Louis native, would be the perfect fit. Only problem was that Red Auerbach, while willing to part with Macauley, wanted St. Louis' first round pick; when the Celtics' patriarch agreed to sweeten the offer by throwing in former Kentucky star Cliff Hagen, the two teams reached a deal. Macauley went on to play just three seasons in St. Louis before retiring. The first-round pick the Celtics received as part of the arrangement? Bill Russell, center, University of San Francisco. You may have heard of him.

Cincinnati Reds Trade Frank Robinson to the Baltimore Orioles for Pitcher Milt Pappas and Prospects Jack Baldschun and Dick Simpson—December 9, 1965

In 1965, the Reds were reaping what they had sowed down on the farm and were calling up brilliant and promising young talent such as Pete Rose, Tony Perez, Bobby Tolan, and Vada Pinson, among others. But they were short on the requisite pitching needed to complement their great young lineup. In one of the worst sports prognostications on record, Reds general manager Bill Dimwit, ahem, *De*Witt rationalized the trade by declaring Robinson to be an "old thirty" and thus expendable. Robinson was coming off a nice year too, having hit .296, sent thirty-three balls out of the yard, and brought 113 men home in 1965. Milt "Gimpy" Pappas was the ace of the Orioles' staff, an All-Star starter, and in nine seasons with Baltimore he never had a losing season. The deal was a classic talent-for-talent swap.

As they usually are, the effects of the trade were felt immediately. Providing a morale boost to aging and decrepit thirty-year-old males everywhere, Robinson won the Triple Crown in his first season with Baltimore. There have been only thirteen players in the history of the game who've managed to pull it off, fourteen if you count Tip O'Neill accomplishing the feat in 1887 for St. Louis of the American Association. (So *that's* what the good senator did before politics. Who knew?) Oh yeah, the Orioles also won the World Series in 1966, and Robinson was named the MVP. That series was the first of four trips he would lead the Birds to in six years.

Queen City fans were horrified by the deal and never accepted Pappas because of it. He would last not even three full seasons with the Reds. In his first year with Cincinnati, he posted the worst ERA of his career (4.29) and went 12–11. He won sixteen games the following year, but after getting out of the blocks slowly in '68, Cincy sent him off to Atlanta in a six-player trade. Pappas's tenure will most be remembered for the infighting he inspired among his teammates, some of whom accused him of not giving it his all.

DEADLINE DEALS

The Deadline Deal is a baseball late-summer ritual—the Rites of July 31—when clubs are willing to do whatever it takes, often well beyond the limits of reason, to acquire the talent needed to go all the way that year. These trades are the ultimate in sacrificing tomorrow for today; clubs often know that what they're giving up is way, way too much . . . but as soft rockers Seals & Crofts say, they may never pass this way again.

Boston Red Sox Trade Jeff Bagwell to Houston Astros for Larry Anderson—July 31, 1990

Needing bullpen help to win the American League East, the Red Sox didn't really want to give up first-base prospect Bagwell, a native of Massachusetts, but felt the short-term results would be worth the sacrifice. On July 31, 1990, Boston traded Bagwell to the rebuilding Astros for thirty-six-year-old setup man Larry Anderson. Anderson came through with a 1.23 ERA and helped the Red Sox win the AL East and go to the playoffs. Oakland swept them in the ALCS. Bagwell went on to hit 449 home runs for the Astros and became the centerpiece of the Houston franchise. Who got the better end of the deal? Ask a Red Sox fan, then duck.

Montreal Expos Trade Randy Johnson, Brian Holman, and Gene Harris
to Seattle Mariners for Mark Langston—May 25, 1989

Les Expos felt as if they were just one experienced left-handed starter
from going all the way in the National League in 1989. So firm were
they in this belief that they were willing to trade Randy Johnson and
Brian Holman, their two top pitching prospects, to the Mariners for
Mark Langston, who was due to be a free agent after the '89 season
and almost certainly wouldn't stay in French Canada. Langston went
12–9 with a 2.39 ERA with the 'Spos and, sure enough, defected to
California in the off-season. Montreal led the NL East in early August but fell apart and finished fourth. Brian Holman won thirty-two
games in three seasons before his career was wrecked by arm trouble.
Randy Johnson turned out all right, eventually going on to horrify
high-def subscribers across the nation.

THIS WILL COME BACK TO HAUNT YOU

It's every fan's worst nightmare: the trade whose doleful results can
be seen live and up close, year after gruesome year. It's bad enough
that the guy for whom you once cheered now just absolutely kills
your team, but it's worse when he makes it personal, telling anyone
who'll listen that he was disrespected and how every time he faces
your team, he takes a direct interest in seeing you suffer for his insult. And the unkindest cut of all? He's right.

Chicago Cubs Trade Lou Brock and Pitchers Jack Spring and
Paul Toth to St. Louis Cardinals for Ernie Broglio, Bobby Shantz,
and Doug Clemens—June 15, 1964

"Brock for Broglio." This trade is baseball's Vietnam: it's repeatedly referred to in morbid and forbidding tones for the sole purpose
of reminding general management of the hard lessons they should
by now have learned. Among the multitude of Chicago's sports misfortunes, this may be the one most responsible for Old Style beer remaining in frothy business even to this day.

At the time of the trade, it looked to be a logical deal and, if anything, a bit of a steal for the Cubbies. Lou Brock had been nothing but a disappointment for Chicago. He was batting .251, and Cubs manager Bob Kennedy found the left fielder to be wholly incapable with the glove, a free-swinging strikeout king, and often irresponsible on the base paths. To the contrary, Cardinals pitcher Ernie Broglio was a twenty-game winner and had had multiple successful seasons hurling for St. Louis. And Bobby Shantz, although in the twilight of his career, was also a twenty-game winner. A good many St. Louis fans *and* players were pissed when word of the deal leaked out, while the Cubs and those inhabiting Wrigleyville were genuinely giddy at the promise of what was as good a pitching staff as any in the league.

Well, things didn't quite pan out as expected. Brock caught fire for the rest of the '64 season, hitting .348 and swiping thirty-three bases en route to a Cardinals World Series victory in seven games over the New York Yankees. Brock would go on to hit .300 six times in his career for the Cardinals, lead the league in stolen bases eight times, and depart baseball as the all-time stolen base leader. He was a no-brainer for the Hall of Fame. But Cubs skipper Kennedy was right about one thing: Brock led the league in errors seven times!

As for Broglio, well, he went 4–7 with the Cubs in '64, developed bone chips in his elbow, and retired after the '66 season with a 7–13 record for Chicago. Ahhh, pitchers.

Chicago Bears Sell Bobby Layne to New York Yankees—July 1949

Papa Bear George Halas had a dilemma prior to the 1949 season: which second-year quarterback should succeed the great Sid Luckman—Notre Dame Heisman winner Johnny Lujack, who had all the physical tools, or Bobby Layne, a tough former Texas star with loads of fire but a lack of great athleticism and arm strength. Halas chose Lujack, and sold Layne to the New York Yankees NFL team. After one brilliant season, Lujack hurt his arm and was forced into premature retirement in 1952. Layne resurfaced in Detroit in 1950, played his entire career without a face mask, and became one of the great clutch quarterbacks of all time, leading the hated Lions to three Western Conference championships in the '50s.

Boston Red Sox Trade Sparky Lyle to New York Yankees for Danny Cater—March 22, 1972

During spring training, seeking outfield depth and punch in their lineup, the Red Sox swapped twenty-seven-year-old relief specialist Sparky Lyle to the Yankees for Danny Cater, a smooth hitter who had batted .301 with the Yankees in 1970. In seven standout seasons in the Bronx, Lyle twice led the AL in saves, made three All-Star teams, and won the 1977 AL Cy Young Award as the Yankees won their first World Championship since 1962. Cater hit a quiet .262 in three seasons of part-time duty in Boston and was out of baseball by the end of the '75 season.

New York Giants Trade Draft Rights to Randy White to Dallas Cowboys for Craig Morton—January 28, 1975

After wasting numerous first-round picks, the Giants decided that what they really needed wasn't another raw rookie, but veteran leadership. So they dealt their 1975 first-round selection (the second overall pick) to the division-rival Cowboys for quarterback Craig Morton. Dallas turned the pick into defensive tackle Randy White. The Manster spent the next fourteen seasons devastating offensive lines, including those of the Giants, who were punished twice a season for eschewing the future Hall of Famer. Morton spent two miserable years in New York before being shipped off to Denver. Trades like these were part of the reason why the Giants had the worst record in the NFL for the decade of the '70s.

WITH THEIR FIRST SELECTION . . .

Nothing excites a sports town like the promise of a gifted rookie. A first-year player, if he's talented and charismatic enough, can transform the fortunes of an entire franchise—as Michael Jordan did for the woeful Chicago Bulls, who were pulling about four thousand per night into the old Chicago Stadium before number 23 showed up. Then there are other times when a team, tantalized by potential, will give up far too much for it. When that happens, look out below.

Philadelphia Flyers Deal Peter Forsberg, Chris Simon, Steve Duchesne, Kerry Huffman, Mike Ricci, and Jocelyn Thibault (Draft Pick), Cash, and Considerations to the Quebec Nordiques for the Rights to Eric Lindros—June 30, 1992

The prodigiously talented Lindros had no desire to play in Quebec, a city with a 98 percent French-speaking population, never mind for a Nordiques franchise that was going nowhere fast. And the Flyers needed a new star to gratify their demanding fan base, who had grown weary of blowing the dust off the club's 1974 and '75 Stanley Cups. On June 30, 1992, Quebec dealt the nineteen-year-old phenom to Philadelphia for a package of players and draft picks. Lindros did win a Hart Trophy as the NHL's MVP in 1995, but his stint in Philadelphia is remembered more for his failure to ever score fifty goals in a season, for his falling out with GM Bobby Clarke, for a series of career-hampering concussions, and for a lone '97 Stanley Cup Finals sweep at the hands of the Red Wings, as opposed to his individual successes.

As for the Nordiques, they went somewhere, all right. First they went to Denver and became the Colorado Avalanche. Then, thanks in large part to the talent heisted from Philly, they went to the top of the NHL, drinking beer out of Lord Stanley's Cup twice, in 1996 and again in 2001.

Saints Trade Two 1999 First-Round Picks, Their Third-, Fourth-, Fifth-, Sixth-, and Seventh-Round Picks, and a 2000 Third-Round Pick for the Rights to Ricky Williams—April 24, 1999

Saints coach Mike Ditka was in love with Ricky Williams, the Heisman-winning, record-smashing back from the University of

Texas, and, as everyone knows, love can make a man do regrettable things. Such as? Such as, in addition to the infamous SI "wedding" cover, giving up eight draft selections for one man who, as it turned out, spent three merely decent seasons in New Orleans before being swapped to the Dolphins for . . . two first-round draft picks. Which means not one, but two teams screwed themselves in acquiring the gifted-but-eccentric tailback.

Golden State Warriors Trade Robert Parish and the Number Three Pick (Kevin McHale) to Boston for the Number One Pick (Joe Barry Carroll) and the Number Thirteen Pick (Rickey Brown)—June 9, 1980

Golden State already had a serviceable center in the Chief, Robert Parish. But the Warriors had their sights set on a big man they believed to be superduper special: Purdue's Joe Barry Carroll. Unfortunately, they owned the third pick in the 1980 Draft and Carroll would almost certainly be long gone by then. Good ole Red Auerbach, the convenient possessor of that year's first pick, was more than happy to offer his help. He offered to deal the pick to the Warriors, along with the number thirteen pick in the first round, for Golden State's selection, the third overall, and Parish in return. Golden State enthusiastically agreed. They proceeded to grab Carroll, the top pick, and the thirteenth, Rickey Brown of Ole Miss. (Who? Where?) Boston took Kevin McHale of Minnesota at number three, inserted him and Parish into its front line alongside Larry Bird, and was off on its 1980s championship run. Joe Barry Carroll, meanwhile, proved to be a lax, overweight sluggard playing for bad teams in Oakland, and owner of one of the better nicknames in sports history: "Joe Barely Cares."

THE JIM KERN SPECIAL

And then there's the Jim Kern Special, named for the flame-throwing, droll relief man from the '70s, who once quipped of a certain employer that he liked to trade "one guy who can play for five guys who can't." A common feature of the Jim Kern

Special is that it's a move made under duress. The player in question costs too much; he's alienated everyone in the clubhouse; he's snorting the yard lines; he's bumping uglies with the owner's wife; whatever. Bottom line, he has to go, and fast. Unfortunately, the team's bargaining position for trade value is diminished. So it's a take-the-first-halfway-decent-offer-and-hope-at-least-a-few-of-those-five-guys-end-up-being-something-other-than-complete-stiffs type of situation.

New York Mets Trade Tom Seaver to Cincinnati Reds for Doug Flynn, Steve Henderson, Dan Norman, and Pat Zachry—June 15, 1977

Tom Terrific's high leg kick and powerful right arm had delivered two pennants and one Amazin' World's Championship to Queens. He was the face of the Mets. But when Seaver grew restless over the shortage of zeros in his checks, team chairman M. Donald Grant was anything but beatific toward his franchise player. He balked at Seaver's salary demands. Days later, Dick Young, one of the city's most influential sportswriters, and father-in-law of a Mets employee, went on a tirade, tearing into Tom on the pages of the New York *Daily News*. On June 15, 1977, the Mets traded Seaver to the Reds, receiving a whole lot of nothing in return. Grant's hopes that the ground for the move had been fertilized by Young's slash-and-burn campaign were dashed quickly. Attendance plunged as fast as the club did in the standings. In fact, in 1979 the franchise finished last in attendance and dead last in the National League.

Milwaukee Bucks Trade Kareem Abdul-Jabbar to Los Angeles Lakers for Elmore Smith, Junior Bridgeman, Brian Winters, and Dave Meyers—June 16, 1975

It wasn't really the Bucks' fault that they traded Kareem to the Lakers, any more than it was their fault that they were located in a humdrum town like Milwaukee. The urbane Jabbar was bored and out of place in Wisconsin, fed up with the local rustics still referring to him as "Lew." He wanted out. The KAJ would only accept a trade to either the Knicks or the Lakers, so, basically, the Bucks were screwed. They just had to get what they could get out of the deal, and be done with it. But they didn't get much out of the deal, didn't escape mediocrity for the rest of the '70s, and could only watch as the Lakers built a dynasty around Kareem and the Sky Hook.

St. Louis Cardinals Trade Keith Hernandez to New York Mets for Neil Allen and Rick Ownbey—June 15, 1983

With his Gold Glove and his run-producing, line-drive stroke, Keith Hernandez's game seemed as if it was designed for manager Whitey Herzog's brand of baseball. But the White Rat suspected that Hernandez was using his nose for more than just a mustache ornament. Midway through the '83 season, the Cardinals traded the suspiciously sniffling first baseman to the Mets for Allen and Ownbey, a pair of pitchers who would deliver a 21–22 combined record with the Redbirds. Hernandez was indeed a regular line blower, as it turned out, but still managed to star for the Mets 1986 World Championship club between "bumps."

WE'RE ONE PLAYER AWAY

It's the siren song that has driven many a team to ruin over the years: the silver bullet, the savior, the one man standing between it and the Promised Land. Too often, it's a mirage.

Minnesota Vikings Trade Five Players and Six Draft Picks (Including the First Pick in the 1991 NFL Draft) to Dallas Cowboys for Herschel Walker—October 12, 1989

All the talented Minnesota Vikings needed was a game-breaking running back. All the untalented Dallas Cowboys needed was an entire roster of skilled players. On October 12, 1989, Minnesota GM Mike Lynn sent five players and six future draft picks to

Dallas for one man: Herschel Walker. The additional picks produced Emmitt Smith, Darren Woodson, and Kevin Smith for the Cowboys, and a trade involving some of the other picks brought Russell Maryland. The Cowboys used the Walker trade as a springboard to three Super Bowl Championships in the '90s. The Vikings won the NFC Central in 1989, were destroyed 41–13 by the 49ers in the NFC playoffs, and fell to last place in 1990.

Walker never even rushed for a thousand yards in Minnesota, and was sent packing to Philadelphia prior to the 1992 season. Lynn's name became mud in the Twin Cities. The trade itself was bad enough, but that it was with, and abundantly benefited, the hated Dallas Cowboys was what was unforgivable. It's debatable who Herschel held back more: the Vikings, or Brian Shimer's Olympic bobsled.

New York Mets Trade Nolan Ryan, Don Rose, Leroy Stanton, and Francisco Estrada to California Angels for Jim Fregosi— December 10, 1971

The Mets had a surplus of power pitchers and needed infield help. They thought they could spare Nolan Ryan, who had been plagued by blister problems and wildness throughout his young career. On December 10, 1971, they sent the twenty-five-year-old Ryan to the California Angels along with some throw-ins for Fregosi, who in a season and a half with New York hit a solid .233 to go with defense charitably described as "atrocious." On July 11, 1973, the Mets unceremoniously sold Fregosi's rights to the Texas Rangers. Four days later, The Express pitched his second no-hitter of the '73 season, on the way to a record seven in a career that seemed to span eons. So much for blisters.

Vancouver Canucks Trade Cam Neely to Boston Bruins with a Number One Pick (Glen Wesley) for Center Barry Pederson—June 6, 1986

The trade of Neely and the third overall pick in the '86 Entry Draft to Boston for Pederson, a two-time hundred-point scorer for the

Bruins, was designed to accomplish two goals: improve Vancouver's anemic attack and get the Canucks out of the Smythe Division basement. When the Canucks dealt an over-the-hill Pederson to Pittsburgh four seasons later, they were still struggling to score goals . . . and they were still in last place in the Smythe. Neely scored fifty-plus goals three times and was one of the stars on Boston's 1990 Stanley Cup finalist squad. An added bit of bile for Canucks fans to swallow: Cam Neely, the Bruins' all-time playoff goals leader and an adopted son of New England, was born and raised on Vancouver Island, British Columbia.

Los Angeles Dodgers Trade Pedro Martinez to the Montreal Expos for Second Baseman Delino DeShields—November 19, 1993

Pedro Martinez, *straight up,* for Delino DeShields. Kind of like Hugh Grant swapping the divine Elizabeth Hurley for a prostitute named Divine.

In the season prior to the trade, the twenty-four-year-old DeShields hit .295 and stole forty-three bases. Over his four full years in the show to that point, he had averaged forty-seven steals and a .277 batting average. The twenty-two-year-old Martinez went 10–5 with a 2.61 earned run average through sixty-five games, including two starts. Pedro's rookie year was 1993, and he struck out 119 in 107 innings. But in Tommy Lasorda's eyes, Pedro was too skinny to handle 200 innings of work as a starter in the bigs. DeShields was a speedy, versatile, and respected leadoff hitter whose reputation was on the rapid ascent, while Jody Reed, the Dodgers current second baseman, was serviceable at best. The Dodgers *had* to have Delino.

Lasorda must've been drunk on Slim•Fast. In his three-year tenure with L.A., DeShields never hit higher than .256. Martinez went on to win three Cy Young Awards—one with Montreal—and establish himself, statistically, alongside Dodger great Sandy Koufax.

THE GRANDDADDY OF THEM ALL

The Babe

So monumentally terrible that it required its own category. It was 1919 and Red Sox owner Harry Frazee had a case of alligator arms when it came to contract negotiations with player Babe Ruth. The Bambino felt that he was underpaid relative to other top players in the League, which he was, and a pissing match ensued. Ruth was eventually sold like a racehorse to Colonel Jacob Ruppert's New York Yankees for $100,000, plus a loan collateralized by Fenway Park. The Babe went to Boston's hated rivals in the Bronx and was even rumored to have built a house while there. As for statistical results, there's not a sports fan on the planet who doesn't know how this one turned out. And if there is, well, they don't deserve to be enlightened.

And the worst trade of all time? It likely hasn't happened yet.

CORPORATE NAMING RIGHTS GONE BUST

The Internet Bubble. Telecom Mania.
Accounting Scandals. Sheer Fan Indifference.
and Even a Little Homicidal Intrigue

ENRON FIELD—HOUSTON, TEXAS

In December 2001, when Enron imploded and became *the* icon for corporate fraud, its employees and shareholders weren't the only ones to suffer the consequences. Houston Astros fans were also left to fret about which company's name would soon replace the crooked "E" outside their ballpark. Enron Field became Minute Maid Park. (Now that that's settled, can something be done about the silly hill and flagpole in center field?)

PSINet STADIUM—BALTIMORE, MARYLAND

Earnings? We talkin' 'bout *earnings*?! If only Allen Iverson was an equity analyst instead of an NBA guard, he might have questioned the conventional wisdom pertaining to Internet companies at the time: only revenue growth was needed—profits were so overrated. PSINet was an Internet service provider pioneer, but it had a very leaky wallet. And in 2001, it filed for bankruptcy. PSINet Stadium became Ravens Stadium, which then became M&T Bank Stadium.

CMGI FIELD—FOXBORO, MASSACHUSETTS

This "technology and venture capital" company's stock soared into the Y2K with contrails, but then it crashed to earth the following year, forcing corporate investment divestitures en masse. When the tulip bubble, er, Internet bubble popped, CMGI's stock went down the flume—from $163 per share in 2000 to a slightly more conservative valuation of $1.66 per share in 2002. It was one of the many companies laid to waste during that time period. As it pertains to the New England Patriots' home field, old industry was more than glad to step in, giggling all the while: CMGI Field became Gillette Stadium.

ADELPHIA COLISEUM—NASHVILLE, TENNESSEE

Adelphia Communications was the fifth-largest cable company in the United States before filing bankruptcy in 2002 due to unscrupulous management behavior. Tennessee Titans fans were thrilled for the next four years as their field of business remained free of corporate sponsor, simply referred to as The Coliseum. But the corporate establishment returned in 2006. Adelphia Coliseum became LP Field.

PAC BELL PARK—SAN FRANCISCO, CALIFORNIA

There was no accounting scandal or unfounded stock appreciation when it came to the renaming of the San Francisco Giants' beautiful ball field. Rather, when Pac Bell became SBC Park and then AT&T Park, the only controversy . . . was that there was none. The change was met with a large dose of fan indifference, as Giants fans simply pretended, and continue to pretend, that the new name doesn't exist. Picturesque Pac Bell became . . . ?

THE SHAWMUT CENTER—BOSTON, MASSACHUSETTS

The Shawmut Center opened its gates to Boston Bruins and Celtics fans in 1995, faced with the hopeless task of replacing the hallowed halls of Boston Garden. Since ground was broken for the "New Garden" in 1993, the arena has had thirty-four different names. *Thirty-four.* A New England regional bank, Shawmut, was on the building's title placard first, but then it merged with Fleet Bank and the arena became the FleetCenter. When Fleet subsequently merged with BankBoston, then with Bank of America in 2004, identity bewilderment ensued.

For nearly a year until TD Banknorth purchased the naming rights, the New Garden was known as "YourGarden." During that year, YourGarden sold naming rights thirty separate times on eBay, among other name-swapping events, donating the proceeds to local charities. On one occasion, a New York City lawyer and Yankees fan won naming rights. Seizing the opportunity, he proposed the name DerekJeterCenter, but team executives rejected the name. On another, the arena was named the YankeesSuckGarden. Team executives relented on that one. The Shawmut Center eventually became the TD Banknorth Garden.

HONORABLE MENTION

When Villanova University constructed its cozy, sixty-five-hundred-seat multipurpose arena in 1986, there were no corporate dollars chasing the naming rights. But there was a generous donation from philanthropist alum John du Pont. The arena was named the du Pont Pavilion in honor of his endowment. But du Pont also dabbled in paranoid schizophrenia. In 1996, he was found guilty of the murder of Olympic wrestling gold medalist Dave Schultz. After the homicidal shooting, du Pont locked himself in his mansion for two days, negotiating his surrender all the while. When the cops cut the power and du Pont scurried outside to fix it, they cuffed him. Shortly thereafter, Villanova picked up the biggest pink eraser the bookstore had to offer and hastily shortened the arena's name. The du Pont Pavilion became, simply, the Pavilion.

THE OLD BOYS' COACHING NETWORK

Round and Round It Goes, When the Carousel Stops ... Er, That's the Point: It Never Does

Perpetuating and preserving an elite inner circle, and doing so without merit, has long been a practice in many areas of the sporting world. Despite the ever-increasing pressure to win and the ever-shrinking window of opportunity in which to do it, team owners, general managers, and athletic directors alike resort to the rapid-fire hiring and firing of familiar-faced coaches—"known commodities"—as a way to placate the vast majority of fans who lust for the quick fix. The average tenure of service for a head coach or manager in the MLB, NBA, and NFL is less than three years. This creates a lot of room for recycling.

Some coaches have pulled careers from this game of coaching hopscotch, and a certain number have managed to do so successfully. Examples of the *best* of the old boys' network of coaches include baseball managers Bill "Deacon" McKechnie and Tony LaRussa. For pro basketball, Pat Riley and Larry Brown come to mind as men who do this fraternal order proud. And Marty Schottenheimer, Chuck Knox, and Bill "The Tuna" Parcells are examples of the best of pro football's old boy system. But this isn't a book about the best of anything. The list of the *worst* coaches of the old boys' network is long, not necessarily distinguished, and much more entertaining.

THE OLD BOYS OF BASEBALL

Dave Bristol

Midway through the 1966 season, when he was hired by the Reds to replace the fired Don Heffner, Dave Bristol, at thirty-three, was the youngest manager in baseball. He wound up spending three more full seasons in Cincinnati, finishing over .500 in each of them. But Reds management, figuring they needed another man to take the talented young team over the top, fired him following the 1969 season and replaced him with Sparky Anderson. Sure enough, Sparky led the Reds to the pennant in 1970. By then, Bristol was in Milwaukee, managing the expansion Brewers, and not doing a particularly notable job of it. The Brew Crew lost ninety-seven and ninety-two games in Bristol's first two seasons, and he was fired when Milwaukee limped to a 10–20 start in 1972.

Yet when the Atlanta Braves needed a new manager following the 1975 season, they went with Bristol, despite the fact that he had already been fired by two clubs. It's possible that new owner Ted Turner picked Bristol because he knew he could "86" him without much of an outcry. Bristol proceeded to chalk up yet another ninety-plus loss season in 1976. On May 11, 1977, with the club mired in a sixteen-game losing streak, the flamboyant Turner replaced Bristol as manager with . . . himself. The media mogul managed exactly one game before being ordered back to the owner's box by Commissioner Bowie Kuhn, who ruled that no man owning stock in a club could manage it. Turner vacated the dugout and Bristol meekly returned to finish what he started, managing out Atlanta's hundred-loss season.

Fired again by Ted Turner, this time permanently, Bristol moved on to San Francisco, where he took a coaching job with the Giants.

Late in the 1979 season, he took over as interim manager after the firing of Joe Altobelli and guided the Giants to a 10–12 record. Given the job on a full-time basis, Bristol's losing ways continued. San Francisco struggled to a 75–86 record in 1980, and Bristol, for the fourth time in his managerial career, was shown the door. He never managed again in the bigs.

In eight full seasons and parts of three more, Dave Bristol compiled a record of 657–764, a .462 winning percentage. He never finished higher than third—and that only once—and in his five seasons, his teams never won more than seventy-five games. The continual hiring, firing, and rehiring of this serial second-division finisher can only be chalked up to the massive lack of imagination on the part of several Major League owners. Or maybe he had pictures.

Pat Corrales

The hot-tempered Corrales, hired and fired by three different clubs in the '70s and '80s, mastered the art of wearing out his welcome in a clubhouse while getting the least out of the talent at his disposal. He had an excellent group of players in Texas, his first stop, but the Rangers were never able to get over the hump under his guidance. In 1979, they finished an uninspiring third in the AL West, and when they sank under .500 in 1980, that did it for Pat Corrales in Arlington.

In Philadelphia he had Pete Rose, Steve Carlton, Mike Schmidt, and a Phillies roster laden with other stars, but was unable to tap this group's potential. In fact, on July 18, 1983, Corrales became the first man to be fired by a first-place team; the Phillies were just 43–42 at the time. Under their new skipper, GM Lee Owens—the man who fired Corrales—the Phillies went all the way to the World Series. And thirteen days after he was fired by Philadelphia, Corrales was hired by the Cleveland Indians, who were in last place in the AL East. It was a midseason penthouse-to-outhouse switch.

Cleveland was the end of the line for Corrales. He went 60–102 in his first full season with the Indians. Then he surprised everyone by lifting the moribund club to an eighty-four-win season in 1986 and was rewarded for the Tribe's rare winning record with what ownership nebulously referred to as a "perpetual" contract. Eighty-seven games into that contract, with the Tribe 31–56 and mired in last place, perpetuity apparently expired. Corrales packed up his 572–634 career managerial record and jumped on the Old Boys' Express to Atlanta, where he assisted Bobby Cox with the Braves powerhouses of the '90s.

John McNamara

John McNamara will be remembered primarily for two things: (a) his Cyrano de Bergerac-esque nose, and (b) his suspect managerial tactics during the 1986 World Series. But the bulk of McNamara's work did not consist of losses in the glare of World Series competition. The year 1986, in fact, was Johnny Mac's only Series appearance. It was the mundane loss in nippy April or steamy July that was his calling card. And over nineteen seasons, four decades, with six clubs, John McNamara lost 1,233 games, good for twenty-fourth highest in Major League history.

Johnny Mac's managerial career began in 1969 with the Oakland A's and ended in 1996 with the California Angels. In between, he managed in San Diego (1974–77), Cincinnati (1979–82), California (1983–84), Boston (1985–88), and Cleveland (1990–91). His greatest misfortune was working for a variety of owners who ranged from the eccentric to the incompetent to the downright demented: McNamara was fired from the A's in 1970, despite winning eighty-nine games and finishing second in the AL West; Oakland owner Charles O. Finley—the man owned a mule named after himself and proposed an orange baseball for night games—believed managers were "a dime a dozen." And, like a drunken best man, San Diego owner Ray Kroc mortified his club and manager in Johnny Mac's first game with the Padres—a loss in the 1974 opener—when the McDonald's tycoon grabbed the house mic and apologized to the fans for the team's "stupid play."

The Pads finished 60–102 that season, one of three seasons Johnny Mac skippered clubs that either lost a hundred games or were on the way to losing as many when he was fired. In Cincinnati, things started off well as he guided the Reds to the NL West title in 1979 before being swept by the (Sing it!) "We Are Family" Pirates in the National League playoffs. But the club's miserly ownership allowed the once-great Reds to decay and McNamara was fired ninety-two games into the 1982 season. It was the first and only year in the franchise's 125-year history that the Reds lost a hundred games. Then in Cleveland he was tossed aside like a bowl of bland baby food when the rebuilding plan he was supposed to mentor went completely sideways, through no real fault of his own.

And then, of course, there was Boston—the one place Johnny Mac had some success. But it doesn't exactly do him any favors with history.

THE OLD BOYS OF BASKETBALL

Kevin Loughery

This feisty Irishman's pro basketball coaching career began in a rather inauspicious fashion midway through the 1972–73 season when, as a guard for the Philadelphia 76ers, he was elevated to head coach to replace Roy Rubin, who had steered the Sixers to a stellar 4–47 record up until that point. Plagued by star player defections to the ABA, poor draft picks, and a roster lacking any talent whatsoever, Loughery was essentially handed the keys in midair to an already-flaming *Hindenburg*. Despite all that, the team's winning percentage improved dramatically: under his stewardship the Sixers won five of their remaining thirty-one games to become the most futile team in the history of the NBA.

Loughery then moved on to the ABA, where he officially began his head coaching career with the New York Nets. This "lively" league's most notable innovations were the three-point shot and the 'fro. And who better to align himself with in the ABA than the most dominant basketball player on earth at the time—Julius Erving, a man who sported both skills *and* a 'fro. Neither he nor his hair required coaching.

In 1973–74, Loughery "coached" the New York Nets to an ABA Championship. He did so again in the 1975–76 season. Over his three seasons coaching in the ABA, Loughery tallied an impressive coaching record of 168–84; 21–11 in the playoffs. This compares favorably to his seventeen seasons as a coach of six different NBA teams, during which he recorded 474 wins and 662 losses. In eight NBA playoff appearances, Loughery-led teams posted a miserable record of 6–21, losing in the first round on *all* eight occasions. The only rational explanations that can be deduced from these numbers are that (a) the Doctor made him a good coach or (b) the plain brown NBA rock just cramped his style.

Gene Shue

Gene Shue coached 1,645 professional basketball games in his career; he lost 861 of them. Shue coached 77 playoff games in that time; he lost 47 of those. In 1977, by far Shue's most successful season as a head coach, he guided the star-laden Philadelphia 76ers to the NBA Finals. But they ended up losing to the underdog Portland Trailblazers, who were led in conquest by part-Sasquatch, part-center Bill Walton.

Shue went about doing things his way for twenty-two seasons. Sometimes it worked. After going 16–40 under Shue in 1967, his first season as their coach, the Washington Bullets, with the help of Earl "the Pearl" Monroe and young Wes Unseld, went on the team's first sustained stretch of success. They even made the 1970–71 Finals, where they were swept by the Bucks.

Sometimes it did not. In 1981, Shue rejoined the Bullets after guiding the Los Angeles Clippers to another predictable stinker of a season. (Note: The Clippers have pretty much always stunk; in the franchise's thirty-six-year history, the team has finished above .500 only six times.) Until he was replaced toward the end of the 1986 season, the Bullets doggy-paddled to a 231–248 record.

Shue finished up his NBA head coaching career back again with the Clippers, his proverbial ex- with the familiar embrace. Their rekindled relationship lasted only one and a third seasons, and

Shue, with a 27–93 record in that final stint, ended his career the way most coaches do: by being axed.

Bernie Bickerstaff

Bickerstaff served as an NBA head coach for three different teams over the course of ten seasons. He's been a president and general manager for seven seasons and also spent twelve years as an assistant coach. Arguably his greatest achievement thus far? Leading the St. Louis Swarm to International Basketball League titles in 2000 and 2001 and earning Coach of the Year honors in both of those seasons. In 914 games as an NBA head coach, his teams won 405 and lost 509. Of the thirty-three playoff games during which he paced the sidelines, Bernie's team won just twelve. He has no division, conference, or NBA titles.

In 1986, Bernie arrived in Seattle for his first head-coaching gig. The Sonics steadily improved in each of the three subsequent seasons, qualifying for the playoffs in all those years. But when they fell to .500 and out of playoff contention in 1990, Bickerstaff was canned. The highlight of his tenure in the Emerald City came in the '87 playoffs, when the Sonics, despite having a losing record in the regular season, managed to fight their way into the Western Conference Finals. Careerwise, Bickerstaff appears to be living off that single, two-decade-old run.

In Denver, he took over as general manager, inheriting a team that had gone 43–39. In his first season as GM, the Nuggets were twenty-seventh out of twenty-seven teams in defense. Bickerstaff addressed the problem, as any good executive would, and the following season the Nuggets' defense improved to thirteenth out of twenty-seven teams. Unfortunately, they fell to twenty-seventh out of twenty-seven teams in *offense* that year. But he did have some success as a GM in Denver; in 1994, the Nuggets pulled one of the all-time NBA playoff upsets when, with their upending of Seattle, they became the first number-eight seed to ever win a postseason series.

After a slow start the following season, Bickerstaff fired Dan

Issel and assumed head coaching duties. The Nuggets were an even .500 and lost in the first round of the playoffs. The following year, the Nuggets slumped and missed the playoffs with a 35–47 record. In late 1996, Bickerstaff departed Denver after his team lost nine of its first thirteen games. The Nuggets went on to win only twenty-one that season, yet their erstwhile coach again found employment, this time with the Washington Bullets. The Bullets won forty-four games that year, twenty-two of them under Bickerstaff's guidance, and went to the playoffs, getting swept in the first round by the juggernaut Bulls. They went 42–40 the following season, missing the playoffs altogether. The year after that, Bickerstaff was let go after the Bullets got off to a 13–19 start. From 2004 to 2007 he coached for almost three seasons with the expansion Charlotte Bobcats. After compiling a 67–161 record he was fired by part-owner Michael Jordan before the end of the 2007 season. He was invited to stay on with the organization in some capacity, of course.

(Note: *Don't sleep on nepotism as another tool by which the old boys further their network. In 2004, the Bobcats hired John-Blair Bickerstaff, who became what was at the time the youngest assistant coach in the NBA at twenty-six years old. Prior experience? J.B. was previously the radio color analyst for the Minnesota Timberwolves. Before that single season of broadcasting work, he served as the director of operations for the University of Minnesota men's basketball program, where he "oversaw all administrative areas of the program." Equipment manager, anyone? John-Blair also worked with Bernie Bickerstaff, a man rumored to be his father, preparing players for predraft workouts in Washington, D.C.*)

Tom Nissalke

Tom.

—Nissalke's response to a reporter's question of how to properly pronounce his name upon being announced as Houston's new coach in 1977

As frightening as that synapse misfire was, it fortunately proved not to be an omen for Nissalke's first year as the Rockets' head coach. Houston went 49–33 that season, winning the NBA's Central Division and advancing to the Eastern Conference Finals. Nissalke even nabbed Coach of the Year honors. However, that response might have been an ominous portent of things to come *after* 1977, as Nissalke-led teams went a combined 186–326 over the next (almost) seven seasons.

Now a much-maligned local radio analyst for the Utah Jazz, Tom Nissalke, like Kevin Loughery, was a head coach in both the NBA and the ABA. His coaching record over thirteen seasons is 371–508. In 1972, he coached the Dallas Chaparrals—quite possibly the worst-nicknamed professional sports team of all time—who eventually moved to San Antonio and became the Spurs. Nissalke was hired in 1973 to coach the Seattle SuperSonics, but was replaced midseason by the happily named Bucky Buckwalter, as the fans and owner Sam Shulman were unsatisfied with the team's 13–32 record. It didn't help that Nissalke was reputedly behind the trade that sent superstar Lenny Wilkens away to the Cleveland Cavaliers.

In '74, Nissalke went back to the Chaparrals, er, the Spurs, but was oddly terminated in his second year with the club, despite starting the season strong at 18–10. It's been reported that ownership was frustrated with Nissalke's conservative coaching style, which encouraged a slower-tempo half-court offense. Translation: even when he was good, he was bad.

Nissalke stayed in the ABA, where he coached the Utah Stars for a little more than a season, then moved back to the NBA. He was with Houston for three years (1977–79); then spent slightly more than two full seasons (1980–82) in Utah, where he earned the proud distinction of being the only head coach fired by the Jazz since they moved from New Orleans in 1979; then moved on to Cleveland for his final two years as an NBA head coach. The Cavaliers, 51–113 in those two years, fired Nissalke with two years remaining on his contract.

THE OLD BOYS OF FOOTBALL

Joe Kuharich

A respected head coach at the University of San Francisco in the postwar years, Joe Kuharich's professional career began in 1952 when he was hired as head coach of the Chicago Cardinals. The Cards went 4–8 in '52, and Kuharich resigned after one season in the Windy City.

This wet fart of a start didn't dissuade Washington owner George Preston Marshall from hiring Kuharich to coach the Redskins prior to the 1954 season. After all, the Cardinals were then, as now, one of the most poorly run outfits in the League. Maybe Kuharich was a misunderstood genius who was caught in a bad situation and just needed the right place for his gifts to shine. Right?

Wrong. The Redskins proceeded to a 3–9 record in Kuharich's first season, giving up a league-worst thirty-six points per game. They improved greatly in 1955, jumping to 8–4 and second place, but that was the high-water mark of Kuharich's tenure in the Capitol. The Redskins dropped to 6–6 in 1956, 5–6–1 in '57, and 4–7–1 in '58, and Kuharich was fired. To be fair, the Redskins endured a run of serious misfortune during his tenure: two players died in off-the-field incidents, star halfback Vic Janowicz's career was ended by brain damage sustained in a car crash, and in 1954 two players who might have been his best—5'8" quarterback Eddie LeBaron and defensive end Gino Brito—defected to Canada. Not to mention Marshall's refusal to sign black players. But Kuharich's 26–32–1 record in D.C. is what it is, all excuses aside.

Kuharich then tried his luck at coaching in the college ranks again, taking the Notre Dame job before the 1959 season. Being a South Bend native was no help; Kuharich failed to break .500 in any of his four seasons under the Golden Dome, and in 1962 he and his 17–23 record were excommunicated.

But Philadelphia Eagles owner Jerry Wolman thought Kuharich was just the man to lead his sorry club back into the League's elite. In 1964, Wolman hired the two-time NFL and onetime Notre Dame reject as coach and general manager. The hiring was an unpopular one

in Philly; Eagles fans were justifiably unimpressed by Kuharich's résumé, and furthermore, the coach alienated fans by trading away several popular players, including Hall of Famer Sonny Jurgenson, who
he dealt to the Redskins for fellow quarterback Norm Snead (see
"The Worst Trades"). Going 11–17 in his first two seasons didn't exactly endear him to the city's passionate fan base, either.

In 1966, however, the Eagles rose to a 9–5 record, their first winning mark in five years and good for a rather distant second in the
NFL's Eastern Conference. The overenthusiastic Wolman, apparently
having never heard the phrase "Second place is the first loser," hastily
signed Kuharich to a whopping fifteen-year contract extension, hailing him as a "savior" and the "coach for life" of the Eagles.

Life is short, as cliché users say. In Kuharich's case, life proved
to be two seasons and an 8–19–1 record.

Kuharich's last season, 1968, was possibly the most exasperating
in the oft-exasperating history of the Philadelphia Eagles franchise.
Finding ways to not get it done week in and week out, the Eagles lost
their first eleven games. Chants of "Joe Must Go!" rang through
Franklin Field throughout the season, and on at least one occasion a
biplane hauling a banner emblazoned with those words buzzed the
old stadium as the beleaguered Kuharich presided over yet another
loss below. The fans' only hope was that the Eagles were bad enough
to secure the following year's top draft pick, which would guarantee
the rights to Heisman Trophy winner O. J. Simpson. But Kuharich's
Eagles mucked up even that. They won two of their last three, dropping them behind Buffalo in the Simpson sweepstakes.

Kuharich ended his career in Philly not with a bang, but with a
"Boo!": it was during his last game, a 24–17 loss to the Vikings,
that Philadelphia fans legendarily heckled and pelted with snowballs a man dressed as Santa Claus as he attempted to bring some
Christmas cheer to a crowd that was in absolutely no mood for it.

Joe Kuharich's career record, in coaching stints with three different NFL teams, was 58–82–3. In eight of his eleven seasons as a
coach, his teams finished at or below .500. And as coach, Kuharich
never sniffed a playoff game. He even helped bankrupt an owner;
Jerry Wolman of the Eagles, who had given Kuharich that fifteen-

year contract, was forced to sell the team in 1969 to keep his kneecaps from being broken. Oddly enough, Kuharich passed away on the same day the Philadelphia Eagles played in Super Bowl XV. Perhaps in his honor, the Eagles lost.

Dave Wannstedt

Dave Wannstedt, the defensive coordinator for the Cowboys championships of the '90s, just couldn't seem to cut it as a head coach. In eleven seasons as head coach with the Chicago Bears and the Miami Dolphins, Wannstedt's teams went 82–86 and made the playoffs just twice, advancing no further than the second round in either trip.

Wannstedt's tenure with the Bears (1993–98) was characterized by a simple lack of talent; in his last five seasons in Chicago, his teams failed to put a single player in the Pro Bowl. His best season in the Midway was 1994, when the Bears went 9–7, squeaked into the NFC playoffs as a wild card, and upset Minnesota in the first round before being destroyed in the second round, 44–15 by the mighty 49ers. (Believe it or not, Wannstedt's 40–56 Bears record puts him third on that franchise's list for victories by a head coach.)

His tenure at Miami (2000–04) was characterized by under-achievement. The Dolphins had talent, especially on defense, but they often teased, then disappointed. They had a winning record in each of their first four seasons under Wannstedt, but they only made the playoffs twice. Other than an overtime win over the Colts in the 2000 wild-card game, the Dolphins put up only token resistance in postseason play, losing to the Raiders and Ravens by a combined score of 47–3.

Wannstedt was quite unpopular in Miami. Prior to the 2003 season, owner Wayne Huizenga attempted to placate grumbling fans by promising that he would fire the coach if the team missed the playoffs that year. Well, it did, but Wannstedt's services were retained anyway. (The old boys have one another's backs.)

In 2004, things really unraveled for the Dolphins. Running back Ricky Williams, the centerpiece of Miami's already-feeble offense, decided to quit the team and go on his now-infamous world cannabis tour, leaving the mustachioed coach in the lurch. After the Dolphins won only one of their first eight games, Wannstedt "resigned."

One would assume that Dave then went back to school, learned a new trade, and pursued an entirely different career. Perhaps real estate. But that's because not everyone's hip to the power of the old boys' network. In December 2004, Dave Wannstedt was announced as the next head coach of Pitt football. In his first two seasons at Pitt, he went 11–12 and failed to make a bowl game. Expect big things in the future from this old boys' rising star.

Mike McCormack

Admittedly, five and a half seasons as a head coach is a limited portfolio in comparison to the relatively greater staying power his old boys' peers have shown. But Mike McCormack's resumé of incompetence takes a backseat to no one one's.

A Hall of Fame lineman under Paul Brown in Cleveland, McCormack's coaching career began in 1962 as an assistant in the annual College All-Star Game, a preseason game played in Soldier Field from 1934 to 1976 between the NFL champions and a team of star college seniors from the previous year. The collegians went 9–31–2 in the series before it was mercifully ended—not that it was McCormack's fault. In fact, perhaps his biggest highlight as a coach came in the '63 College All-Star Game, when he assisted in the All-Stars' shocking victory over Vince Lombardi's Packers.

In 1973, McCormack was hired as head coach of the Philadelphia Eagles. It's been debated whether a helmet change or the makeover of the team's logo was the most exciting thing that happened on his watch. What can't be debated is that McCormack's three-year tenure in Philly was a disaster. Early in the 1975 season, after a 15–13 loss to the Chicago Bears, McCormack remarked sourly that there were "two dogs" on the Eagles roster. That little quip pretty much wiped out any good feeling between the coach and his players, every one of whom knew that he could very well be the "dog" in question. McCormack was fired following the season. His record in Philly was 16–25–1.

After spending several seasons as an assistant, McCormack was hired in 1980 as head coach of the Baltimore Colts. He got the Colts off to a 4–2 start in his first season before the team collapsed to a 7–9 finish. The meltdown became wholesale in '81, as the Baltimore season became a haze of never-ending losing, atrocious attendance, players sleeping in meetings, players getting hurt on the way out to the coin toss (no, seriously), and quite possibly the worst defense in the history of pro football. The '81 Colts went 2–14 and gave up 533 points, still a league record. Needless to say, McCormack was fired following the season. His record in Baltimore was 9–23, including 5–21 in his last twenty-six games.

Amazingly, Mike McCormack resurfaced in a head coaching capacity in 1982, when he took over the Seahawks as interim coach following the firing of Jack Patera. McCormack guided Seattle to a 4–3 record during the strike-marred '82 season. Not bad, but not good enough for the Seahawks, who prudently hired Chuck Knox, a more accomplished member of the old-boy network, to coach the team in 1983. McCormack's head coaching career, thankfully, was over.

In his five and a half seasons as a head coach, McCormack compiled a record of 25–48–1. In his nearly twenty-year professional coaching career, McCormack made it to the playoffs only once: in 1970 as an assistant to Paul Brown with the Cincinnati Bengals. Yet his career in football lasted well into the late '90s, when he retired in 1997 from a front office position with the Carolina Panthers.

Marion Campbell

Marion Campbell, a renowned defensive mind as an assistant for several teams, was no dummy as a football man. But his acumen didn't translate into victories throughout his career as a head coach. In all or parts of nine seasons with three different teams, Campbell compiled a sickly 34–80–1 record. Not only did he never make it to the playoffs, he never had a winning season. His highest single-season winning percentage was a dismal .400.

Campbell's first head coaching gig came with the Atlanta Falcons during the 1974 season. He began as an interim coach, but by the time he was handed the keys, the team was 2–6, having imploded under his volatile predecessor, Norm Van Brocklin. Campbell guided the punchless Falcons (who averaged fewer than eight points per game) to a 1–5 finish. Not really an improvement, but the Falcons made him the regular head coach anyway, perhaps figuring that his name recognition—Campbell was an outstanding linebacker at nearby University of Georgia in the '50s—would beef up the sparse crowds at Fulton County Stadium. After a 4–10 finish in 1975 and a 1–4 start in '76, Atlanta went ahead and fired the coach, name recognition be damned.

Campbell moved on to Philadelphia, where he coached Dick Vermeil's great defenses for the rugged Eagles teams of the late '70s and early '80s. Vermeil thought highly of him, and for good reason: under Campbell's guidance, the Eagles were number one in the NFL in scoring defense in 1980 and '81, and went to the Super Bowl in the first of those years. When Vermeil resigned because of burnout and reputed tear dehydration in 1982, Campbell was the natural choice to succeed him. The Eagles flew straight to the basement of the NFC East under Campbell in 1983, and stayed there in 1984. With one game remaining in the 1985 campaign, and the Eagles going nowhere, Campbell was fired.

Even after all this futility, the Falcons went back to the well, hiring Campbell for his second stint as head coach with the team in 1987. The defensive guru watched as his Falcons unit, second in the league in 1986, dropped to dead last the following season. In fact, the 1987 Falcons pulled off a relatively rare feat: they finished last in total offense, last in total defense, last in scoring offense, and last in scoring defense. It may be redundant to say that they also had the worst record in the league at 3–12.

Two years later, with the Falcons well on their way to their third last-place finish in a row, the organization finally gave up the home-boy-makes-good dream and pulled the plug on Marion Campbell. Campbell's record with the Falcons, '70s and '80s combined, was an excruciating 17–51. They say that you can't go home again. Maybe you can, but sometimes you just shouldn't.

THE ALL-BAD FREE-AGENT PITCHING STAFF

Men Who Weren't Worth the Paper on Which Their Outrageous Contracts Were Printed

A club can't win a championship without good pitching. Yet, thanks in large part to the dilution of talent brought about by expansion, there just isn't that much good pitching out there. The laws of scarcity kick in and, as a result, some very large dollar amounts are thrown at players who plain don't deserve them. This leads to a pitiful domino effect: money better invested elsewhere is tied up in one albatross of a contract. Other needs go unattended, flexibility in signing other players is lost, the other guys in the clubhouse resent the would-be superstar for stealing their paychecks, and so on. In a nutshell, it sucks for everyone, except for maybe the guy who got paid.

The All-Bad Free-Agent Pitching Staff is merely a snapshot of the grisly history of high-priced signings that have gone terribly, terribly wrong. Unfortunately, this staff of woe stands no chance of serving as a cautionary tale for owners of big-league teams, who will continue to throw good money after bad in the ever-desperate attempt to shore up this most important and elusive element of a good ball club.

HIDEKI IRABU, NEW YORK YANKEES

A massive star in Japan, Irabu high-handedly refused to play with any American club other than the Yankees. So New York traded with the Padres for his rights, then signed him to a four-year, $12.8 million contract. Irabu went 29–20 with the Yankees from 1997 to 1999, but had an ERA (4.96) as chubby as his 240-pound body. Thanks to manager Joe Torre's reluctance to use him in any situations perceived as actually meaningful, Irabu was also useless in the postseason, appearing just once for the Yankees and piling up a 13.50 ERA.*

MIKE HAMPTON, COLORADO ROCKIES

In his first six full seasons (1995–2000) as a starter in Houston and New York, Mike Hampton's highest ERA was 3.83. Prior to the 2001 season, he signed an eight-year, $121 million contract with the Rockies. Hampton's ERA ballooned to 5.41 in his first season in Denver, then to 6.15 the following year. For good measure, he also threw in a 7–15 record. Just two years into his ginormous contract, Hampton, yet another casualty of that thin Colorado air, was bundled off to Atlanta. His ERA promptly went on a diet and slimmed back down to 3.84.**

JAIME NAVARRO, CHICAGO WHITE SOX

Early in 1997, the Pale Hose penned Navarro to a four-year, $20 million contract following a couple of excellent seasons with the rival Cubs. In three seasons on the South Side, Navarro went 25–43 with a hideous 6.06 ERA, all while being the second-highest-paid

* Irabu gave up sixty-eight home runs as a Yankee, which gave birth to Stuart Scott's home run call: "Iraaaaaa-BOO-YAH!" As it happens, this is officially the only slightly amusing catchphrase Stu has ever uttered in his *SportsCenter* career.
** Hampton, an outstanding hitter for a pitcher, hit .315 with ten home runs and a .552 slugging percentage in 143 at-bats with the Rockies. So he took back at least a little of what he so often gave out.

player on his team. These two fun facts didn't sit well with the White Sox faithful.

WAYNE GARLAND, CLEVELAND INDIANS

The Tribe signed Garland, fresh off a twenty-win season in Baltimore, to a ten-year, $2.3 million deal in 1977. That's right, you read correctly, *ten* years. In his first spring training with the Indians, Garland tore his rotator cuff. He went 28–50 with Cleveland, and had been out of baseball five years when he received his last paycheck from the contract in 1986. Making matters worse, Garland squandered much of the money on schemes that were worse investments than he had been for the Indians.

Garland, in a 1990 *Sports Illustrated* story on the first free-agent class, complained that Cleveland fans seemed to think he was actually a millionaire, even though his contract only paid roughly $200,000 per annum. "People would see me on the street and say, 'There goes the millionaire.' "

CHAN HO PARK, TEXAS RANGERS

Arlington has long been a graveyard for pitchers, but Chan Ho Park's Ranger headstone is a bit pricier than most. Signed to a lucrative deal in the winter of 2002, Chan spent three and a half seasons in Texas: he won twenty-two, lost twenty-six, had a 5.80 ERA, and spent long stretches on the disabled list. He made more than $50 million doing so.

MATT YOUNG, BOSTON RED SOX

Historically not known for shrewd thinking when it comes to pitchers, the Red Sox signed Young, a 51–79 lifetime hurler who had lost eighteen games the previous year in Seattle, to a three-year, $6.4 million contract on December 4, 1990. That he was a dismal stinker in Boston, going 3–11 with a 4.91 ERA in two seasons, shouldn't have been a surprise to anyone with any inkling about the game, which may or may not describe every single person in the Red Sox front office at the time.*

RUSS ORTIZ, ARIZONA DIAMONDBACKS

In 2003, Ortiz was a twenty-one-game winner for Atlanta. He'd won at least fourteen in six consecutive seasons before signing a four-year, $33 million deal with the D-Backs in 2005. In a nightmarish season and a half in the desert, Ortiz went 5–16 with a 6.99 ERA before Arizona designated him for assignment and then traded him to Baltimore, not even two years into his meaty contract.

CARL PAVANO, NEW YORK YANKEES

Appropriately enough, the Yankees have two pitchers on this All-Bad staff. In the winter of 2005, they signed Pavano, a twenty-nine-year-old righty coming off an eighteen-win season in Florida, to a four-year contract worth just under $40 million. The Yankees thought Pavano was becoming the top-of-the-rotation stalwart the Pin-striped Ones had craved for years. What he turned out to be was a black hole of wildly expensive injuries.

After a truncated 2005 in which he went 4–6 with a 4.77 ERA, Pavano was a tenured member of the disabled list for all of the '06 season with, among other ailments, two broken ribs from a motorcycle accident. New York's thin and aging staff was a major contributor to the Yankees playoffs defeat in both of those seasons. Meanwhile, $17 million of George Steinbrenner's money disappeared into the pocket of a pitcher who wasn't doing any pitching.**

---

* Matt Young pitched a no-hitter for the Red Sox in Cleveland on April 12, 1992. But he still lost 2–1, mainly because he walked seven batters and allowed six stolen bases.

** Red Sox fans revel in their rival's misfortunes, and Carl Pavano has made a career out of benefiting New York's bitter enemy in Boston. In 1998, the Red Sox traded Pavano, then a stud prospect in their farm system, to Montreal for Pedro Martinez, who became the best pitcher in the history of the Red Sox franchise.

DON STANHOUSE, LOS ANGELES DODGERS

In Baltimore, they called Stanhouse "Full Pack," because that's how many cigarettes Earl Weaver nervously puffed through watching the frizzy-haired fireman eke out another save for the Orioles. In 1979, the Dodgers needed to rebuild their bull pen, so they signed Stanhouse to a five-year, $2.1 million contract that November. In one season in Los Angeles, he transformed from Full Pack to Full Platter. That was how much comfort food Tommy Lasorda needed in order to withstand seeing Stanhouse win two games, save just seven, and run up a 5.04 ERA, all the while working in one of baseball's most pitching-friendly ballparks. On April 15, 1981, just one year into his contract, the Dodgers cut Stanhouse. "Somewhere the guy just lost his stuff," shrugged team president Al Campanis. Yeah, maybe on the transcontinental flight from Baltimore.

MARK DAVIS, KANSAS CITY ROYALS

It took a then–Major League record four-year, $14 million contract to bring Mark Davis, the 1989 NL Cy Young Award–winning closer, to Kansas City. Davis had saved forty-four games in '89. In parts of three seasons with the Royals he had a total of seven saves, along with a 9–13 record and a 5.31 ERA.*

* In 1990, the Royals—yes, the Royals—had the highest payroll in baseball.

Jean Van de Velde gets his footsies wet as he implodes and gift wraps the 1999 British Open. *AP Images/Ben Curtis*

CHOKERY

The world of sports brings pressure to bear, and the worth of an athlete is measured by how well he or she responds to it. Some step up to the challenge; some do not. And when the meltdowns do occur, the resulting spectacle warrants official documentation and subsequent discussion, ad nauseum.

* ★ SELF-DESTRUCTION!
* ★ GREAT INDIVIDUAL MELTDOWNS OF THE '90s
* ★ THREE BAD CALLS
* ★ DEMOLISHED AT THE GATES
* ★ AND ONE VERY, VERY *FORTUNATE* COLLAPSE

SELF-DESTRUCTION!

The '95 Angels and Their Surge of Incompetence

Through the first few weeks of the 1995 season, it looked like business as usual in the feeble American League West, the worst division in baseball. Only the 1994 players' strike kept the division from being won by a team below .500, and with all four West clubs at a seemingly uniform level of mediocrity, it looked as if 1995 would be another year of forgettable baseball in the division.

Then the California Angels, who had finished a sickly 47–68 in 1994, began to win in bunches. A seven-game winning streak propelled California into first place in late May. Texas and Oakland hung tough, and on July 1 the Rangers were on top of the division by a game over the Angels and a game and a half over the Athletics. Then the Angels got hot again. They went 20–6 in July while the Rangers and Athletics slumped. By the end of the month, California was twenty-one games over .500 and held a ten-game lead, distinguishing itself as a new power to be reckoned with in the American League.

A marriage of a good base of experience and an explosion of youthful talent made great things possible, as a number of promising Angels hit their career strides in '95. Twenty-seven-year-old first baseman J. T. Snow blossomed in the field and at the plate. Twenty-five-year-old Jim Edmonds became one of the game's top center fielders. Twenty-six-year-old power hitter Tim Salmon was having the best season of his young career. Twenty-two-year-old rookie Garret Anderson barreled onto the scene with a .321 batting average and sixteen home runs. Thirty-six-year-old Tony Phillips arrived from Detroit and provided versatility and veteran leadership.

And the glue that held it all together was shortstop Gary Di-Sarcina. The twenty-seven-year-old had never hit above .260 in his career, but was playing like a man possessed in '95, hitting over .300, solidifying the infield defense, and rounding out the powerful lineup with back-of-the-order punch.

Starting pitching was an area of concern. Other than the one-two southpaw combo of Chuck Finley and Mark Langston, the rotation was shallow. But the Angels got by on the combined efforts of a number of journeymen—Shawn Boskie, Brian Anderson, and Jim Abbott—to fill the remaining starts, let the offense pound out the lead, and safely deliver games to their dynamic bullpen duo of Troy Percival and gritty old Lee Smith.

California continued to streak as August opened. On August 3, in the seventh inning of a 10–7 loss to the Mariners, Gary DiSarcina tore ligaments in his right thumb sliding into second base and was lost for several weeks. Employing a ramshackle platoon at short, the Angels kept playing solid ball, going 8–4 in the first twelve games after the loss of DiSarcina. But the loss was a crucial one.

By August 15, the Halos were in cruise control, gliding along with a ten-and-a-half-game lead in the West. California's 64–38 record was second-best in the AL to Cleveland's 67–33, but the Angels were leading the league in runs scored, were third in runs allowed, and had the best run differential in the league by a fairly wide margin. By many a measure they looked like the best team in the league, and a likely pick to represent the AL in the World Series that fall.

Even if the Angels played .500 ball in their last forty-two games, the second-place Mariners would have to close out with a 32–11 spurt just to get a tie at the end of the season.

On August 16, 1995, at Comiskey Park, starter Brian Anderson and two Halo relievers were rocked for fourteen hits in a 9–2 White Sox romp. Over the next eight games the Angels sputtered, going 3–5. On the night of August 24, after a victory over Baltimore, their lead stood at eight and a half games. But after months of sunny skies, the storm arrived—with a vengeance.

Starting with an 11–2 flattening at the hands of the Orioles, California lost nine straight games by a combined score of 71–23. Everything collapsed at once. Angel hurlers were blowtorched, posting an 8.62 team ERA during the skein of horror, and the young hitters were all cooling off at the same time. Finally, on September 4, the Halos stopped the bleeding with a 5–3 win over Baltimore. Since August 15, California was 4–15. Yet their lead was still a relatively solid six and a half games. Seattle wasn't playing inspired baseball either, going just 8–10 since California's slump began. If the Angels could regroup, the division was still theirs.

The club muddled along, going 5–3 in the next eight days. On September 12, they defeated the White Sox to maintain their six-game lead over Seattle. The worst seemed behind them. There were only sixteen games left in the regular season. Surely they would hold off the Mariners, who still weren't playing particularly consistent ball. The Angels had four games to go on their current home stand and faced an interdivisional road trip that would take them to Oakland, Texas, and finally, Seattle, for a two-game series in the Kingdome. A split in the ten games preceding the Seattle series would guarantee the Halos at least a one-game lead going into the Emerald City.

California proceeded to drop the last four games of the home stand—a 6–1 loss to the White Sox and a three-game sweep at the hands of the Royals, in which Kansas City bombarded the Angels staff for twenty-two runs. Seattle finally began to heat up. The Angels headed to Oakland just three games ahead of the Mariners, with two weeks to go in the season. The race was slipping away, and it was happening quickly.

In Oakland, the A's Doug Johns kicked them while they were down, befuddling the Angels with a two-hit shutout. The following night, DiSarcina finally returned as a pinch runner, and the Halos scored two in the ninth to tie the game 2–2. But Oakland extended the losing streak to six with a run in the tenth. The Athletics completed the sweep and made it seven in a row by scoring the game's first nine runs and hanging on to win despite a six-run Cali rally in the ninth. Seattle, meanwhile, got its ninth win in eleven games, rolling over the Rangers 11–3. It was September 20. After seventy-nine uninterrupted days at the top, the Angels had fallen out of sole possession of first place.

Having blown the lead, the Angels now proceeded to fall behind. An 8–3 California loss in Arlington, coupled with a Seattle win over Oakland, put the Mariners out in front by a game. The losing streak reached nine and the deficit two before one-armed Jim Abbott stepped up and delivered a three-hit shutout that temporarily stopped the bleeding. One week remained, and the Angels were in Seattle, needing to take both games just to restore a division deadlock.

It didn't happen. On September 26, in a rare weekday game played before forty-seven thousand hooky-playing, bandwagon Seattle fans, the Mariners jumped all over the dimming Halos, pounding out a 10–2 rout that stretched their lead to three games with five to play. Since the high-water mark of August 15, California was 9–28 with not one but two nine-game losing streaks, and had lost thirteen and a half games in the standings.

With all seemingly lost, the Angels got hot. They won their last five, salvaging the final game of the Seattle series and taking four straight from the Athletics. Seattle still led by two with two to play, and lost them both. California forced a tie on the final day of the regular season, routing the Athletics, 8–2, while Seattle was losing in Texas. A playoff was necessary.

It went down on October 2, 1995, in the Kingdome. The Angels competed valiantly against Randy Johnson and the partisan crowd. Mark Langston and the Big Unit dueled through four scoreless innings. In the fifth, a Vince Coleman single gave the Mariners a 1–0 lead.

The bottom of the seventh brought the killer blow to the Angels. Seattle's Mike Blowers opened the inning with a single, Tino Martinez beat out a bunt, and a sacrifice moved the runners along. Langston hit Joey Cora with a pitch, loading the bases with one out. A flyout held the runners. But one batter later, Luis Soho opened the floodgates with a bases-clearing double down the right-field line. When the unnerved Langston let the relay get by him, Soho, an ex-Angel, came all the way around to score, beating the throw to the utter delight of the crowd. The Little League grand slam made it 5–0, M's.

The Angels were comatose. Seattle tacked on four more in the eighth. With two outs in the ninth and the score 9–1, Tim Salmon was all that stood between the Angels and oblivion. Salmon became the Big Unit's twelfth strikeout victim, and it was all over. The California Angels, arguably the best team in the American League in the first four months of the season, would watch the playoffs from home.

Late-season pennant-race collapses are overrated, because they focus too much on the demerits of the "collapsing" team and not enough on the merits of the team that comes from behind. The '51 Dodgers didn't play badly late in the season (26–22 in their last forty-eight games), but the '51 Giants went a ridiculous 37–7 down the stretch and simply gobbled up a thirteen-game deficit. The '78 Yankees went 51–21 after July 19 to catch the Red Sox, who went 37–35 in the same span. The '93 Braves erased a nine-and-a-half-game August 7 deficit to the Giants by going a mind-blowing 39–11 to San Francisco's good, but not good enough, 29–22. Countless pennant-winning teams have built up big late-summer leads and lazily cruised home. What usually makes for a historic "collapse" is another team, a wild card that gets very, very hot.

And that team didn't really exist in 1995. Seattle went just 25–18 in its last forty-three games. That's good baseball, but it should have taken great baseball to overcome a double-digit deficit in the last month and a half. Given Seattle's real progress, the Angels would have needed to go only 15–27 after August 15 to hold on to the lead and win the West. Achieving that exceedingly modest task should have been easy for any contending team. But it was not. It took the greatest late-season collapse in baseball history to lose the division. The Mariners didn't run the Angels down from behind. The Angels ran them down from ahead.

For California, the aftershock was as powerful as that of a Golden State earthquake. The 1996 Angels lost ninety-one games and finished last in the division. Prior to the '97 season, the franchise changed its surname to the "Anaheim" Angels—anything to erase the stain of the greatest month-and-a-half meltdown in baseball history.

GREAT INDIVIDUAL
MELTDOWNS OF THE '90S

From Kurt Cobain to the video for Pearl Jam's "Jeremy" to pretending that swing music was cool, self-obliteration was all the rage during the '90s. And the trend carried over into sports, as athletes male and female made like a Vietnamese monk and immolated themselves in front of the masses.

BLACK SUNDAY—GREG NORMAN, 1996 MASTERS

Greg, old boy, there's no way you can f— this up now!
—Old friend of Greg Norman's, Saturday night at the '96 Masters

In building a reputation as a man who always found a way to lose at Augusta, Greg Norman, to a certain extent, was a victim of the fates as much as his own play. It wasn't his bad play that cost him the Masters in 1986 so much as Jack Nicklaus's brilliant back nine. Norman couldn't have run out onto the course and blocked Larry Mize's tournament-winning chip the following year. Defenders of the hale Australian could have pointed to the fates as the ultimate culprit in his haunted history at Augusta, and had they done so, they would have had a point. Until 1996.

Right from the opening day of the '96 Masters, when he shot a tournament-record 63, Greg Norman was brilliant. He built his lead relentlessly, warding off all comers. Striking and charismatic, he was always popular, and as he built a six-stroke lead over two-time winner Nick Faldo through Saturday, the galleries roared their approval. They wanted to see the Shark close it out this time. Yet under the elation was a whisper of anxiety—after all, this was Greg Norman at Augusta.

Norman opened Sunday with a bogey on 1 to see his lead drop immediately to five strokes. He bogeyed on 4, and like a Wrigley Field playoff crowd, the galleries began to see and feel the ghosts. Norman bogeyed on 9. He bogeyed again on 10, bogeyed *again* on 11, and finally double-bogeyed the par-three twelfth hole, dunking his tee shot in Rae's Creek and with it a share of the lead. Going into the ninth hole, Norman had still been four strokes ahead of Nick Faldo. By the time the Shark meekly holed out on 12, he trailed by two.

Faldo (who shot a sensational 67) was watching Norman's struggles with more horror than elation. He wanted his third green jacket—but not like this. There was agony in the galleries and among the millions watching on television who identified and empathized with the pathos of Norman, hunched obsessively over his ball, visibly crumbling under the strain.

The dying Shark kept pace with Faldo through the next three holes, barely missing an eagle chip on 15. When his tee shot hooked into the water on 16, he was finished. Leading by six going in, Norman's final-round 78 had put him into second place—by five full strokes.

After holing out on a funereal 18 for the win, Nick Faldo hugged Norman and apologized for what had happened. The Englishman knew his third Masters championship was destined for afterthought status. Norman was the real story, the garrulous, ruddy Australian, a larger-than-life figure with very platinum hair, laid low by a lil' old golf course in Georgia . . . and the most frustrating freaking game on the face of the earth.

"FAULT!"—JANA NOVOTNA, 1993 WIMBLEDON FINALS

Jana Novotna finally seemed on the verge of a long-awaited tournament victory as the 1993 Wimbledon Championship wound down. The twenty-five-year-old Czech, who was always at her strongest on grass courts, fought her way through the draw in Cinderella form. In the semifinals, she Novot-knocked out Martina Navratilova to reach the championship, where she met the best female tennis professional of the day—Steffi Graf, who was cruising toward a third straight Wimbledon crown as if it were scripted.

But Novotna was ready for a fight, and it turned out to be a good old-fashioned European blood feud in front of the privileged. For two exhausting hours and fourteen grueling minutes, Graf and Novotna traded volleys. Graf fought off the challenger in an 8–6 pitched battle of a first set. Novotna took the second easily, 6–1. It was down to one set: winner take all.

Novotna dominated the third set right from the start. As she built her lead, confusing the German champion, onlookers saw a classic upset unfolding. Novotna built her lead up to 4–1. She had taken ten of the last twelve sets from Graf, and wasted no time building up a 40–15 lead in this one. Holding serve, she was one swing away from being one point away from victory at Wimbledon.

That's when everything went sideways.

First she double-faulted. Graf stormed back to take the game and cruised to the next one as well. Novotna again double-faulted, couldn't hold serve, and again Graf was victorious. The set was tied, 4–4. The Novotna who had performed splendidly throughout the tournament and for most of the final match had suddenly vanished. Her replacement was a nervous, jittery wreck who looked like she'd known how to play tennis for about a week. From serves driven into the net to return volleys knocked wildly in every direction except the correct one, the newbie's repertoire was on full display—except that this newbie had been on the verge of winning Wimbledon just a few minutes earlier.

Graf swept the next game to make it 5–4 and proceeded to routinely, coldly dispatch her shell-shocked opponent. It was over, just like that. Steffi Graf raised the enormous piece of dinnerware over her head for the third consecutive year. The Duchess of Kent held a weeping Jana Novotna in her arms. Five years later, on the verge of retirement, she would finally win her Wimbledon title.

A VACANT LOOK IN HIS EYES—JOSE MESA, 1997 WORLD SERIES

Even in the best of times, nobody ever called Jose Mesa stable. Even during his brilliant 1995 season, when he saved forty-six games for the Indians and had a 1.12 ERA, he bore the markings of an emotional wreck. Tony Pena, Cleveland's grizzled backup catcher, would occasionally stalk to the mound and slap Mesa upside the head with his glove to get him to focus.

But the man fans referred to as "Joe Table" was the closer, and when the Tribe entered the ninth inning with a lead, the burly Dominican was always the choice, for better or for worse. So manager Mike Hargrove didn't hesitate to call on Mesa in the bottom of the ninth of Game Seven of the 1997 World Series, with his team holding on to a 2–1 lead over the Florida Marlins.

What followed became history, and not the good kind. Moises Alou, a Cleveland killer the entire Series, opened the Florida ninth with a clean single up the middle. Eschewing his trademark fastball for the slider, Mesa struck out Bobby Bonilla, setting up a possible game-ending double play. But on a 1–2 pitch, he threw a slider that Charles Johnson dumped into right, sending Alou all the way to third. Craig Counsell followed with a long fly to right, driving Manny Ramirez deep for the catch and bringing home the tying run.

And with that banal little sequence, one that would have been quickly forgotten had it happened in, say, Kansas City in April, Mesa and the 1997 Cleveland Indians became the first team ever to blow a ninth-inning lead in Game Seven of the World Series. They would lose in the eleventh, on Counsell's single over the head of Charles Nagy, who was probably thinking that he shouldn't have even been there that day.

Jose Mesa was booed out of Cleveland early the next season and, as if wearing the mark of Cain, embarked on an off-and-on tour of baseball's less prestigious outposts. No logical explanation can be found for why he abandoned his bread-and-butter fastball in the biggest inning of his career. Several years later, Tribe shortstop Omar Vizquel wrote an autobiography entitled *Omar!* (yes—*with* the exclamation point) in which he claimed Mesa had "a vacant look in his eyes" during that ninth inning in Miami. Mesa responded by threatening to kill Vizquel and, not satisfied with empty threats, throwing at him every time the two faced each other—as ever, one unstable table.

LIKE SEDAN ALL OVER AGAIN—JEAN VAN DE VELDE, 1999 BRITISH OPEN

I'm definitely going to start thinking, because my IQ is a little bit over 10.

—Jean Van de Velde

With a three-stroke lead over Paul Lawrie and Justin Leonard, course leader Jean Van de Velde had it all going his way as he stepped to the eighteenth tee on Sunday of the 1999 British Open at Carnoustie in Scotland. Lawrie (who had shot a tournament-best 67 on Sunday just to get within screaming distance) and Leonard were already in the clubhouse. All Van de Velde had to do was double-bogey, at worst, and the Open was his.

The eighteenth hole was a 487-yard par-four. The Barry Burn, a deep ditch with a creek at its bottom, ran along the left side of the fairway before tacking right to form a moat separating the fairway from the green. With the burn and its wild roughs, 18 was a typical shrieking bitch of a Scottish golf hole. But Van de Velde had tamed it thus far, saving par on Thursday and dropping birdie putts on 18 the next two days as he built his lead. His Saturday birdie was a thing of beauty—a 45-footer that he dropped in with an eight-iron from off the green.

The birdies were a result of *cojones* not seen on a Frenchman since the days of Marshal Pétain. While most golfers used an iron off the tee at 18, playing for a par, Van de Velde had used a driver, aggressively going for the pin on his second shot. It was a high-risk, high-reward strategy given the numerous hazards, especially the Barry Burn. It had served Van de Velde well thus far. But daring was not needed here. After all, he just needed a double bogey. Everyone expected Van de Velde to play it safe this time with an iron shot off the tee.

Out came the driver. Van de Velde's tee shot went slicing way off to the right, coming to rest on the neighboring seventeenth fairway. He still had five strokes to give, and two options for his second shot. The first—the reasonable, sensible option—was to simply get back onto the eighteenth fairway and play it from there. The second, clearly ludicrous option was to go directly for the green, which Van de Velde couldn't even see from where his ball was located.

Van de Velde went for the green. The ball sliced again, ricocheted off the grandstand to audible screams from the gallery, bounced off a wall of the Barry Burn, and somehow hopped back onto dry land, coming to rest in the rough just in front of the Burn. It was a huge break for Van de Velde; he was just thirty yards from the green, and even after two awful golf shots, he still had four strokes to give. It was still easy money.

Van de Velde's third shot chili-dipped directly into the burn, once more to gasps from the crowd. Knowing a penalty would leave him with just two strokes to give for the victory, he took off his shoes and socks, rolled up his pantaloons, climbed into the burn, and set up to somehow lay up from where his ball sat, about an inch deep in the little brook. There was none of the visible, red-faced strain of Greg Norman. Instead, a small, enigmatic smile sat on Van de Velde's Gallic face. He seemed to be the embodiment of a French existentialist fantasy. "The British Open? *Injustifié!* Pointless! As is all existence!"

Dissuaded from laying up from the burn, Van de Velde took the penalty stroke and made his drop. His fifth shot dropped blandly into the rough. He finally made it to the green with his sixth, leaving himself with an eight-footer to force a three-way playoff.

He nailed it. Perfect. More torture. *Pourquoi pas?*

The following day, Paul Lawrie, Justin Leonard, and Van de Velde slogged through a wet, hideous, four-hole playoff that for the Frenchman was little more than a formality. Lawrie, a native Scot, continued his hot streak and shot even par for the victory, to the delight of his countrymen. Leonard finished a distant three strokes back. So did Jean Van de Velde, who missed the chance to become the first Frenchman to win the British Open since 1907.

"There are worse things in life," Van de Velde said. True. But there aren't any worse collapses in golf—ever.

THREE BAD CALLS

The Worst of Coaching Decisions in a Championship

ince it takes a pretty good coach to win a championship, it stands to reason that it takes a pretty good coach to *lose* one. The three men on this list were all highly accomplished and well respected in their fields, and on the vast majority of occasions made the right moves to help their teams win. In these three cases, however, um, no.

SLOW IT DOWN!—GUY LEWIS, HEAD COACH, UNIVERSITY OF HOUSTON, 1983 NCAA BASKETBALL CHAMPIONSHIP GAME

Guy V. Lewis coached for thirty-two years and won 592 games at the University of Houston, leading his team to five Final Fours. He never won a championship. And in his dream shot, he may have coached himself right into a loss.

The number-one-ranked Houston Cougars came into the 1983 Championship game riding a twenty-five-game winning streak and had just buried number two Louisville in the semifinal, the brothers of Phi Slamma Jamma devastating the Cardinals with a 21–1 second-half run. North Carolina State had to win the ACC Tournament just to get into the NCAAs, needed two overtimes to beat little Pepperdine in the first round, and came into the title matchup at the Pit in Albuquerque an overwhelming underdog to Clyde Drexler, Hakeem Olajuwon, and Co.

N.C. State flipped the script. Employing a slowdown game to frustrate the high-scoring Cougars and getting free help from Drexler's early foul woes, the Wolfpack jumped out to a 6–0 lead and led 33–25 at halftime. But the Cougars were a second-half team, and right out of the halftime locker room they embarked on a 17–2 run to roar by N.C. State. It was exactly the kind of run that had destroyed Louisville two nights earlier, and it looked to end in Houston's first-ever NCAA basketball title.

With nine minutes left, the Cougars led 42–35 and had everything going their way. The Houston players, accustomed to getting up and down the floor in a hurry, were eager to keep running and put away the panting Wolfpack. But Guy Lewis wanted to burn some time in those pre-shot clock days and force N.C. State out of its zone defense and into a man-to-man defense that would create layup and dunk opportunities. Lewis ordered his team to spread the floor and sit on the basketball.

If the move distressed the Houston players, it must have elated N.C. State coach Jim Valvano, who had talked before the game of his desire to slow down the Houston fast break and keep the final score in the 40s or 50s. Lewis's decision to stall played right into N.C. State's hands. The Wolfpack began to creep back into it, aided by some outstanding long-distance shooting and Valvano's successful strategy of intentionally fouling the Cougars, who were a terrible free-throw shooting team. Still trailing 52–46 with three minutes left, N.C. State scored the game's last eight points, winning it all on Lorenzo Charles's put-back slam over Olajuwon at the buzzer. After the game, Jim Valvano famously ran around the University Arena floor, looking for someone to hug. He should have found Guy V. Lewis.

"SCREEN!"—JOE GIBBS, HEAD COACH, WASHINGTON REDSKINS, SUPER BOWL XVIII

There were twelve seconds left in the first half of Super Bowl XVIII, and things were not going well for the Washington Redskins. The Los Angeles Raiders were shutting down Washington's record-breaking offense, stonewalling John Riggins and harassing Joe Theismann on his pass attempts. As if that wasn't enough, L.A. scored its opening touchdown by dealing Washington its first blocked punt of the season. With time almost gone before recess, Washington, trailing 14–3, had the ball on its own twelve-yard line.

With eighty-eight yards to traverse and twelve seconds in which to do it, your average mortal would elect to take a knee and get to the locker room posthaste. But the fertile mind of Joe Gibbs flashed back to his team's dramatic win early in the season over these same Los Angeles Raiders. The Redskins had been backed up on their end of the field in that game and had run a quick screen pass to Joe Washington that popped for a sixty-seven-yard gain. Sensing that his struggling team needed a boost, Gibbs sent Little Joe and his old-fashioned face mask into the ball game and called for the screen.

Raiders defensive assistant Charlie Sumner remembered that earlier play too, though, and while Gibbs across the way dreamed of a quick dose of "mo," Sumner laid plans for an ambush. He yanked starting linebacker Matt Millen and replaced him with backup Jack Squirek, who was taller and faster than Millen. Sumner instructed Squirek to shadow Joe Washington.

Sure enough, when Theismann faded back and Joe Washington drifted out to the left, Squirek was ready. He broke on the softly thrown pass, yanked it out of the air, and was in the end zone before he touched the ground. The Redskins had been losing, 14–3. Now they were getting their asses kicked, 21–3. What might have been a salvageable situation became unsalvageable in the amount of time it took for the call to be made. The Raiders rolled to a 38–9 rout, in what was then the largest-ever margin of victory in a Super Bowl. It was a stunning end to the season for the mighty Redskins, who had been a three-point favorite going into the game.

YOU'RE GOING TO START WHO?—JOE McCARTHY, MANAGER, BOSTON RED SOX, 1948 AMERICAN LEAGUE PLAYOFF

The Red Sox had just finished a bitter, yearlong American League pennant fight in a flat-footed tie with the Cleveland Indians. The two clubs met to decide the league championship the day after the regular season—a winner-take-all showdown in Boston's Fenway Park. Now Boston manager Joe McCarthy would earn his salary and pick a starting pitcher for the most important game of his club's season.

Ellis Kinder and Mel Parnell, two of Boston's four top-line starters with a combined 25–15 record, were rested and ready to go. Either man expected to get the call and take the hill against the Indians. But McCarthy had a surprise in store. He selected as his playoff starter Denny Galehouse, a thirty-six-year-old spot starter who had gone just 8–7 during the '48 regular season.

The move didn't make much sense. McCarthy had better options at his disposal. The last time Galehouse had started against Cleveland, on August 25 at Fenway Park, the Tribe had romped over the ex–St. Louis Brown, 9–0. Maybe McCarthy got cocky and decided to save his top-of-the-line starters for the upcoming all-Hub World Series against the Boston Braves.

Whatever the reason, McCarthy's choice of a mediocre journeyman produced mediocre journeyman results. The Indians hounded Galehouse to the showers in a four-run fourth inning that broke the game open, and cruised to an 8–3 victory. Cleveland's shortstop manager, Lou Boudreau, having a far better day than his counterpart, went 4-for-4 and blasted two home runs over the "Mawnstuh" in left. The Tribe then beat the other Boston team in the World Series, ruining the winter of every single baseball fan in the Old Town and beyond.

DEMOLISHED AT THE GATES

The Worst of Team Performances in a Championship

It happens. Sometimes a talented, experienced, smoothly running team will come out for a game or series . . . and get waxed. The explanations for these brutal performances aren't complex. Hell, everyone has a bad game. But it's the timing and the stage that makes a championship breakdown stand out.

THE 3–0 CHOKERS

In the history of modern sport's postseason play, only two teams had lost a best-of-seven playoff series after cruising to three-love: the 1942 Detroit Red Wings and the 1975 Pittsburgh Penguins. That is, until 2004, when the New York Yankees joined this forsaken club and made it a threesome with their storybook collapse to the Boston Red Sox in the American League Championship Series.

1942 Red Wings

The 1941–42 hockey season is considered the last year before the "modern" NHL began. The following season, the "Original Six"—

Canadiens, Maple Leafs, Bruins, Red Wings, Blackhawks, and Rangers—became the core and only teams in professional hockey, staying that way until 1967, when the NHL commenced its over-expansion/hyperdilution strategy.

If it was going to be the last year of premodern hockey, the Red Wings were seemingly determined to have the season remembered for something—they just took a while to get motivated. Detroit struggled to a 19–25–4 record and fourth-place finish, barely edging the Brooklyn Americans for cellar-dweller honors, and thus, the odd team out of the playoffs. Having snuck into the playoffs by the hair of their chinny-chin-chins, however, Detroit was energized. Facing the Bruins in the semifinals, the Red Wings picked up their first upset of the postseason, winning the best-of-three set, two games to one. They would face second-seeded Toronto, who had already knocked off the favored New York Rangers, in the finals.

The Red Wings, riding a scoring flurry—twelve goals in the first three games—stormed to a commanding 3–0 lead. They then folded like loose leaf at an origami convention. The Maple Leafs woke up, realized they were playing the hapless Wings, and forced the series to a deciding seventh game, the first in NHL history. They won, 3–1, giving the Wings some dubious history of their own. Detroit went back to the finals in 1943 and this time finished off a sweep of the Boston Bruins.

1975 Pittsburgh Penguins

The Penguins got off to a fast start in the '75 Stanley Cup playoffs, defeating the St. Louis Blues 2–0 in the best-of-three opening round, and advanced to meet the New York Islanders in the quarterfinals. Although the teams had been only one point apart in the standings in the regular season, Pittsburgh looked dominant early in the series, winning the first three and not trailing for a single second in those games. An all-Pennsylvania Cup semifinal between the Pens and the Philadelphia Flyers looked imminent. Then the young Islanders, an embryonic version of the team that would terrorize the NHL in the early '80s, struck back. They swept the last four, outscoring the Pens 12–4 (ironically, not trailing for a second of those games) and clinching the comeback with a 1–0 white-knuckler in front of a mournful Civic Arena crowd. The Igloo proceeded to melt: the following season the Penguins declared bankruptcy and creditors padlocked their front offices. Although a white knight investor syndicate saved the team from bankruptcy court, by that time one of the sadder sagas in Pittsburgh sports history had already been recorded.*

2004 New York Yankees

The Yankees roll-over-and-play-dead embarrassment in the 2004 ALCS is and will remain one of the most discussed events in the history of games. From Big Papi's repeated heroics to A-Rawd's improbable drop on the loser barometer, it was a collapse for the ages. The Red Sox would go on to win the World Series for the first time in eighty-six years, going from fan favorite to bandwagoner's flypaper. Considering the stakes—"1918!"—their subsequent sweep of the Cardinals was one of the biggest World Series afterthoughts of all time. As time passes, the 2004 baseball season will mostly be remembered for the big choke in the Big Apple.

FRONT-RUNNERS—WASHINGTON REDSKINS, 1940 NFL CHAMPIONSHIP GAME

Late in the 1940 season, the first-place Chicago Bears came to D.C. to take on the first-place Redskins in what everyone knew would be a preview of the NFL Championship Game. Living up to its advance billing, the battle between conference leaders was tight and low scoring. Washington won 7–3, in a game marked by the unhappiness of the Bears with the quality of the officiating.

---

* In the '75 Cup semifinals, the Islanders fell behind the Flyers 3–0, rallied to tie the series, but were finally subdued in Game Seven by a combination of the Broad Street Bullies, the rowdy Philadelphia faithful, and Kate Smith belting out "God Bless America."

Washington owner George Preston Marshall once raised ticket prices without notice on the day of a game, and before he moved his team from Boston played a home NFL Championship Game at New York's Polo Grounds to thumb his nose at the lukewarm Beantown fans. So he wasn't the kind of guy who minded stirring things up. His club had the best record in the NFL and had the title game at home in Griffith Stadium against an opponent they had beaten just a couple of weeks earlier. Prior to the Championship Game, Marshall decided to spice things up by laying down some smack on the Bears. Responding with disdain to the Bears' complaints about the refs in the earlier matchup, he called them "crybabies" and "front-runners."

"They're not a second-half team" was Marshall's analysis.

Papa Bear George Halas went through the motions of distributing Marshall's words throughout his locker room, but he had something more tangible and lethal than garden-variety motivation in store for the Redskins. Working closely with Stanford coach Clark Shaughnessy, the offensive innovator who served with the Bears as a voluntary assistant, Halas added brand-new wrinkles to the team's already-cutting-edge T-formation, devising an offensive game plan for which the Redskins had no answer.

The Bears came out ready. On the second play of the game, fullback Bill Osmanski ran left on a sweep and rambled sixty-eight yards for a touchdown. The last two Redskins defenders with a chance to make a tackle were wiped out by tackle George Wilson's vicious block. The game was effectively over right there. Chicago took a 21–0 lead in the first quarter, stretched it to 28–0 by halftime, then completely buried Washington with a forty-five-point second-half outburst. So much for Chicago not being a second-half team. Not only did the Bears pile up 381 rushing yards and 519 overall, their defense intercepted eight passes, returning three for scores. Ten Bears scored touchdowns. On their last two scores, the Bears passed for the extra point; so many footballs had been kicked into the stands and spirited away by fans that there was a shortage.

When the blood stopped flowing, Chicago had won 73–0. It is still by far the biggest margin of victory, regular-season or postseason, in NFL history. After the game, Redskins quarterback Sammy

Baugh was asked what the score might have been had Washington converted its one real scoring opportunity, in the first quarter. "73–7" was Baugh's reply.*

DESERT MASSACRE—THE UNIVERSITY OF FLORIDA, 1996 FIESTA BOWL

Florida coach Steve Spurrier could be forgiven for feeling confident as he brought his undefeated, number-two-ranked Gators into Tempe to take on the undefeated, number-one-ranked Nebraska Cornhuskers. Florida barely had to break a sweat during the regular season, winning all of its games by at least eleven points and emerging from a rugged Southeastern Conference schedule with its record unscathed.

Granted, Nebraska was even more dominant—aside from a 35–21 beating of Washington State, Tom Osborne's sometimes-lawless crew won all of its games by at least twenty-four points and was averaging more than fifty-two points per game. Nebraska had won twenty-four straight games and thirty-five of its last thirty-six. The one loss was by two points to Florida State in the '94 Orange Bowl. But Spurrier thought his explosive "Fun 'n Gun" offense would be able to keep pace with the Huskers' devastating option attack. The experts agreed, making Nebraska a bare three-point favorite and predicting a back-and-forth shootout.

Which is exactly how it started. Florida opened the scoring with a field goal. Then, after a Cornhusker touchdown, Gator quarterback Danny Wuerffel returned his team to the lead with a one-yard touchdown sneak. It was 10–6 Florida at the end of the first quarter. Then the roof caved in on the Gators, much to the joy of the gigantic Cornhusker contingent in the Sun Devil Stadium stands.

Nebraska exploded for twenty-nine points in the second quarter

---

* Late in the fourth quarter, with Washington trailing by ten touchdowns or so, the Griffith Stadium PA announcer picked this perhaps inconvenient time to remind the fans that 1941 Redskins season tickets were on sale. The response from the remainder of the crowd can be imagined.

to take a 35–10 lead at the half. The Huskers' run-heavy scheme was physically abusing Florida, and so was the Blackshirt defense, which terrorized Spurrier's offense with a tactic that was at the time almost unknown at the college level—the zone blitz. Danny Wuerffel was sacked seven times and picked off three more. During the hellish second quarter the Gator quarterback was dropped for a safety and had an interception returned forty-two yards for the score that put the game out of reach.

Deciding that Florida and the abrasive Spurrier just hadn't been beaten enough, Coach Osborne kept his foot firmly planted on the gas pedal in the second half. Nebraska rolled up another 27 points, including the signature play of the game—quarterback Tommie Frazier's seventy-five-yard touchdown run during which roughly every member of the Florida traveling squad attempted to tackle him, but couldn't. Coach Spurrier, who bragged about how he liked to put "half-a-hundred" on opposing defenses, watched his own get literally run over for sixty-two points and a bowl-record 524 rushing yards. Final score—Nebraska 62, Florida 24. Smackdown.

Spurrier was candid in defeat: "They were just better than us, a lot better than us." Florida wide receiver Chris Doering agreed: "If Nebraska played us ten times, they'd probably beat us ten times." Ya think?

INDIAN WIPEOUT—THE 1954 WORLD SERIES

Indians fans like to claim that their team would have won the '54 World Series if only the first two games had been played in Cleveland and not New York. After all, Vic Wertz's 460-foot drive in Game One, the blast Willie Mays turned into the most famous catch in baseball history, would have been a three-run homer in Municipal Stadium.

But when a team wins 111 games in the regular season and gets swept in the World Series, the reasons are a little more complex than a simple matter of the Giants playing in a ballpark, the Polo Grounds, with 250-foot foul lines and a 483-foot chasm in center. What the Tribe experienced was nothing less than a total team breakdown.

In the four-game series, the Indians hit 4-for-41 with runners in scoring position and stranded thirty-seven runners. They had a chance to win both of the first two games in New York—they took a first-inning lead in both contests and lost Game One in eleven innings—but went 2-for-28 with men in scoring position, leaving twenty-six men on base. That kind of inefficiency will lose games anywhere. The anemic offense hit .190 for the Series overall.

The Tribe's vaunted pitching staff went the way of the hitters. Cleveland's "Big Three" of Bob Lemon (23–7, 2.72), Early Wynn (23–11, 2.73), and Mike Garcia (19–8, 2.64) went 0–4 with a combined 5.68 ERA in the World Series. And as the offense dragged the team down in New York, the pitching dragged it down in Cleveland. Garcia, needing to hold the line in Game Three with his club down two games to none, was routed out of the box in the fourth inning of a 6–2 Cleveland loss. Bob Lemon started Game Four (to the enduring regret of fans, who wished to see thirty-eight-year-old legend Bob Feller get the ball) and was knocked out in the fifth inning of the 7–4 loss that wrapped the Series for New York.

The offensive collapse, coupled with the mound problems, gave Cleveland, which had a single four-game losing streak during the regular campaign, its second such streak at the worst possible time. Despite winning an AL record number of games, the Indians had to fight off the stiffest of challenges from the Yankees, who had won 103 themselves. After finishing a frustrating second to the Bombers the previous three seasons, topping Casey Stengel's boys was the Holy Grail. But by the time the World Series rolled around, the Indians may have had nothing left in the tank.

THE UNEXPECTED SWEEP—WASHINGTON BULLETS, 1975 NBA FINALS

During the 1974–75 NBA season, the Boston Celtics and Washington Bullets had finished tied for the best record in the league at sixty wins and twenty-two losses. No other team in the NBA had even won fifty. They were the mightiest forces in the Association, by far.

As expected, they met in the Eastern Conference Finals. When Washington toppled Boston in six games, most observers assumed that the Bullets were out of the woods and that the NBA Finals would be a mere formality.

The Western Conference Champion Golden State Warriors, winners of only forty-eight games in the regular season, begged to differ. It quickly became apparent that they had no intention of being the foil in Washington's fairy tale when they jumped out to a fourteen-point halftime lead and took Game One, 101–95, in front of a sullen crowd at the Capitol Centre.

The series moved west to San Francisco's Cow Palace, home of the Grand National Rodeo,* for Games Two and Three. The tone was already set. Golden State edged Washington in both games, 92–91 and 109–101. Expected to dominate, the Bullets suddenly found themselves one game from being swept.

And indeed, the sweep went down back in Landover, Maryland, on May 25, 1975, when the Warriors battled back from a thirteen-point deficit and pulled out a spine-tingling 96–95 victory. Golden State hadn't been overwhelming—they won two games by a point apiece each—but they didn't have to be. Putting the broom to a team that hadn't had a losing streak longer than three in the regular season was arresting enough.

For Washington, the collapse defied explanation. The Bullets really were an outstanding team; they won three Central Division titles in six years, captured three Eastern Conference titles, and hoisted an NBA Championship banner in 1978. They had two of the bigger stars in the league in Elvin Hayes and Wes Unseld and a deep and talented supporting cast, and they had gone 3–1 against the Warriors in the regular season. The sweep just happened.

---

* The old Cow Palace wasn't G-State's regular venue, but a scheduling conflict had forced the team out of the Oakland Coliseum Arena for the balance of the Finals. Washington coach K. C. Jones was given a choice—play the first game on the road, get the next three at home, and alternate from then on, or play the first game at home, the next two on the road, and alternate from then on. K.C. chose the former, because he wanted to open the series at home. The move backfired.

0-FOR-12—ST. LOUIS BLUES, 1968–70 STANLEY CUP FINALS

The National Hockey League took a rather curious approach to expansion in 1967. That year the league doubled itself, adding six new franchises to match the venerable Original Six. Though the new entries—Philadelphia, Pittsburgh, Minnesota, St. Louis, Los Angeles, and Oakland—were spread throughout North America, the league didn't create two geographically oriented divisions. Instead, the Original Six were placed in the East Division, while all six expansion clubs were placed in the West. The placement guaranteed a Stanley Cup Finals matchup between an established team and an expansion outfit. Considering the disparity in talent between your average expansion team and a championship-caliber club, it made winning the West a fairly thankless task right out of the gate.

Stepping up to the dubious challenge in 1968 was Scotty Bowman's St. Louis Blues. Although they finished only third in the division during the regular season, the Blues fought their way through the all-expansion West playoffs, edging the Philadelphia Flyers and Minnesota North Stars in respective seven-game battles to win a spot in the Stanley Cup Finals.

Once there, the Blues matched their one-year pedigree and losing record with that of the mighty Montreal Canadiens, winners in the East. As expected, the Finals were a quick affair. Montreal swept St. Louis in four straight games, taking all four by a goal apiece.

Down but by no means out, the Blues regrouped and won the West Division title again in 1968–69, finishing with the first-ever winning record for an NHL expansion team and sweeping the Flyers and Los Angeles Kings to storm back into the Stanley Cup Finals. For the second straight year they met the Canadiens. Again it was a sweep, only this time it was worse—Montreal outscored the Blues 12–3 in the four-game whitewash.

In 1969–70, St. Louis again finished with a winning record, again won the West, and again advanced through the playoffs, defeating the North Stars and the Penguins in six games apiece. This time the Blues had a new Finals opponent—the Boston Bruins. It was the same Finals result. Boston swept to victory in four straight, outscoring the Blues 20–7 and clinching the Cup on Bobby Orr's famed leaping goal in the Game Four overtime.

Following the season, the NHL reexpanded, putting teams in Buffalo and Vancouver. It also moved the established Chicago Blackhawks to the West, putting an end to the all-expansion division. For the Blues, losers of twelve straight Stanley Cup Finals games by a combined score of 43–17, the realignment came three years too late.

AND ONE VERY, VERY
FORTUNATE *COLLAPSE*

Boston College Football, November 28, 1942

Powerful Boston College was on a roll going into their last game of the '42 season. Top-ranked and winners of their first eight games (five by shutout), the Eagles needed only a win over their archrivals, the Holy Cross Crusaders, to clinch their second undefeated season in three years and, with it, a berth in the Sugar Bowl. So confident of a victory were the Eagles over the mediocre Crusaders that they scheduled their celebration in advance at one of Boston's hottest nightspots—the Cocoanut Grove on Piedmont Street.

But Holy Cross, a docile .500 team going into the game, turned buzz kill and buzz saw at the prospect of spoiling their rivals' party. In front of a beyond-capacity crowd of forty thousand at cold and rainy Fenway Park, the Crusaders dominated right from the start. Led by halfback Johnny Bezemes, who accounted for four touchdowns with his legs and arm, Holy Cross built a 20–6 halftime lead and put the game away with a twenty-one-point third quarter. Expected to win handily, Boston College found itself on the wrong end of a 55–12 rout. The game still stands as one of the great upsets in college football history.

For Boston College, the loss was catastrophic, an embarrassment to a proud program. The number-one ranking and Sugar Bowl invite went up in smoke. The victory party at the Cocoanut Grove was canceled, and the disheartened B.C. players either stayed in their dorms or did whatever it was college kids did for fun on a Saturday night in 1942.

At about 10:15 that night in the Cocoanut Grove's Melody Lounge, a busboy trying to find a light socket in the dark lit a match and accidentally set fire to an artificial palm frond. Before anyone could stop it, a blaze—fed by the acres of flammable paper and cloth decorations that festooned the interior of the club—traveled corridors and staircases and exploded onto totally unsuspecting partiers in the club's main ballroom and dining room. Hundreds of terrified patrons were trapped in the inferno. Their attempts to escape were thwarted by the club's single front exit—a revolving door that quickly jammed and became a death trap. By the time the fifteen-minute fire was extinguished, 492 people were dead. It remains the second-deadliest building fire in American history. Boston was scarred for eternity. To this day, all public buildings and businesses in the city are equipped with doors that open outward, and all eating and drinking establishments in the Old Town to this day are forbidden from using the name "Cocoanut Grove."

Stanley Tomaszewski, the sixteen-year-old busboy who accidentally started the fire, survived without being so much as singed.

The Boston College Eagles had just been humiliated, in perhaps the biggest game in the history of the program, by their number-one rival. The undefeated season was gone, and in shattering fashion. The New Year's trip to New Orleans for the Sugar Bowl was gone. But on November 29, 1942, every member of the squad was able to wake up in the morning, healthy and whole, and bitch about it, if they so chose.

Mayflower moving trucks leaving Baltimore as the Colts flee to Indianapolis under the cover of darkness and snow—March 28, 1984. *Courtesy of the Baltimore Sun Company, Inc., All Rights Reserved.*

TEAM ISSUES

Authors included, we sports fans put our hearts and souls into supporting our teams. More often than not, our teams reward this passion by whipping up a nice big crap sandwich for us to munch on. And boy, do we chew and chew and chew. Why? Because unless you're a Phillies fan, regardless of whether your team is good, bad, or just plain awful, they're still your squad.

★ WHEN THE ALL-TIME BEST WAS THE ALL-TIME WORST
★ THE WORST TEAMS
★ THE CURSE OF JEFFREY MAIER
★ THE WORST FRANCHISE-KILLING LOSSES
★ THE BALTIMORE COLTS 1975–83

WHEN THE ALL-TIME BEST WAS THE ALL-TIME WORST

A Brief History of the Pittsburgh Steelers . . . Before the Dynasty

When you think about the Pittsburgh Steelers, what comes to mind?

Chances are, you think of Franco Harris picking the ball off his shoe tops against the Raiders in '72 . . . *and it's caught out of the air by Franco Harris! Franco is going for a Steeler touchdown!* Or maybe you think of the Steel Curtain, or Lynn Swann devastating the Cowboys in Super Bowls X and XIII, or jut-jawed Bill Cowher spraying words into Greg Lloyd's face: *Rush the quarterback,* or toothless Jack "Splat" Lambert shoving the face of Cleveland's Cleo Miller into the turf.

All of that = victory. Sure, the Steelers had a tough time winning AFC Championship Games at home in the '90s and early '00s, but three of those four defeats were to eventual Super Bowl Champions, and at any rate they were playing in the Championship Games to begin with. The mild stench of those repeated failures didn't linger, and was blown away completely by Pittsburgh's horribly officiated Super Bowl XL victory over the Seahawks. The overwhelming image of Steelers Football remains one of success. Hell, Mean Joe Greene even nailed that Coke commercial.

But there is a reason why all those Pittsburgh highlights are in color. Back in the black-and-white era, in the formative years of the National Football League, it was constantly and thoroughly inappropriate to put the words *Steelers* and *success* in the same sentence. For the balance of Pittsburgh's first four decades as a franchise, the Steelers, quite simply, sucked dry the conflux of the Ohio, Allegheny, and Monongahela, mustering up just seven winning seasons in their first thirty-six as a team. When the Steelers won the AFC Central Championship in 1972, their fortieth season, it was the first-ever title of any kind for the franchise.

The bad old days of the Pittsburgh Steelers are almost lost in the wake of the success the team has experienced in the last three-odd decades. And that's unfortunate, because the early history of the team is filled with as much color as their schedules were with losses.

IT STARTS AT THE TOP: THE CHIEF

Art Rooney is a legit legendary character in pro football history—the salty, bighearted, cigar-chewing former amateur boxer who won his fortune in a single day at the racetrack—the benevolent patriarch of the Pittsburgh Steelers.

He's a legend, all right, and deservedly so. But for forty years, he was the most unsuccessful owner in the National Football League. Rosters changed, coaches changed, but the Steelers remained out in the cold. The common denominator was Arthur J. Rooney. That he meant well is beyond contestation. But that he didn't do well is also. To put a twist on the 1983 Tom Cruise movie filmed in nearby Johnstown, Rooney, decade after dismal decade, made all the wrong moves. It took the shrewdness of his sons, Dan and Art Jr., along with that of Chuck Noll, to finally bring the Steelers out of their own version of the Dark Ages.

1934: JAILBIRDS

The Pirates (as originally known), like their cross-state rival the Philadelphia Eagles, opened for business in 1933, upon the legalization of Sunday professional sports in the Keystone State. But Art Rooney's new creation sartorially looked a lot like it was still violating the law the following year. The Pirates came out in horizontal-striped jerseys that more closely resembled a chain gang's uniform than that of a football team. The punishment for the fashion faux paus was a last-place finish. (In 1994, the Steelers breathed new life into the "Jailbird" jersey in what were by far the ugliest of that season's throwback uniforms.)

1936: ART ROONEY 1, PITTSBURGH STEELERS 0

With one week remaining in the 1936 season, the Pirates were tied with the Boston Redskins for first place in the Eastern Division and needed a win at Boston in the final week to win the title and, with it, their first berth in the NFL Championship Game. Winning on the road with the stakes set so high was a challenge in itself, but Art Rooney had added boldly to the degree of difficulty. He had scheduled his team to play an exhibition game the week of the Boston game . . . in Los Angeles.

It wasn't uncommon for Rooney to send his team barnstorming; he had done so in the past. An earlier trip to New Orleans had foundered, according to Jack Clary's book *Pro Football's Great Moments*.* As it was 1936, there was no luxurious, four-hour flight to carry the Pirates to the West Coast. They dutifully boarded a train, rocked to and fro on rails across the country, and played the exhibition game. Then they got back on board the train and rattled three thousand long miles from L.A. to Boston for the showdown with the Redskins. Not surprisingly, the Pirates lost 30–0. They probably would have lost anyway. The fatigue-inducing transcontinental round-trip didn't help.

---

* The mayor of the city, who was supposed to set up the game, turned out to be completely clueless about the professional status of the Steelers; he thought they were a college team in town to play Tulane. But the trip to L.A. proved exceptionally untimely.

1938: TOO SMART FOR STEEL TOWN

Even the occasional bold move failed to work out for Rooney, like in 1938 when he shelled out a pro record $15,800 contract to college phenom Byron "Whizzer" White. The heralded halfback from the University of Colorado responded by leading the league in rushing as a rookie. But unlike most of his fellow players, the young litigator–ballcarrier had choices, and White preferred the leafy greens of Oxford to the valiant but foolhardy—not to mention physically taxing—task of carrying a horrible team in Pittsburgh, Pennsylvania. After one season, the future Supreme Court associate justice decamped to England on his Rhodes Scholarship. The Chief sold his rights to the Lions. But hey, it was a nice try.

1944: THE "CARPETS"

Rooney experienced modest success in 1943 when, faced with roster attrition from World War II enlistments, he combined his team with Bert Bell's Philadelphia Eagles. The "Steagles," as they were known, went a respectable 5–4–1 and finished third. Sensing that he had a good thing going, Mr. Rooney the following season merged his roster with that of the Chicago Cardinals, creating an amalgamation officially known as "Card-Pitt."

But this time his luck—with Art Rooney, winning was nearly always more a product of luck than design—ran out. The "Carpets" finished 0–10, yielding more than thirty-three points per game. Seven of their losses were by three touchdowns or more. Card-Pitt's Single Wing quarterback, Johnny Grigas, decided to call it a season early and walked out just before the final game, an eventual 49–7 loss to the Bears. Unhappy with the merger's "synergies," the teams decided to go their separate ways for the 1945 season, each finishing last in its respective division.

1947: THEIR ONE CHAMPIONSHIP SHOT

Dr. John "Jock" Sutherland was a driving, acerbic taskmaster and an adherent of the archaic Single Wing offense; the Steelers were the last team in the NFL to utilize the Single Wing, running it long after every other club had switched to the T-formation. Sutherland was a tough man to get along with—his problems with the great Bill Dudley forced Rooney to trade the Hall of Fame tailback to Detroit prior to the 1947 season—but he could definitely coach, and he had the Steelers in the thick of the Eastern Division race throughout the '47 season, even without Dudley.

Pittsburgh finished the season with an 8–4 record (the franchise's best season winning percentage until the Chuck Noll years) and a tie for the Eastern Division title with the Philadelphia Eagles. A one-game playoff, scheduled for the friendly confines of Pittsburgh's Forbes Field, was all that stood between the Steelers and a spot in the NFL Championship Game.

The week before the playoff, the Steelers players briefly went on strike, demanding to be paid bonuses for the game. Though it wasn't his money, Sutherland was displeased to say the least to find his players more focused on their wallets than on the matter at hand. He expressed this displeasure by whipping them through a long and torturous practice in brutal weather conditions just a few days before the game. The dissension-plagued Steelers were a dead team walking by the time of the playoff contest, and the Eagles took advantage. Philadelphia cruised to a 21–0 shutout and the Eastern Division championship. Rooney paid the bonuses, by the way. That's just the kind of guy he was.

The following spring Sutherland died of a brain tumor, and the Steelers slid quietly back into the lower reaches of the standings. The Doctor was a revered figure in the city, mainly due to his brilliant tenure as coach of the University of Pittsburgh. To this day, his untimely, sudden death is quite possibly the worst blow the Steelers franchise has ever experienced.

1955: TOO DUMB FOR JOHNNY U.

The Steelers pulled off a rare draft-day coup in 1955 when in the ninth round they selected Johnny Unitas, a Pittsburgh-area native who had starred at quarterback for the University of Louisville. But despite his impressive showing in training camp, the Steelers cut Unitas before the regular season. The rationale: Johnny U. was "too dumb" to be a good NFL quarterback. As it turned out, the Pittsburgh organization was simply too dumb to recognize a good player when it saw one. For the price of an 80-cent phone call, the out-of-work Unitas was obtained by the Baltimore Colts, and immediately proceeded to embark on what is arguably the greatest career any NFL quarterback has ever had.

Two years after the Unitas fiasco, Pittsburgh passed on Jim Brown in the first round of the 1957 Draft, then selected Len Dawson and got rid of him after three seasons, the vast bulk of which he spent welded to the bench. The sorry Steelers got a total of seventeen pass attempts from the two Hall of Fame signal callers.

1965: BUDDY PARKER—AN HONEST MAN

Raymond J. "Buddy" Parker, a two-time NFL Champ in Detroit, was one of the best coaches of his era, and perhaps its most volatile. In 1957, piqued by the sight of his players drinking with ownership, he impulsively quit as coach in Detroit during a speech at a "Meet the Lions" banquet. Rooney immediately hired Parker to coach the Steelers. He didn't win any championships, but under Parker Pittsburgh experienced its greatest period of sustained success up to that point, garnering four whole winning records in his eight seasons. In 1964, the team slipped to second-to-last place and Parker, reading the tea leaves on his aging, mediocre team, decided it was time to get out of Dodge. Just a few days before the 1965 season opener, he walked into Rooney's office and handed the Chief his resignation. His reason was short, simple, and painfully direct: "I can't win with this bunch of stiffs."

Coaching responsibility went to assistant coach Mike Nixon, who had amassed a record of 4–18–1 in an earlier stint as head coach of the Redskins. The Steelers proved they were, indeed, a bunch of stiffs, going a pro football–worst 2–12 under the hapless Nixon in '65. In the last five years of the '60s, Pittsburgh went

14–53–3 and finished in last place four times. Even by the radically lowered standards of the Black-and-Gold, this was atrocious football.

1950–69: UM, WHAT RIVALRY?

Right from the start, the two games played each year between the Steelers and the Cleveland Browns were the pro football equivalent of the Kansas–Missouri pre–Civil War border feud. But while the fistfights in the stands were anyone's game, the results on the field were wholly predictable, and turned Pittsburgh's claim to "throw out the records" rivalry stands into a laughable farce. The Browns finished ahead of Pittsburgh in the standings in all but one of their first twenty-two seasons in the league together. The Black-and-Gold lost its first eight games to the Orange-and-Brown and in the first two decades of the series went a Washington Generals-esque 8–32.

Since the early 1970s, Pittsburgh has been, with the exception of a few lean years late in the Chuck Noll era, a consistent player among the league's elite. Bill Cowher (a former Cleveland linebacker and assistant whose jaw jutted farthest after a win over his old team) was 22–6 against the Browns, including a pair of playoff victories. Only the Cowboys and 49ers can match Pittsburgh's five Lombardi Trophies. Meanwhile, in the same span the Browns have gone through twelve head coaches and two completely different franchises, and haven't played in a Super Bowl.

Yet for all of this, the Steelers didn't actually tie the all-time series with the woebegone Browns until 2006. It took thirty-four seasons for Pittsburgh to excavate itself from a hole it had taken twenty for Cleveland to dig; a good long time for the Steel Curtain, Swanny, Franco, the Bus, Big Ben, and the Sixty-Minute Men to cash the checks their lousy predecessors wrote in the first place. And most of the digging has come recently, thanks to the fact that the real Cleveland Browns play in Baltimore, and the new team in Cleveland is a wretched insult that should publicly apologize for sullying the proper good name of the old one.

1969: THE NADIR

In 1969, determined to turn over a new leaf for his franchise, Rooney hired as his head coach a young defensive assistant from Baltimore named Chuck Noll. The Steelers beat Detroit 16–13 in Noll's first game. Kool-Aid drinkers got excited. Cynics waited for the other shoe to drop, which it did. In fact, it dropped thirteen times in a row to close out the 1969 season. Some were close losses (10–7 to the Giants and the Cowboys; 38–34 to the Packers; 14–7 to the Redskins). Some were routs (52–14 to the Vikings; 47–10 to the Cardinals; 41–27 to the Eagles). All combined to give Chuck Noll's first team the longest in-season losing streak in NFL history at the time. The Steelers also lost their first three games of the 1970 season, extending the losing streak to sixteen games. Hard to fathom but true: at one point in his coaching career, Chuck Noll's record was 1–16.

One of those losses, though, brought with it the kind of twist of fortune that finally allowed the Steelers to break out of perpetual suck. There was another 1–13 team in the league in 1969, the Chicago Bears. For a team to have Gale Sayers on offense and Dick Butkus on defense and win only one stinking game is beyond disgraceful. But Chicago put it all together in its only victory—a 38–7 rout of the Steelers at Wrigley Field—and the tiebreaker allowed the Steelers to select first in the 1970 Draft. They took Terry Bradshaw.

Slowly but surely, led by Bradshaw (at least, starting in about 1975 or so) and the many other skilled young players drafted by Noll, the fortunes of the Steelers turned for the better. In '72 they won their first championship, and in the playoffs against Oakland officially and permanently turned things around with the Immaculate Reception, a miracle play that should, in fact, have been ruled an illegal touch and waved off, negating Franco Harris's touchdown. (Rooney never saw the play. He was in a Three Rivers Stadium elevator, on his way down to thank his players for their valiant effort, when Bradshaw threw his blind heave downfield and Oakland's

Jack Tatum predictably decided to go for the big hit instead of the interception.)

In 1974 the Steelers put it all together, winning their second AFC Central title, powering through the playoffs, and shutting down the Minnesota Vikings to win their first Super Bowl. The transformation of the Steelers from forgotten losers to famous winners was complete, cast in the medal of the Vince Lombardi Trophy.

Yet the bedraggled past shouldn't be forgotten for at least one good reason: as bad as they were, the Steelers were never physically intimidated. They didn't win, but they hit, they had no problem employing a style that was at least a little dirty, and no matter what the result on Sunday, the opponent always had a tough time getting out of bed on Monday morning. Chuck Noll's and Bill Cowher's teams maintained that philosophy of physicality to this day. "Winning the battle of the hitting" is the essence of Steeler Football. It is the one invaluable legacy the sad-sack Steelers passed on to their lordly successors.

THE WORST TEAMS

Fun Facts About What Bad Teams Do Best: Lose Often

LONGEST LOSING STREAK

NCAA Football

Eighty Games: Prairie View A&M, 1989–98: The mother, father, sister, and brother of losing streaks, Prairie View's skein of failure began on October 28, 1989, against Langston University, and didn't end until September 26, 1998—a month short of nine full years.

While it does boast former Kansas City Chiefs great Otis Taylor as an alumnus, Prairie View is a tiny southern college—a college where the band is more popular than the football team. So a little bit of shabbiness on the field is forgivable. But to go longer than the stay of a two-term president without winning was a wee bit excessive.

During their early years of misery, which mostly consisted of lopsided defeats, Prairie View had company. In 1991–92, A&M's football team, men's basketball team, and women's basketball team went a combined 0–65. There may have existed a bit of a "culture of losing" on the campus.

For the football team, the losing continued. On November 6,

1994, Prairie View tied Columbia's Division I-AA record with its forty-fourth straight loss, a 70–20 Homecoming whaling at the hands of Division II Tarleton State. That's right, *the* Tarleton State University. Six years after it began, Prairie View's winless streak hit fifty-one with a 64–0 blowout by Grambling, making it the longest in the history of college football. The end was nowhere in sight— the streak had another twenty-nine games and three years left to run.

It finally ended in somewhat anticlimactic fashion, when the Panthers jumped out to an early lead and hung on to defeat Langston University, the team that started the streak, 14–12. They got another win later in the season and steamrolled to a 2–9 record. The Prairie View A&M Marching Storm was outstanding, as always.

NFL

Twenty-six Games: Tampa Bay Buccaneers, 1976–77: The Buccaneers were placed in the AFC West for standings purposes in their inaugural season, but played a round-robin schedule—a game against each of the other thirteen AFC members, plus a game with their expansion brethren, the Seattle Seahawks. When the Bucs were moved to the NFC in their second season, the same schedule applied: one game against each conference member, and the Expansion Bowl with Seattle. Simply put, this meant that almost every team in the league had an opportunity to beat Tampa Bay—and for nearly the first two years of the franchise's existence, that's just what they did.

To say the least, Tampa Bay was a friendly matchup. The team was as potent as your granddaddy's libido after too many glasses of Johnnie Walker. The punchless Buccaneers were shut out thirteen times in their first twenty-six games as a franchise, losing by an average score of 24–7. Seven different quarterbacks threw interceptions for John McKay's team during the streak. During the entirety of the fourteen-game 1977 season, the Tampa "offense" mustered a grand total of seven touchdowns.

In the next-to-last week of the 1977 season, and with the franchise at 0-for-26, Tampa's defense did what its offense had been unable to do: score on multiple occasions. Tampa's D came up with three touchdowns on interception returns, outscoring both offenses in a 33–14 rout of the Saints at the Superdome. When the team returned home to Tampa, it was greeted by thousands of fans at the airport. Taking a liking to winning, the Bucs did it again in the final week, beating the St. Louis Cardinals 17–7 in front of a delirious crowd at the Big Sombrero.

NBA

Twenty-four Games: 1982–83 Cleveland Cavaliers: Ted Stepien's first love was softball; he once dropped softballs off Cleveland's Terminal Tower as a publicity stunt to promote his professional league and wound up getting sued when a woman had her arm broken by one of the plunging projectiles. Stepien's main claim to fame as an NBA owner, aside from practically destroying the Cleveland Cavaliers, was his freewheeling habit of trading high draft picks for nothing players. (David Stern eventually forced Stepien to agree not to make any trades without the explicit permission of the league office; the NBA's "Stepien Rule," which forbids teams to trade first-round picks in consecutive years, still exists to this day.*)

The 1981–82 season marked the nadir of Stepien's reign of terror over the denizens of Richfield Coliseum, located halfway between Cleveland and Akron (in other words, nowhere). Reasoning (insanely) that the ramshackle Cavaliers should be in the thick of the playoff race, Stepien went through four head coaches in 1981–82, including Chuck Daly. He only succeeded in driving his team further into irrelevance. On March 13, 1982, the "Cadavers" moved to 15–48 in the season with a victory over the Utah Jazz.

---

* Cleveland had traded its 1982 number-one pick to Los Angeles for some bench player named Don Ford. On Draft Day '82, the Lakers GM stepped to the podium—undoubtedly grinning like the Cheshire Cat—and selected James Worthy, becoming the first and last team to pick numero uno in the NBA Draft following a World Championship.

The next victory came eight months later. The Cavaliers lost their final nineteen games and their first five of the 1982–83 season before ending the agony on November 10, 1982, with a 132–120 win over the Golden State Warriors. They then lost seven more in a row, giving them thirty-one losses in thirty-two games.

Angered by the shortage of fans willing to brave the slick, winding country roads to see his terrible team, Stepien threatened to transfer the Cavaliers to Toronto. He went so far as to unveil a new uniform and name (the Toronto Towers) in anticipation of the move before he relented and sold the team in 1983.

NHL

Seventeen Games: Washington Capitals, 1974–75: The Expansion Capitals are the '76 Buccaneers of the NHL, winning fewer games (eight), scoring fewer points (twenty-one), and giving up more goals (446) than any team in league history. They were 6–47–5 on February 18, 1975, when they started the streak with a 6–1 loss to the Los Angeles Kings, and 6–64–5 when they ended it on March 28, 1975, topping the California Golden Seals 5–3 at the Coliseum Arena in Oakland. So it didn't exactly come out of nowhere.

Opposing players with scoring in mind licked their chops at the sight of Washington's patriotic red, white, and blue uniforms. Capital netminders allowed a veritable flood of goals during the streak—115 to be exact, an average of nearly 7 per game. The Caps also lost their first thirty-seven road games of the season; in fact, the win over the Seals was their first and only road "W" for this long, long season.

To their credit, the Washington players had a sense of humor about their plight. When the clock hit zero on their streak-breaker in Oakland, the Capitals skated around the ice holding up a green trash can—a sardonic, last-place twist on the Stanley Cup.

MLB

Twenty-three Games: Philadelphia Phillies, 1961: It started innocently enough: a 4–3 loss on July 29, 1961, at Connie Mack Stadium to the powerful Giants. It was just another defeat in a season full of them. The Phillies had already suffered five losing streaks of five games or more, including a ten-game stinkeroo that marred both April and May. They were eleven games out of seventh place in an eight-team league. But this streak was different. It was longer . . . much, much longer. It didn't stop until August 20, at Milwaukee's County Stadium, when the Phillies broke open a close game with a four-run eighth and held on to beat the Braves 7–4. At times it must have seemed to the Phillies and their Phanatics, who were Phew and Phar between at that point, as if it would never end.

Even chances to stop the bleeding were few and far between. The Phillies held the lead past the sixth inning twice for the duration of the losing streak and at one point went twenty-one innings without scoring a run. It didn't help that, as the streak continued and gained publicity, teams began "getting up" to play Philly, each of them engaged in a desperate fight not to be the team that allowed the Phutile Phils to get healthy.

Oddly enough, the Phillies followed the twenty-three-game whopper with a four-game winning streak, the longest for the club in 1961. They still finished sixty games under .500, good for a distant last in the NL.

LONGEST WITHOUT A CHAMPIONSHIP

MLB

Ninety-nine Years: Chicago Cubs (1908–): Even with all the attention this ever-growing record gets, it's still a little hard to believe a major sports franchise can go so long without winning a championship. Believe it: the last time the Cubbies won it all, Arizona and New Mexico were territories, Civil War vets marched by the thousands in Fourth of July parades, international politics featured czars, kaisers, emperors, and sultans . . . and it would be another six years before Wrigley Field was built.

But, despite the collapses in 1984 and '03, despite the talk of curses, despite the sheer stupefying length of time it's been since the Cubs won it all, this God-awful streak is fully legit. The year 1908 happens to be the last year the Cubs had the best team in baseball. That's why they haven't won a World Championship or, to paraphrase a World Series–winning White Sox manager's explanation for his own club's long lack of a "sausage": *They've had too many shitty players.*

NFL

Sixty Years: Chicago/St. Louis/Phoenix/Arizona Cardinals (1947–): On December 28, 1947, on the icy surface of Comiskey Park, the Cards' "Million-Dollar Backfield" of Charlie Trippi, Elmer Angsmann, and Pat Harder gashed Greasy Neale's famed Eagle Defense for 282 rushing yards and, with a 28–21 victory over Philly, brought an NFL Championship home to the South Side of Chicago for the first time.

And . . . that's been just about it for this vagabond franchise, which has won a grand total of one postseason game since '47* and hasn't even gotten to within a game of the Super Bowl, let alone appeared in one. The Cardinals might want to be content with aiming for a ten-win season; they haven't had one of those since 1976. But now they have a really cool field that can be wheeled outside for sun and watering. That's gotta count for something, right?

NBA

Fifty-six Years: Rochester/Cincinnati Royals/Kansas City/Omaha/Sacramento Kings (1951–): While their downstate rivals, the Los Angeles Clippers, collect the accolades for general stinkiness, this franchise quietly

---

* Not counting St. Louis's 24–17 victory over Vince Lombardi's Packers in the 1964 Playoff Bowl. The what? The Playoff Bowl was a postseason consolation game held at the Orange Bowl between the second-place teams in each conference. Lombardi referred to the game as "the Shit Bowl," an attitude that may explain his team's performance against the Cardinals in '64.

continues to build on a record of futility that it began three time zones, two thousand miles, and more than five decades ago. The Kings haven't played in an NBA Finals since '51, let alone won the whole kit and kaboodle. The Oscar Robertson–led Cincinnati Royals teams of the early '60s lost twice to the Bill Russell Celtics in the Eastern Division Finals. In 1981 the Kansas City Kings, just 40–42 in the regular season, got to the Western Conference Finals before losing to another 40–42 team (Houston). And in 2002, the Sacramento Kings had home court in the West Finals against the Lakers but crumbled in the face of Robert Horry's shooting, their lack of shooting, and a general tightening in the throat region. Wherever the road has gone—Rochester, Cincinnati, Kansas City, Omaha, Sac-Town—it's been paved with frustration.

But give the Royals/Kings credit—on the one shot that they had, they scored. In their one and only Finals appearance, in 1951, the Aristocrats by Any Name defeated the New York Knicks, four games to three.

NHL

Forty Years: Toronto Maple Leafs (1967–): In the last year of the Original Six, the Maple Leafs, a third-place finisher in the regular season, rousted up a great postseason effort, upsetting the Blackhawks and then stunning the archrival Montreal Canadiens in six games to bring Lord Stanley's Cup back to Toronto.

We hope the Leafs Nation partied long and hard in those halcyon days in the spring before the Summer of Love, because it was their last celebration to date. Plagued by the incompetence of owner Harold Ballard, Toronto ceased to be a championship contender and, despite an upswing in on-ice results in the '90s and the new century, hasn't been back to the Stanley Cup Finals yet—the only Original Six member to be locked out of the Finals since the league expanded to twelve teams in 1967. It's been a tough four decades for one of the more blindly loyal fan bases in all of North American sports.

LONGEST BETWEEN WINNING SEASONS

NCAA Football

Twenty-eight Years: Oregon State (1971–98): On November 21, 1970, on what was probably a cold, wet day in Corvallis, Coach Dee Andros's Beavers trounced Oregon 24–9 in the Civil War, locking down a 6–5 season. It was OSU's fifth straight winning year. It would be their last, for a long, long time. Not once during the streak, which took place under the stewardship of six head coaches, did the Beavers go into the last game of the season against Oregon with even a chance to go .500.

Though there was only one winless season among the twenty-eight—in 1980, under Joe Avezzano—Oregon State was, in terms of consistently losing more than it won, the worst team in big-time college football. And unfortunately, OSU didn't have the "We're an academic school in an athletic conference" argument that Rice, Duke, Northwestern, and Vanderbilt could fall back on to explain away piss-poor results. The Beavers just stank.

The misery didn't end until 1999, when Mr. Fix-It coach Dennis Erickson imported some mercenary speed and led the Beavers to a 7–5 record and their first bowl appearance since 1965.

NFL

Twenty Years: New Orleans Saints (1967–86): On Opening Day of the 1967 season, rookie receiver John Gilliam took the very first kickoff in the history of the New Orleans franchise and ran it ninety-four yards for a touchdown, giving the spanking new Saints a 6–0 lead over the Los Angeles Rams.* It was all downhill from there. In their first nineteen years, the Saints burned through nine head coaches, including Hank Stram, Dick Nolan, and Bum Phillips. None managed anything better than an 8–8 record. The Saints never won more than five games in any of their first eleven seasons and, during this streak

* George Allen's Rams came back to beat the Saints in that opening game, 27–13.

from hell, finished last in the NFC West as many times as Ferris Bueller had absences (which is to say, nine).

When the streak ended, it ended emphatically. Led by Rueben Mayes and LSU product Dalton Hilliard in the backfield, the "Dome Patrol" linebacker corps, and the emotive Jim Mora (the team's tenth head coach), the Saints rolled to a 12–3 record and their first-ever playoff berth. After their team was destroyed 44–10 by Minnesota in its first-ever playoff game, the sellout crowd in the Superdome gave the Saints a long, rousing ovation. They'd seen worse.

MLB

Eighteen Years: Philadelphia/Kansas City A's (1950–67): This streak spanned eras. When it began with 102 losses and a last-place finish in 1950, the A's were still playing in Shibe Park and eighty-three-year-old Connie Mack was still seated on the bench in street clothes, occasionally calling for Chief Bender to get warmed up in the bullpen. When it ended with a mighty eighty-two-win effort in 1968, the A's were in Oakland, wearing dandified green and white uniforms and white shoes, stocked with young players like Joe Rudi, Bert Campaneris, Sal Bando, Catfish Hunter, and Reggie Jackson—the nucleus of the powerful mustachioed, white-shod '70s A's—and the legendary Mack had been replaced by the infamous Charlie O. Finley. In between was a lot of bad baseball and shady business.

NBA

Fifteen Years: Kansas City/Sacramento Kings (1983–98): The scoring of Eddie Johnson and Mike Woodson, the floor leadership of Larry Drew, and the shrewdness of the late Cotton Fitzsimmons led the Kansas City Kings to a 45–37 record in 1982–83. When the Kings suffered the ignominy of being chased from their home city by a Major Indoor Soccer League franchise two years later, their streak of sub-.500 seasons was already under way, and it would continue

remorselessly for the first thirteen seasons they played in Sacramento. Included in the string were eight straight seasons of more
than fifty losses and, somewhere in the morass, an NBA-record
forty-three-game road losing streak. Long known for consistently
selling out Arco Arena to watch awful basketball, Sac-Town fans
were finally rewarded in the lockout-shortened 1998–99 season,
when the revamped young Kings went 27–23 and became a team
that won just enough to make losing really sting.

NHL

Fifteen Years: Vancouver Canucks (1976–91): For fifteen seasons, the
Vancouver Canucks failed to manage a winning regular season
record. What they were often very good at for many of those years,
however, was tying. In the 1980–81 season, for example, the
Canucks hit the showers having tied their opponent twenty times.
Twenty. That's one quarter of the season. But after all, they played
in the NHL, a league where the simple fact that you're a member
entitles you to a spot in the playoffs. Of those fifteen consecutive
losing seasons, Vancouver found themselves skating in the playoffs
on nine occasions, and in the 1981–82 season, they made it all the
way to the Stanley Cup Finals before the New York Islanders
sobered up and swept them in four games.

THE CURSE OF JEFFREY MAIER

The Orioles' Contribution to a Sport Long Fraught with Superstitious Pestilence

The hex formerly known as the Curse of the Bambino. The Curse of the Billy Goat. Both are well established in baseball lore. They've been blamed for altering the course of history and have been belabored for decades. But the Curse of Jeffrey Maier is as neglected as a redheaded stepchild. It's the new face at the party for the damned, and no one knows its name. While it may be a bit premature to even declare the existence of such a thing, the Baltimore Orioles' tangled web of misfortune over the past decade at least warrants the contemplation of it.

On the evening of October 9, 1996, the New York Yankees and the Baltimore Orioles squared off in Game One of the American League Championship Series. It was the bottom of the eighth inning, the bases were lonely, and the Yankees were trailing the Birds 4–3. To the giggly delight of the ladies in the crowd, Derek Jeter completed his patented routine of ass-bends, bubble-gum pops, and practice swings in the on-deck circle, then strutted to the dish. As the Yankee shortstop dug in, Orioles reliever Armando Benitez delivered to the plate and Jeter hit a "deep" fly ball to right field—

deep being a relative term, as Yankee Stadium's right field seats are only an effortless Mickelson flop shot away—sending right fielder Tony Tarasco scrambling back onto the warning track. As Tarasco extended the leather high above his head in an attempt to haul in the fly, someone else's leather reached the ball first. And it wasn't a teammate's.

A twelve-year-old boy from Old Tappan, New Jersey, by the name of Jeffrey Maier, had reached over the fence from his seat and managed to deflect the ball into the stands. *Mr. Jeter, you may now commence your fist-clenching . . . because it's a home run!* Or at least that's how right field umpire Rich Garcia ruled the play. But the Orioles felt otherwise. Manager Davey Johnson and Tarasco, among others, protested vehemently. And they had a case. Fans are permitted to catch balls hit into the stands, but Major League Baseball's rulebook clearly states that if a spectator reaches out of the stands, or goes onto the playing field and touches a live ball, then the umpire must call interference. Garcia's call was one of the worst in baseball playoff history.

The shell-shocked Orioles never recovered. The Yankees went on to win Game One in the eleventh inning on a Bernie Williams walk-off home run. New York feted Maier as a hero, and the boy was summoned to the front row of George Steinbrenner's box as a special guest of the owner-in-turtleneck for Game Two. The Yanks happened to lose that game, but overcame this slight bout with karmic retribution and cruised to win the pennant in five, ultimately recording the franchise's twenty-third championship in a World Series victory over Atlanta. To this day, most Orioles players claim that Tarasco most certainly would have caught the ball and they most likely would've won the game. Baltimore's manager, Davey Johnson, has even inferred that that single play eventually cost him his job. The fallout of that memorable Game One of the 1996 ALCS is widespread, and since then the paths of the two organizations involved have diverged wildly. The Yankees installed the "Jeffrey Maier bar" to prevent fans from reaching over the wall, and then proceeded to win six American League pennants and four

World Series. The Orioles, on the other hand, filed a grievance in protest of the Maier play after the conclusion of the game, only to have American League president Gene Budig deny the motion, as judgment calls cannot be protested. Upon review of the videotape and in a public admission (read: confession) that would turn D.C.-area stomachs, umpire Garcia stated that he'd blown the call, as there was indeed adolescent interference on the play.

The O's appeared to recover from the Game One controversy and ultimate series loss the following regular season, going 98–64 and winning the division. But they would go on to lose to the Indians in the 1997 ALCS. Then Davey Johnson "resigned." Since that time, they've stumbled to nine consecutive seasons under .500 through 2006 and haven't finished higher than third in the AL East. The organization's management under owner Peter Angelos has been rife with missteps. And repeated distractions both on and off field have plagued the clubhouse, putting to the test the loyalty and commitment of the fan base.

RAFAEL PALMEIRO

I have never used steroids. Period.

While pointing at elected U.S. officials for melodramatic effect, the Baltimore Orioles' Rafael Palmeiro made this most memorable assertion during testimony to the House Government Reform Committee on steroid use in baseball. Five months later, in an ironic twist so ridiculous it simply couldn't have been made up, Raffy was suspended for violating Major League Baseball's steroids policy. He tested positive for the anabolic steroid stanozolol, made famous by Canadian sprinter Ben Johnson. The failed test also came just fifteen days after Palmeiro collected his three thousandth career hit, thus tarnishing one of the rare shining moments in recent Orioles history.

Palmeiro's positive test caught many by surprise. Granted, the Orioles' sweet-swinging 1B/DH was not the stereotypical muscle-bulging, vein-popping poster boy for steroids. But upon review of his career stat lines, the reader's eyebrow should immediately rise. Why? Because Palmeiro didn't start putting up Hall of Fame–type numbers until after the age of thirty, at which point he burst out with a sudden streak of thirty-five-plus home runs and one hundred-plus runs batted in over nine consecutive seasons (1995–2003). That's oddly prolific for an aging veteran playing a young man's game.

ALBERT BELLE

When "Affable Albert" signed with the Chicago White Sox for five years and $55 million in 1996, he became the highest-paid player in baseball. There was a rare, inflation-indexed clause in his contract stating that he could file for free agency if he wasn't one of the three highest-paid players in the game. So in October 1998, Belle filed for free agency after the White Sox balked at giving him a raise. The Orioles swooped in to save the day and offered Belle a five-year, $65 million deal, again making him the highest-paid player in baseball and thereby restoring the natural order of things.

Belle's statistics prior to signing with the Orioles were incredible. With the White Sox in '98 he batted .328, hit forty-nine ding-dongs, rattled off forty-eight doubles, and delivered 152 RBI. But Belle was a notorious prick. It's a recurring theme in the front offices of professional sports teams: overestimate the value of a "good clubhouse guy" and drastically underestimate the baggage brought and havoc wreaked by the "clubhouse cancer." Orioles general manager Frank Wren and owner Peter Angelos made this very miscalculation when they signed the surly and combative Belle.

In '99 and '00, Belle's first two years under contract with Baltimore, his numbers were way down, but still very respectable. Not $13-million-a-year good, but certainly good enough for an Oriole in the hard-luck era brought about by Jeffrey Maier. But after only two seasons that were chock-full of controversy both on and off the field, Belle ended his career in Baltimore, retiring at age thirty-four because of degenerative osteoarthritis in his hips. He was kept on the team's active forty-man roster for the next three years.

THE MOOSE

Mike Mussina was the Orioles best pitcher since Jim Palmer. In his first career start with the Birds on August 4, 1991, Moose lost a 1–0 decision to the White Sox, on a stellar, four-hit performance. It was a demoralizing foreshadowing of things to come. Despite the franchise rifling through pitching coaches like the White House through press secretaries, Mussina managed to put up fantastic numbers in his ten seasons with the team, and twice helped the Orioles to the playoffs. He was a five-time All-Star with the Birds, on five occasions finished in the top five in Cy Young voting, and was one of the decade's best pitchers.

In 1997, the Orioles re-signed Mussina to a three-year, $20.45 million contract extension. In a rare act of hometown favoritism by a professional athlete, Mussina effectively cut Angelos a break by re-signing with his team at a discount. Moose would come to regret it. The contract was widely criticized by the league's pitchers and the Players Union's Donald Fehr for undercutting the market.

In 1999, fellow Orioles starter Scott Erickson signed a longer-term deal to the tune of five years for $32 million. While he had a couple of exceptional years with Minnesota and a few acceptable years with the O's, Erickson was no Mussina.

At the end of the 2000 season, Mussina's contract was up. During that year, Angelos was unloading many of the team's big-name players at the deadline (B. J. Surhoff, Will "The Thrill" Clark) while showing no sincere commitment to retaining arguably the most productive pitcher of the decade. Angelos's initial bid was five years at $50 million. Mussina didn't need to call on his Stanford economics degree in valuing this offer. He was aghast and indicated that free agency was likely the following season. Angelos upped the ante a few times throughout the year, but was noticeably gun-shy each and every step of the way. Could it have had anything to do with the fact that fellow starter and big-time earner Scott Erickson was on his way to a nightmare 5–8, 7.87 ERA season? We think so.

In what turned out to be his final start for the Birds, Mussina beat the Yankees, 9–1. New York's management liked what they

TEAM ISSUES ★ 141

saw—probably not at the time, but after the season when they were reviewing film, anyway. In 2000, Mussina led the AL in innings pitched (237.3) and was dominant in key moments with runners in scoring position. In November 2000, the Yanks signed Moose to a six-year, $88.5 million contract.

The Orioles haven't had a number-one guy since.

JAVY LOPEZ

Following the 2003 season, the Orioles fell for Javy Lopez's contract year chicanery. Lopez's numbers at the plate exploded in his last season with Atlanta, thus dramatically increasing his free agent market value in advance of 2004. It's not an unusual phenomenon (players often suddenly seem a bit more dedicated to plying their trade in the final year of their contracts), and it's akin to the owner of an old Chevelle buffing his baby up with Armor All and Turtle Wax before putting the FOR SALE sign in the rear window.

Since that anomalous year, Lopez has frequently been hurt and has been only a shell of his 2003 self. At the expense of the Orioles and their fans, Co-General Managers (Co-GMs??) Jim Beattie and Mike Flanagan just had to have Lopez's bat.

THE 1997 ALCS

The Orioles thought they had caught a break in the '97 ALCS when, instead of the Yankees, they met an eighty-six-win Cleveland team that Baltimore had beaten in the previous year's Division Series. But somehow, despite outscoring the Tribe and holding them to a .193 team batting average, the Orioles dropped the series, with all four of their losses coming by a single run. In Game Two, Baltimore, already up 1–0 in the Series, cruised into the eighth with a 4–2 lead. They handed the ball to Armando Benitez, who promptly gave up a three-run homer to Marquis Grissom. In the twelfth inning of Game Three, Orioles catcher Lenny Webster failed to chase after a passed ball, thinking it was foul-tipped, and Omar Vizquel raced home from third with the winning run. In Game Four, the O's tied the game with a run in the top of the ninth, only to promptly give up the game on Sandy Alomar's RBI single in the bottom of the ninth.

After winning Game Five to stay alive and send the series back to Baltimore, the O's sent the pride of Montoursville, Mike Mussina, to the mound in Game Six. Mussina was superlative, giving up just one hit and striking out ten in eight innings of masterful work. His teammates rewarded him by stranding fourteen men on base, hitting into two double plays, going 0-for-11 with runners in scoring position, and allowing the game to remain scoreless into extra innings. Once there, Big-Game Benitez dry-humped the pooch again, coughing up the go-ahead home run to Tony "Fungo" Fernandez in the top of the eleventh—the same Tony Fernandez who, in seventeen seasons, averaged slightly more than one home run every one hundred at-bats. Robby Alomar took a called third strike with two outs and a man on in the bottom of the inning to send the Birds home with one of the more shocking defeats in postseason history. Serving up a go-ahead homer to Tony Fernandez? Who said anything about a curse?

THE WASHINGTON NATIONALS

Salt in the wounds. Kicking a man when he's down. Pick an old, cynical saying, and most likely it could be used to describe September 29, 2004, the day Major League Baseball announced that the Montreal Expos would move from French Canada to Washington, D.C., the following season. The proposal was overwhelmingly approved by baseball's owners, 29–1. Any guesses as to who cast the lone dissenting vote? Survey says: Baltimore Orioles owner Peter Angelos! Not that anyone should blame poor Peter for his disdain for the deal. The Orioles had been the only team in the Baltimore–D.C. area for more than three decades. Commissioner Selig acknowledged the impending hardship and conceded somewhat, giving the Orioles broadcast rights to the Nationals games through their own network. But if the Curse of Jeffrey Maier keeps working its magic, and as Orioles fans begin to defect en masse to the Nats, all those broadcasts will serve to do is remind the Baltimore faithful of a time when their seats used to be filled, too.

SAMMY SOSA

Sosa's character was first questioned in 2003 when he grabbed a corked bat "by mistake" and used it during a game. Curiously, baseball fans let that episode slide. But in March 2005, while testifying to Congress and sitting behind the same table as the finger-pointing fibber Palmeiro, Sosa played the "no hablo ingles" card. What happened to the endearing "I'm so 'appy to be here's" for which he'd become famous? This pathetic and disrespectful display came three months after the Orioles had signed themselves yet another clubhouse cancer. Despite injuring himself sneezing the year prior and walking out on his Chicago Cub teammates just after the start of their final game of the year, Baltimore just had to have Sosa's (corked?) bat. In his only season with the Orioles, Sosa averaged .221 at the plate and hit a paltry fourteen home runs in 102 games, which equated to approximately $775,000 per round-tripper. This coming two seasons after a five-year stretch during which Sammy averaged an eye-popping fifty-five home runs per year. Speaking of 2005 . . .

THE 2005 REGULAR SEASON

For the first sixty-two days of the season, the Orioles held sole possession of first place in the American League East. Not the Yankees, not the Red Sox, but the Baltimore Orioles. But then the team suffered a string of injuries, the most disheartening coming to their scrappy second baseman, Brian Roberts, who had started the All-Star Game after enjoying a career first half. He, like so many other Orioles, was not able to insulate himself from the rest of the team's unraveling. Lopez, Palmeiro, the perpetually whiny Miguel Tejada, M.A.D.D. poster boy Sidney Ponson, and Sosa were all major contributors to the snowball effect. After playing .600 baseball for nearly half the year, the Orioles imploded and went 32–60 in the second half. Manager Lee Mazzilli lost his job and, following one of the least memorable seasons in Orioles history, owner Peter Angelos was quoted as saying, "We are coming back strong next year. I know you have heard that tune before, but this time it will literally come true." The Orioles went 70–92 the next year, winning four fewer games than they did in the season that guilt-tripped Angelos into puking out that regrettable comment.

Considering the level of hardship endured by the Orioles organization and their fans since the mid-'80s and *especially* since that October night in 1996, Angelos's quotes nearly a decade later in a June 2006 *Washington Post* piece were unnerving to say the least. The article concerned a standout senior ballplayer from Wesleyan University, a Division III program located in Middletown, Connecticut. The outfielder/third baseman had just become the school's all-time hits leader and had hopes of making the jump to professional ball. But what was so noteworthy about a first-team all-NESCAC selection that made it fit to print on the sports pages of the *Washington Post*? The 5'11", 190-pound Wesleyan senior was none other than Jeffrey Maier.

Upon news of Maier's record-setting double, *Post* staff writer David Sheinin called the Orioles owner for a reaction to Maier's achievement. And he got one, with Angelos going on record to say: "I wouldn't be at all opposed to [drafting Maier]. In fact, I'd say it's a very interesting development. You can say the Orioles are very seriously considering him. I know this much: I was at that game, and he certainly did seem to be a heck of an outfielder. Sure, we'd take him. In fact, I like the idea more and more, the more I think about it." Baltimore never actually ended up drafting Maier, as many news outlets erroneously reported, but the simple fact that Angelos blurted out that they were even considering doing so is a microcosm of all that's gone wrong during his administration's tenure.

THE WORST FRANCHISE-
KILLING LOSSES

A particularly nasty defeat can be like Chernobyl, with the fall-out lingering for years, decades—forever. The loss can be so debilitating, so demoralizing, that the loser is unable to come back from it.

5. ST. LOUIS CARDINALS: 1984 WEEK SIXTEEN VERSUS WASHINGTON REDSKINS

What Happened: If victorious over the Redskins in RFK, the Cinderella Cardinals would win the NFC East and host a playoff game for the first time ever in St. Louis. A loss meant no playoffs at all. The Cardinals spotted Washington a 26–7 lead, but the passing combination of Neil Lomax and Roy Green brought St. Louis roaring back. The Cardinals briefly led, but a field goal gave Washington a 29–27 lead with fewer than two minutes remaining. A last-second St. Louis field goal attempt missed, and the Cardinals' season was over.

The Aftermath: The Cardinals collapsed in 1985 and '86, going a combined 9–22–1. Neil Lomax, who threw for 4,614 yards in '84, went into a premature career decline. Popular coach Jim Hanifan was fired. Football fan support, always tenuous in St. Louis, dwindled. After the 1987 season, owner Bill Bidwell packed up the Cards and moved them west to greater Phoenix.

4. ORLANDO MAGIC: GAME ONE, 1995 NBA FINALS

What Happened: With its superstar duo of Shaquille O'Neal and Penny Hardaway, fifty-seven-win Orlando was expected to roll in the Finals against the Houston Rockets, who had won just forty-seven regular-season games. The Magic led Game One by three with ten seconds left when Orlando guard Nick Anderson was fouled. Needing to make just one free throw to clinch the game, he missed them both. Then, after grabbing the offensive rebound, he missed two more. Houston tied the game with a three-pointer and won in overtime, 120–118.

The Aftermath: The Rockets rolled to a shocking four-game sweep of the stunned Magic. Nick Anderson developed a mental block at the charity stripe that pretty much ruined his career. In 1996, Michael Jordan and the Bulls slammed the window of opportunity shut on Orlando with an Eastern Conference Finals sweep. Shaq left for Los Angeles, Penny Hardaway's career was sidetracked by injuries, and Orlando ceased to be a serious contender.

3. PORTLAND TRAIL BLAZERS: GAME SEVEN, 2000 WESTERN CONFERENCE FINALS

What Happened: Portland led the Los Angeles Lakers 75–60 with 10:28 left in the fourth quarter, then missed thirteen straight shots, gave up a game-tying 15–0 run, and lost 89–84. The Blazers had to scramble back from a three-games-to-one deficit just to force a seventh game. All it earned them was notoriety and embarrassment.

The Aftermath: In a rash response to the series loss, young Jermaine O'Neal was traded to Indiana for Dale Davis, who was aging in dog years. Portland met the Lakers again in the 2001 and '02 playoffs, and was swept both years. Eventually age and character issues overtook the "Jail Blazers." In 2004–05 they had their worst season in more than thirty years, and to this day, things aren't exactly looking up in Rip City.

2. HOUSTON OILERS: 1992 AFC FIRST-ROUND PLAYOFF GAME

What Happened: The Oilers had a history of playoff chokes, but this was the mother of them. Leading the Buffalo Bills 35–3 early in the third quarter, Houston gave up four touchdowns in about seven minutes and ended up losing in overtime, 41–38. It is the biggest comeback, and biggest blown lead, in NFL history.

The Aftermath: The following year the Oilers won the AFC Central but again blew a second-half lead to lose in the playoffs, this time to the Chiefs. The year 1993 was marred by turmoil, especially in the coaching staff, where defensive coordinator Buddy Ryan tried to wring the neck of offensive coordinator Kevin Gilbride in the middle of a game. In 1994 Houston dumped Warren Moon—who was the least of their problems—and won two games with "Commander Cody" Carlson under center. Fans threw up their hands and walked away. In 1995 the team announced plans to move out of Houston. A "Save the Oilers" rally in the city's downtown drew roughly sixty-five people. Today, the franchise plies its trade in Nashville as the Tennessee Titans.

1. PITTSBURGH PIRATES: GAME SEVEN, 1992 NATIONAL LEAGUE CHAMPIONSHIP SERIES

What Happened: After rallying from a three-games-to-one deficit to tie the series, the Pirates took a 2–0 lead into the bottom of the ninth inning of Game Seven. The Braves then scored three runs, winning the game and the series on Francisco Cabrera's two-out, two-run single off Stan Belinda. Both runs were unearned.

The Aftermath: Everyone knew at the time that 1992 was the last chance for the Pirates. The core of their early '90s teams was breaking up. Bobby Bonilla was already gone, and Barry Bonds and Doug Drabek also became ex-Pirates following the 1992 season. Pittsburgh fell below .500 in '93 and, thanks to a combination of a lack of revenue and a lack of management brains, has remained a permanent denizen of the National League's murky depths ever since.

THE BALTIMORE COLTS, 1975–83

From Ray May to Mayday: The Worst of Team Declines

The story of the Colts and their last years in Baltimore touches on just about every aspect of the Worst of Sports as it applies to franchises. Postseason failure, devastating injuries, lousy ownership, poor player evaluations, debilitating addictions, wholesale betrayal of a fan base—you name the malady, it pops up at one point or another in this woeful story of the final plunge into the abyss of a team whose last years resembled a computer rendition of a plane being brought down by its own pilot.

The Colts were one of the best teams in football for years. From the late '50s into the '70s they won a Super Bowl, three NFL Championships, five conference championships, and two division titles. But the core of the great teams of the 1960s suddenly got old all at once. For a time there was no adequate talent in Baltimore to replace the departed stars of previous years, and the team languished. From 1972 through '74, the Colts had a three-year record of 11–31. In 1974 they hit rock bottom, finishing with the worst record in the league.

But in 1975 came a revival. After starting the season 1–4, the Colts exploded, winning their final nine games and dethroning Don

Shula's Dolphins as champions of the AFC East. The keys to the Baltimore renaissance were many, including a talented young front four, the development of Lydell Mitchell into one of the league's most versatile backs, top-flight young receivers such as Roger Carr and Raymond Chester, unexpected late-round finds like Bruce Laird and Stan White, and others. But the pièce de résistance of the brave new Colts was quarterback Bert Jones.

Bert Jones isn't remembered like some of his contemporaries, such as Terry Bradshaw, Roger Staubach, and Ken Stabler. His prime years shortened by injuries, Jones isn't a Hall of Famer and never will be. But for a time in the mid-'70s, there wasn't a better pure passer in football than the country boy from LSU. Jones was a talent similar to the soon-to-be star John Elway not only in the number 7 on his jersey, but also in size, running ability, and a cannon of an arm. And much like Elway was the Denver franchise in the 1980s, so was Jones for Baltimore in the '70s. With Bert Jones went the Colts.

And with Jones healthy and firing heat-seekers all over Memorial Stadium, the Colts were very successful—to a point, anyway. Baltimore won three straight AFC East titles in 1975–77. In one thirty-three-game stretch lasting from Week Six of the 1975 season through Week Ten of the '77 campaign, the Colts won twenty-nine games and lost four.

But for all this success, the faint sulfuric whiff of failure hung over the franchise. The Colts weren't just masters of the AFC East, they were also masters of horrible timing. Their rise to power coincided with the dynastic peak of the all-conquering Steelers. Baltimore's reward for its remarkable 1975 turnaround was an all-expenses-paid trip to Pittsburgh's Three Rivers Stadium for a divisional playoff game against a Steelers team that was for all intents and purposes unbeatable. Pittsburgh briefly knocked Jones out of the game with a knee injury and cruised 28–10, scoring the clinching touchdown on a ninety-three-yard fumble return by Andy Russell. Legend has it that this game saw the invention of the Terrible Towel, meaning that Baltimore's failure in essence gave birth to the doleful phenomenon of thousands of yinzers waving yellow rags while Myron Cope gratingly intones, *"And look at dis, da Terrible Towels are all over da place, dare flyin' everywhere."*

Anyway, the beat-down in Pittsburgh, while not surprising, was an unpleasant way to end a magnificent season. But it didn't get better. The springtime turned out to be just an Indian summer, and the catalog of Worsts began. Perhaps they weren't the Worst in every area but they were a good contender for any top-five list.

THE WORST PLAYOFF DEFEAT

In 1976, the Colts won the AFC East for the second straight year and sailed into the playoffs riding an offense that had averaged almost thirty points a game in the regular season. Bert Jones had his greatest season in '76, throwing for 3,104 yards, twenty-four touchdowns, nine interceptions, and a 102.5 QB rating. Lydell Mitchell finished third in the NFL in rushing yardage and in receptions. Roger Carr piled up 1,112 yards on just forty-three receptions (an average of nearly 26 yards per catch) and twelve touchdowns.

The high-powered Colts were at home in the divisional playoffs, and played the Steelers again. Like the Colts of the previous year, Pittsburgh had started the year 1–4 and closed out with nine straight wins, five of them by shutout, outscoring their opponents 234–32 in the process. The Colts were a good team; the Steelers were a great team, and one that was hitting on every possible cylinder. Baltimore never really had a prayer, although it probably thought it did—at least until Pittsburgh's opening possession when, on the third play, Bradshaw took advantage of double coverage on Lynn Swann and hit Frank Lewis straight down the middle of the field for a seventy-six-yard touchdown.

Pittsburgh rolled up 526 total yards, holding Baltimore to 170, and trashed the Colts in Memorial Stadium, 40–14. Bradshaw completed fourteen of eighteen passes for 264 yards and three touchdowns, running up a perfect quarterback rating of 158.3. Jones went eleven of twenty-six and was picked off twice. Pittsburgh stole Baltimore's offense—and kept its own defense to go along with it.

Although there are far worse defeats in terms of margin, you'd have to look pretty hard to find another team that got thrashed as comprehensively as this, in its own building, in a playoff game.

THE WORST FAN STUNT

Appropriately enough, it came on the same day as the loss to the Steelers in the '76 playoffs. Twenty minutes after the final gun, a Colts fan and licensed pilot crashed his small plane into the upper deck of Memorial Stadium. No one, including the pilot, was hurt— the stands had cleared out in a hurry after the game, as downcast Colts fans were in no mood to hang around the scene of their team's evisceration. The crumpled Cessna dribbled fuel over the empty seats of the upper deck, but fire crews were on the scene and, unlike Baltimore's secondary, Memorial Stadium was saved from going up in flames.

Baltimore bounced back to win the AFC East for the third consecutive year in 1977. This time the Colts avoided the Steelers in the first round of the playoffs. They had a new opponent in the Raiders, and found a new way to lose, as Oakland came from behind late in the fourth quarter and defeated the Colts in double overtime, 37–31. Three straight division titles; three straight first-round losses in the playoffs; two at home, one humiliating, one gut-wrenching. And that was as good as it got for the Colts.

THE WORST FRANCHISE-DEVASTATING INJURY

Bert Jones suffered a separated shoulder in a meaningless preseason game in 1978 and spent most of the next two seasons lamed up, watching other quarterbacks pilot the team. All in all, he started seven out of the thirty-two games Baltimore played in those two seasons. The Colts were 5–2 in those games. In the other twenty-five games, they were 5–20. After 1977, the Colts never had another winning season in Baltimore, and Bert Jones never regained his preinjury form, although later he did make a pretty good foil for L. C. Greenwood in those old Lite Beer From Miller commercials.

THE WORST START TO A SEASON

The Colts opened the 1978 season with backup quarterback Bill Troup at the helm. Tall, lanky, and possessing a drooping mustache and a curly white-guy 'fro, Troup more resembled Donald Sutherland's character in *Animal House* than a competent NFL quarterback. The offense suffered. But the horror that was the team's first two games was a total team effort. Baltimore opened the '78 season in Texas Stadium with a Monday Night contest against the defending World Champion Cowboys. Dallas ran up a club-record 587 total yards and shut out the Colts, 38–0. The avatar of Baltimore impotence appeared in the second quarter, when Dallas's Tony Dorsett caught a screen pass and went ninety-one yards for a touchdown. Baltimore's defensive pursuit on the play was so nonexistent that Dorsett was able to jog the last twenty yards, exchanging old-school *right on, brother*–style low-fives with teammates.

The next week, Baltimore opened its 1978 home schedule against Miami. Bill Troup's first pass of the game resulted in a fifty-three-yard interception return for a touchdown by Dolphin cornerback Norris Thomas. Miami intercepted five more Colt passes, took a 28–0 halftime lead, and won 42–0. The '78 Colts were outscored 80–0 in their first two games, as they and their fans were brutally initiated into the world of football irrelevance.

THE WORST OWNER

On July 13, 1972, Illinois air-conditioning magnate Robert Irsay traded the ownership of the Los Angeles Rams to Carroll Rosenbloom in return for that of the Colts. With the exception of the brief run of success in the middle of the '70s, Irsay's ownership in Baltimore was an almost unmitigated disaster, and even the turnaround was tarnished by association with its engineer, GM Joe

Thomas, a gifted talent evaluator and rampant megalomaniac who was roundly disliked around B-More for selling Johnny Unitas to the Chargers before the '73 season.

Irsay was a born meddler. In 1974 he fired head coach Howard Schnellenberger following a game in Philadelphia because Schnellenberger refused to change quarterbacks at halftime. Two years later, Irsay triggered a squad mutiny when he canned Ted Marchibroda following a preseason game in 1976. Irsay was what they used to call a "toper," and he ran the Colts with the fuzzy-headed aplomb of Joseph Hazelwood at the wheel of the *Exxon Valdez*. The erratic nature of the team's ownership bore sour fruit on the field. When Baltimore went into its late-'70s tailspin, there was no one around competent enough to reverse it.

THE WORST PASS PROTECTION (GAME)

Midway through the 1980 season, Bert Jones was back in the huddle, and the Colts were a relatively healthy 4–3 going into their matchup against St. Louis. Jones had been sacked just nine times in the first seven games of the season. In Week Eight, the Cardinals drove the former LSU star and future lumber mill operator into the painted dirt of the Memorial Stadium field twelve times, setting an NFL single-game record for sacks that has been tied but never broken. Baltimore lost, 17–10, and skidded to a 7–9 record, a mark Colts fans would soon look back on with nostalgia.

THE WORST SINGLE-SEASON NFL NONEXPANSION TEAM

The '81 Colts went 2–14, beating only the Patriots in the first and final weeks of the season, by a total of three points. Twelve of their defeats came by at least eleven points. Their fourteen consecutive losses came by an average score of 35–15, meaning, in a nutshell, that Baltimore simply was not competitive when it took the field. The 533 points surrendered by the Colts remains an NFL record; Baltimore gave up at least 21 points in every single game during the 1981 season and got torched for a league-record 424 yards per "contest." Opposing quarterbacks stood tall in the pocket against a Baltimore pass rush that netted thirteen sacks for the entire season. Baltimore deep men returned a total of twelve punts for 56 yards in 1981. Players fell asleep in film sessions and got hurt running out for the opening coin toss. It was a poor season.

THE WORST OPPONENTS IN NFL HISTORY

This distinction belongs to the finale of the 1981 season, when the 1–14 Colts met the 2–13 New England Patriots in a game later dubbed "The Stupor Bowl" by Chris Berman. The 3–27 combined record for the two teams was the worst ever for teams meeting in a regular-season game. The 1981 Patriots were a funny team—maybe the best two-win team in NFL history, for whatever that's worth. This was the only losing season for the Patriots between 1975 and 1989. New England's –48 points scored/allowed differential belonged to a team with six or seven wins—a decent team having an off-season, not a 2–14 basket case. But this Patriots team excelled at finding ways to lose. They were 0–8 in games decided by seven points or less, including two overtime defeats. One of those fourteen L's came on a Hail Mary against the Bills. It isn't your year when Buffalo is getting over on you in the karma department.

The historic nature of the Stupor Bowl didn't seem to impress Baltimore fans. On a cold, pre-Christmas day, an intimate gathering of 17,073 watched the Colts edge the Patriots 23–21 behind three Bert Jones touchdown passes.[*]

THE WORST FIRST-ROUND PICK

Seeking a replacement for Jones, who had been exiled to the Rams to finish his career, the Colts drafted Ohio State quarterback Art Schlichter with the fourth overall pick in 1982. Schlichter wound up with six times as many stints in jail (eighteen) as career touchdown passes (three), and the number of the former is still growing.

---

[*] From Week Fourteen of 1980 until Week Four of 1983, the Colts were 3–27–1: 3–1 against New England, 0–24–1 against everyone else.

When it was revealed that Schlichter had spent his entire six-figure signing bonus paying off bookies, the NFL suspended him for the 1983 season. Baltimore would have been better off taking BYU quarterback Jim McMahon, who went to the Bears with the next selection. (True, the Punky QB wasn't great, but he also didn't have to go to Nicky Santoro to get the heat turned back on.)

THE WORST FIRST-ROUND PICK (REDUX)

The reaction of the front office to the failure of Schlichter only deepened the grave the franchise was energetically digging for itself. The 1982 Colts went 0–8–1 in the strike-shortened season. It was the first winless season in the NFL for a nonexpansion team since World War II.

One positive aspect about not winning a single stinking game all season was getting that first overall pick. But Stanford quarterback John Elway, the consensus number one in the draft, had a clearly stated and oft-repeated lack of desire to play in Baltimore. This was due mainly to the condition of the team and its coach, Frank Kush, former Arizona State boss, a whip-cracking, face mask–grabbing screamer that Elway and his father, Stanford coach Jack Elway, knew and disliked from their days in the Pac-10. The Colts drafted Elway. Believe it or not, he refused to report.

GM Ernie Accorsi claimed he could have eventually persuaded Elway to report to Baltimore. Like Joe Johnston's claim that he had a plan to save Atlanta from Sherman in 1864, it was an easy one to make. Six days after the draft, without consulting Accorsi or anyone else in his front office, Robert Irsay dealt Elway to the Broncos for tackle Chris Hinton, quarterback Mark Herrmann, and Denver's 1984 first-round pick. Elway's first of forty-six career fourth-quarter comebacks? December 11, 1983, when he rallied the Broncos from 19 down to beat . . . Baltimore.

THE WORST FRANCHISE SHIFT

The Colts finished last in the NFL in attendance in 1983. On March 28, 1984, Irsay loaded his franchise onto the Mayflower trucks and decamped under the cover of darkness for Indianapolis. Baltimore went without professional football for twelve seasons, unless you count the experiment with the silver-helmeted CFL "Colts," which we sure as hell don't. Neither did Baltimore, which is why eventually the city colluded with Art Modell to heist the Browns from Cleveland in 1995 and bring pro football back to Maryland. Speaking of Worsts.

Coaches Larry Brown and Mike Fratello have both undergone mysterious transformations over the course of their careers. One for the better, the other not so much. You decide which. *Larry Brown photos: Heinz Klutemeier/Sports Illustrated; AP Images/Paul Sancya. Mike Fratello photos: Copyright 1982 NBAE, by Scott Cunningham NBAE/Getty Images; AP Images/Douglas C. Pizac*

LOOK AWAY

From the power and pageantry of NFL Films to the glorious vision that is the USC cheerleaders, the world of sports is quite often a bountiful feast for the senses. But where lies beauty, so lurks the beast: Hideki Matsui in high definition; the vertical-striped socks worn by the original Denver Broncos; Lou Carnesecca's sweaters; sunburns on NASCAR fans; the Vet. You want to look away, but you can't. Neither can we.

★ EVOLUTION VERSUS DEVOLUTION
★ THE ALL-ROTUND PITCHING STAFF
★ "BLOOD IN THE WATER"
★ THE WORST OF GROTESQUE INJURIES
★ UNIFORM VIOLATIONS
★ THE NATIVE AMERICAN CONUNDRUM
★ THE MINNESOTA MASSACRE

EVOLUTION VERSUS DEVOLUTION

Larry Brown's Sartorial Progression: Mike Fratello's Follicle Regression

If clothes do indeed make the man, then much can be deduced from Larry Brown's historical patterns of dress. Throughout the course of his career, Coach Brown has led two very distinct fashion lives. In both cases, his definitive style choices were the by-product of conformity of the highest order.

An individual's closet naturally evolves over time, ebbing and flowing with the passing trends. But from his first basketball-coaching stop with the ABA's Carolina Cougars in 1972 to his brief but tumultuous tenure with the NBA's New York Knicks ending in 2006, Larry Brown's sartorial proclivities underwent a drastic, New England Patriots- and/or Dallas Mavericks-esque transformation. And as it was with those once-pitiful franchises, change was most certainly welcome when it pertained to Brown's attire.*

* Phil Jackson was another coach who needed to do some work on himself before making it big. Then a top CBA coach, Jackson interviewed for the Bulls job in 1986, but mortified owner Jerry Reinsdorf when he walked into the room wearing a beard that is described in Sam Smith's book *The Jordan Rules* as looking like he was eating a muskrat. Doug Collins, who was clearly unstable yet clean-shaven, got the job. When Jackson reinterviewed in 1989, he wore only a mustache and was hired.

Coach Brown's current Chairman of the Board-like appearance is a classic look and one that demands respect, conveys responsibility, and bespeaks a man who feels compelled to represent himself and the NBA in a professional manner. But the sidelines have not always been patrolled by Brooks Brothers Brown. There was once a very different-looking Larry Brown, one with a sense of style so outlandish he became known as "The Modfather" among his peers. Never has a moniker been so appropriate at one point in time, and so ironic at another.

The American Basketball Association commenced play in 1967 as a league created to compete head-to-head with the established National Basketball Association. The ABA knew its only chance for survival was to pursue a differentiation strategy, one that focused on providing spectators with what their more conservative rival league often lacked: pizzazz. And the ABA did just that, with forward-thinking and innovative modifications to Dr. Naismith's brainchild, such as the three-point shot; a red, white, and blue ball; and a lively style of play compared to the more staid NBA game. And yes, there were gorgeous 'fros too—lots of them!

The ABA was a microcosm of the '60s and '70s counterculture movement, and Larry Brown, who was cutting his coaching teeth at the time, embraced it with both arms. More important, he championed all that it stood for via his wardrobe. The Modfather loved to shop for new getups, and he incorporated the entirety of the Roy G. Biv continuum into his accoutrement: wildly bright and colorful striped sweaters that would've made Bert, Ernie, and Bill Cosby jealous; multicolored bell-bottom overalls that would've left the Little House on the Prairie's wardrobe director speechless; nut-hugging checkered leisure pants that would've brought Clark W. Griswold's cousin Eddie to tears of joy; and broad-collared, flower print shirts that would've made either Tony Manero or Austin Powers green with envy. And please don't forget the Willy Wonka-ish billowy bow ties, or the clodhopper platform shoes. In an era when styles got more than a bit out of hand, Larry Brown was a fashion demigod.

The ABA folded in 1976, not for a lack of popularity, but because of financial losses exacerbated by the lack of a national television contract. Four of its teams managed to avoid extinction by folding into the NBA: the New York Nets, the Denver Nuggets, the Indiana Pacers, and the San Antonio Spurs. Brown was coach of the Nuggets at the time and, while he fought the status quo initially (he felt the ABA players were treated as second-class citizens and hated the aesthetically boring brown ball), he would soon concede and conform to his new environment and undergo a makeover of biblical proportions. While he wasn't ready to go full-on corporate just yet, Larry's style grew muted in comparison to his fabulous outfits of ABA yesteryear. Stints as head coach of UCLA and Kansas in the 1980s saw Coach Brown sporting a brand-new bespectacled look, which we have reason to believe may have inspired PGA golfer Tom Kite's nerdy choice of eyewear a few years down the road.

When he returned to the NBA for good in 1988 as coach of the San Antonio Spurs, Brown's evolution from ABA rebel to Brooks Brothers fit model was near completion. Over the next eighteen years, Brown would go on to coach five more NBA teams, ending his coaching career in New York in 2006 (maybe) after a controversial season with the train wreck that was the Isiah Thomas-misled Knicks. But unlike in the past where even the most fashion-forward would cringe at his offensive uniforms, the controversy swirling around Brown had nothing to do with his dress. He had evolved.

There's a flip side to every coin, and in the case of Mike Fratello's own personal *devolution,* let's associate him with "heads," for reasons about to become obvious. Coach Fratello's sad story of follicular decline, while less complex than Coach Brown's aforementioned attire evolution, will sound familiar to a large percentage of the male population. His desperate course of action, however, will only ring true with a much smaller subset of pitiable individuals.

Born in 1947 in Hackensack, New Jersey, Mike Fratello was a professional basketball coach in the NBA with the Atlanta Hawks, the Cleveland Cavaliers, and the Memphis Grizzlies for seventeen seasons. In the years between the Atlanta and Cleveland jobs and then the Cleveland and Memphis gigs, while waiting for a call from his old boys' coaching network placement officer, Fratello did what many out-of-work coaches do: he got behind the mic and in front of the camera. It was during his stint with NBC in the early '90s that fellow talking head Marv Albert dubbed the 5'7" Fratello the "Czar of the Telestrator."

Short + Balding = Confidence Constrained. Fratello has had a growing forehead for almost his entire coaching career. But even his original curly-topped 'do, a familiar sight in the 1980s NBA, showed signs of recession from an early stage. When he resurfaced as the head coach in Cleveland in the '90s, the curls were still there, but the baldness continued to encroach.

Aside from the superficial shortcomings, in looking at Fratello's coaching career there's a fair bit of failure that may also be part of his root bed of insecurity. While his overall record is a respectable 572–465, Fratello's postseason performance has been wretched. Only once in seventeen seasons has his team won a division—the Atlanta Hawks in 1986–87—and in ten of the eleven years his squads made the playoffs, they were eliminated in either the first or second round. He has never won an NBA championship. His emphasis on defense was a mixed bag—it never took with the high-flying Hawks, and although the strategy boosted the less-than-talented Cavaliers of the '90s to several playoff appearances, all of them were short-lived. What's more, the deliberate, slow-it-down style sapped fan interest in Cleveland despite the relative success of the team. His teams in Memphis made the playoffs as well, but went 0–8 in a pair of first-round sweeps. Although admired for his acumen, the Czar has never ruled the NBA.

Taking all of these confidence-eroding factors into consideration, and sprinkling in the self-conscious nature inherent to network broadcasting, it's understandable that Coach Fratello would make the decision to artificially rectify his scalp situation. It's never been confirmed or officially acknowledged in public, but sometime toward the end of his stint with the Cleveland Cavaliers in the late

'90s, Fratello had some construction work done up top. Whether he had a little grafting done, got some plugs thrown in, or went with the "hair-in-a-can" solution à la Beau Bridges in *The Fabulous Baker Boys* has never been determined. What is known, however, is that when the little guy embarked on the latest stage of his coaching career with the Grizzlies, he did so sporting a weird, sandy-colored straight-haired look that in no way, shape, or form resembled the tight curly 'do of his Atlanta days.

The devolution of Coach Fratello's hair paralleled that of his NBA coaching career—from mastermind of Dominique Wilkin's prodigiously talented Hawks, to overachieving string-puller in Cleveland, to interim coach in Memphis. Although most of the blame for Fratello's firing from Memphis in late 2006 should be centered on the Grizzlies' 6–24 record at the time of the dismissal, the corrosive effect of his brand-new 'do can't be ruled out as a contributing factor.

Larry Brown is an NBA fashion icon. Mike Fratello stands for something less distinguished. Their strikingly divergent evolutionary paths would twist even Darwin's noodle.

THE ALL-ROTUND PITCHING STAFF

These Pitchers Would Welcome the Chocolate-covered Ball Back from Engelberg

Baseball will always have its Cecil Fielders and late-career Tony Gwynns lumbering around the dugouts, but for the most part, its players are relatively fit. Pitchers, however, hold down a higher rate of outsized waistlines. And while the frequency of chubbiness relative to other positions on the diamond is a curious phenomenon, statistics flesh out the notion that big pitchers have a proven record of prosperity and durability.

Ahh, the plight of the gluttonous hurler. When he's pitching well, management, the media, and the fans all wonder how effective he'd really be if only he could slim down. And when he's not getting batters out, the consensus is that it's because of the weight problem. But has anyone ever considered that maybe, just maybe, in order to surmount the stereotypes he faces, a rotund pitcher has to be exceptionally good? The following five starters and five bullpen members were exceptionally good—most of them at least. They also were exceptionally sized. Coincidence? We think it would be small-minded to say so.

THE STARTING ROTUND ROTATION

Fernando Valenzuela

In 1981, this Mexican southpaw became an international phenom-enon and planted the seeds for NAFTA when he won Major League Baseball's Cy Young Award—the only rookie pitcher so honored. His Rookie of the Year selection that season was a foregone con-clusion. And the pristine sod of southern California's Chavez Ravine could not have been a more fitting home for Fernando. He was a favorite son in that region of the country, beloved by his brethren in the barrios and adopted by the gringos in the Valley.

Through a six-season stretch running from 1981 to 1986, Fer-nando mania was at its peak, and so was "El As Gordo"'s game. His "eyes to the gods" windup and vicious screwball helped him average more than 250 innings per season and a 2.95 ERA through-out that span. He was a National League All-Star selection in all six of those years. In three seasons he struck out two hundred or more, led the league in shutouts in the magical year of 1981, was a three-time NL complete games leader, and won World Series rings with the Los Angeles Dodgers in 1981 and 1988. He could swing a bat well for his position, too, twice winning the Silver Slugger Award. And—giving credence to our theory of the durability of the chubby pitcher—Valenzuela, after his retirement from the MLB in 1997, continued to pitch in the Mexican Pacific League, even teaming up with his son, Fernando Jr., in 2006.

Mickey Lolich

Another fantastic southpaw who never missed a meal, Mickey Lolich dealt in the Major Leagues from 1963 to 1979. But a quick scan of the stat lines on the back of his baseball card reveals that Mickey was out of the game for the entire 1977 season. Was he in-jured? Playing in Japan? Nope. It was time to make the dough-nuts—literally. In 1977, Mickey Lolich decided to forgo pitching for the Detroit Tigers and instead opened a doughnut shop in Lake

Orion, Michigan. Whether or not the intent was to wiggle his way out of a contract with the New York Mets, a pitcher with a known weight problem skipping a year to open a doughnut shop is the height of hilarity—and secured Lolich's place on the prestigious *All-Rotund Pitching Staff.*

Always self-effacing, Lolich once described himself as a "beer drinker's idol" and keeping his epic bowlful of jelly under control was a cross he was forced to bear throughout his entire career. What a career it was, though. In the '68 World Series, the big man lifted the Detroit Tigers onto his weighty shoulders and carried them to the title, winning three games (all complete games in which he yielded only five runs total) and outdueling St. Louis Hall of Famer Bob Gibson in the deciding Game Seven. Another durable glutton, Lolich's name became synonymous with the complete game (195 in total), and he won fourteen or more games in ten con-secutive seasons. At retirement, he had whiffed more batters than any other lefty in Major League Baseball history* (2,679), employ-ing his four-seam fastball to record two hundred or more K's on seven occasions. During his thirteen seasons with the Tigers, Lolich was a three-time All-Star. His career year was 1971, when he pitched a staggering 376 innings, recorded 29 complete games, and fanned 308 batters.

Charles "Sid" Fernandez

A fifteen-year Major Leaguer who wore number 50 in honor of his native Hawaii, the fiftieth state, "El Sid" is yet another left-handed addition to the butterball staff. In Fernandez's first year in the Bigs, he was the model of efficiency, leading the league in both hits al-lowed (5.71) and strikeouts (9.51) per nine innings pitched. He was a two-time All-Star selection (1986, 1987), the former year winning a World Series ring as part of the "Amazin'" Mets pitching staff, whose members (Bob Ojeda, Dwight Gooden, El Sid, Ron Darling) boasted the four best ERAs in the National League that season.

* Lolich was eventually surpassed by Steve Carlton and Randy Johnson.

While there were many stretches of brilliance, however, Fernandez's pitching was inconsistent, sometimes fading over the course of a season, other times fading as it wore on. And he was a much better pitcher at home than he was in visiting ballparks, which we attribute to the known difficulty of eating well on the road. But in a display of versatility, some of his best work was done in relief roles: appearing twice out of the pen in the '86 World Series, Fernandez was particularly effective in Game Seven, retiring seven Red Sox in a row, four by strikeout.

Pinstripes are known to be slimming, but in all his years on the rubber for the Mets, El Sid's rump never met a set of stripes it couldn't stretch.

Rick Reuschel

"Big Daddy" Reuschel embarked on his nineteen-year Major League pitching career with the dreaded skinny–fat guy body. But he persevered, and by the time his twilight years on the mound came to pass, Reuschel's hard work with the utensils had earned him a respectable double chin, a couch potato's paunch, and a gluteal region to be reckoned with.

Continuing the trend inherent to most on the *Rotund Staff,* Reuschel was also a long-lasting pitcher, recording an impressive 102 career complete games, 26 of which were shutouts. He was a three-time All-Star and made World Series appearances with the Yankees in '81 and with the Giants in the earthquake-disrupted Bay Bridge Series of 1989. On both occasions his teams lost. In his final All-Star appearance in '89, a forty-year-old Reuschel started the game and surrendered memorable back-to-back bombs to the AL's Bo Jackson and Wade Boggs in the top of the first inning.

Fred Fitzsimmons

In a nineteen-year career with the Giants and Dodgers, "Fat Freddie" (that really was his nickname—they didn't pull punches in those days) pitched in three World Series, winning one of them with the

New York Giants in 1933, and won fifteen or more games on eight separate occasions. In nine straight seasons spanning the Roaring Twenties and the subsequent Depression, Fitzsimmons used his heft and his knuckleball to log more than two hundred innings pitched. He was also cheered by peers and fans alike for his adept fielding, often putting his wide body to use as might a catcher with a chest protector. Proclaimed to be the first pitcher to gain control over the pitch, the chunky Fitzsimmons relied heavily upon his knuckleball and a variety of deliveries to get batters out. His typical windup was unorthodox in that Fat Freddie would turn his back to home plate in an attempt to hide the ball from the hitters (à la Luis Tiant), then uncork it with a grunt that would make Monica Seles jealous.

THE ROTUND RELIEF CORPS

Rich Garces

El Guapo!

In a ten-year career, Rich Garces compiled a 23–10 record and struck out 296 batters in 341 innings, holding opposing hitters to a .227 batting average. His most misleading statistic was his weight, which was listed at 250 pounds in the Red Sox media guide. Only the original budget for Boston's Big Dig could compare in terms of gross underestimation.

Owner of one of the best nicknames in the history of sports, El Guapo became somewhat of a mythical figure and cult hero, despite his erratic performance, during his stint with the Red Sox at the turn of the century. His best year came in 1999, the same season Pedro Martinez walked on water against the Cleveland Indians in the ALDS. El Guapo posted a 1.55 ERA in '99 over forty innings in thirty appearances, but twice got shellacked by the Yankees in the ALCS.

Terry Forster

The zaftig Forster was a fine relief man for five teams in the '70s and '80s despite recurring arm problems. The first-ever free agent signed by the Los Angeles Dodgers, he pitched in two World Series for that franchise (losing in 1978 to the Yankees and returning the favor by beating them in 1981), giving up zero runs in six total innings of work. While his most prolific closing years were in the early '70s with the White Sox, his most efficient work out of the pen came with the Atlanta Braves in the mid-'80s when Forster weighed in at a cumbersome 270 pounds. In three seasons with the Bravos, his ERA was a minuscule 2.38, a sequence of digits Braves management wouldn't have minded seeing when Forster stepped on the scale as well.

After laboring in relative anonymity for five teams throughout the course of his sixteen-year career, in June 1985 Terry Forster became a household name and somewhat of a national celebrity when *Late Night* host David Letterman referred to him as a "fat tub of goo" during one of the show's opening monologues. But Forster knew his proportions were outsized and rolled with it, once remarking, "A waist is a terrible thing to mind."

Bob Wickman

The Wickster is a round man. Neither he nor his cadre of devoted fans would dare deny that fact. There isn't a league bowler on earth with a worse body than the beefy Green Bay, Wisconsin, native. But that matters not. After all, Wicky is a pitcher. And in his profession he is a two-time All-Star, led the American League in saves in 2005 with 45, is the Cleveland Indians all-time save leader, and has racked up more than 250 career saves. Beloved by his fans for his blue-collar aura, his cool head in nerve-racking ninth-inning situations, and just his general Bob Wickman-ness, the big bratwurst-lover is a welcome addition to the All-Rotund staff.

Bob Stanley

Stanley's career numbers scream durability, longevity, and reliability. Surviving for thirteen years with the Red Sox during the fickle, chaotic, and often disastrous Harrington/Yawkey regime proves that fact even without statistical backup. A sinker ball specialist, the Steamer is the club's all-time saves leader (132) and a member of the Red Sox Hall of Fame. During his career he tallied 693 strike-outs, 21 complete games, and seven shutouts, and he was a two-time American League All-Star. His best season came in 1983, when he led the Sox with 33 saves and posted a 2.45 ERA.

But many remember him only for that fateful jog from the Shea Stadium visitor's bull pen in Game Six of the 1986 World Series when he replaced Calvin Schiraldi, no Adonis in his own right. It looked as if there was an attempted jailbreak from Midget Prison transpiring underneath Stanley's uniform—breasts and ass in per-petual motion. With two outs in the tenth inning, Stanley's wild pitch allowed Kevin Mitchell to score and the Mets to tie the ball game. As the cliché-sayers say: the rest is history.

Charlie Kerfeld

Most sports almanacs, encyclopedias, biographies, and broadcasters speak in special p.c. code when discussing an athlete's characteris-tics, makeup, and shortcomings: "athletic"=dumb; "undersized"= too short; "methodical"=slow; "limited range"=can't shoot for shit; "control problems"=walks everybody; "intelligent"=unathletic; and so on and so forth. But for whatever reason, when Charlie Kerfeld is remembered, the kid gloves come off and the word *obese* invari-ably accompanies his name.

This is probably because the smart-talking Kerfeld dished it out as well as he took it. Another Major League lard-ass pioneer, Ker-feld once had thirty-seven boxes of Orange Jell-O written into his contract, and in 1987 he was caught literally red-handed, devour-ing a plate of ribs in the bull pen. His best year was his rookie sea-son, when he went 11–2 and posted a 2.69 ERA for the NL West Champion Astros. But when he ballooned to over 275 pounds the following year, Kerfeld was sent down to the minors due to "con-trol problems" of an entirely different sort.

FUTURE STARS

These slovenly pitchers' respective bodies of work (pun absolutely intended) have yet to be completed, but their *All-Rotund Pitching Staff* aspirations are no secret: Bartolo Colon, C. C. Sabathia, Livan Hernandez, Carlos Zambrano, Sidney Ponson, Runelvys Hernandez, and Bobby Jenks.

NOTABLE EXCLUSIONS

The Babe clearly had intentions of making this staff, as he ate and drank himself to a respectably portly state by the end of his career. But the Bambino wasn't a natural fat man. In his days with the Red Sox as the best young lefty in the game, Ruth was 6'2" and a shade under 200 pounds—big, fast (yes, fast), and obviously very powerful. He always had a round face, which made him look heavier, but early in his career the inspiration for most of the taunts directed at Ruth wasn't his weight. Instead, it was his looking like he had "black blood," which people were ruthless about back then.

Other notables who didn't quite make the cut include Johnny Hutchings, the heaviest baseball player of the '40s according to Bill James; David Wells, whose water is due to break any day now; the rubber-armed knuckleballer Wilbur Wood, who is best remembered for being the last Major League pitcher to start both ends of a double-header in 1973 (he lost both); and lastly, the man Yankees owner George Steinbrenner once referred to as a "fat pussy toad," Hideki Irabu.

"BLOOD IN THE WATER"

An Olympic Water Polo Battle Royale that
Embodied the Cold War Struggle

The tension was palpable when the Hungarian and Soviet water polo teams splashed into the pool for their 1956 Olympic semifinal match in Melbourne. Soviet tanks sat in Budapest and a Hungarian populist revolt had just been put down with unrestrained brutality. Thousands of Hungarians lay dead in the street and hundreds more would soon be tried and summarily executed, including Prime Minister Imre Nagy. With this violent political struggle as backdrop, two of the most powerful teams in the sport took to the water. What was supposed to be spirited Olympic competition soon turned into something less, and something more—the blood of Budapest coloring the water of a swimming pool in Australia.

The sport of water polo has a violent history of its own: the overt tackling and pulling in plain view of the spectators pales in comparison to the roughhousing that transpires below the surface. During water polo's formative years in the late 1800s, players often came to the surface gasping for air and nearing loss of consciousness after a long struggle below. At the time, the sport was considered so barbaric it was banned from university campuses in the

United States. The match between the USSR and Hungary in 1956 brought water polo back to its violent roots, and then took it to a level never before seen.

Near the conclusion of World War II, the Soviet Red Army sent Hitler's boys packing and "liberated" Hungary, among other countries. Having run roughshod over the Nazis throughout most of Eastern Europe, the Soviets grew fond of their new digs and decided to stay awhile. The war-ravaged natives had been flipped from Hitler's frying pan into Stalin's fire. They were not consulted on the matter, and a reluctant satellite began to turn in the Soviet orbit.

The Magyars had long been reluctant to accept anyone's dominion—especially Russia's—and when Stalin took a dirt nap in 1953, the winds of change began to blow. The year of Stalin's death there were riots against the Communists in East Berlin that were put down brutally. But the secret speech of new Soviet premier Nikita Khrushchev to the twentieth Party Congress, in which he denounced the crimes of Stalin, set a spark. In 1956, Poland upped the ante with an anti-Communist workers' revolt. Although it was quickly squashed where it began, the uprising spread to the south. On October 23, 1956, the students and workers of Hungary rallied peacefully in support of the Poles, marched en masse to various symbolic points throughout Budapest, and recited their list of demands: a multiparty system, free elections, withdrawal of Soviet troops from their country, and revocation of the Warsaw Pact.

With or without Stalin, the country formerly known as the CCCP was not an ideal negotiating partner. The next day the Soviets entered the dialogue with the rumbling of tank treads and the methodical beat of the boots of 200,000 soldiers. By November 4, the Hungarian Revolution was terminated in bloody fashion.

At the time of the uprising, Hungary's water polo team was training on the outskirts of Budapest before departing for the Melbourne Olympic Games. They were largely unaware of the extent of the unrest, unaware that their countrymen were serving as speed bumps for Soviet armor. Not until they arrived in Australia weeks later did they comprehend the scope of what had happened. But by the time they faced their Communist oppressors in the semifinals the first week of December,* Hungary's team had had plenty of time to digest the atrocities that had occurred in their homeland. The Olympics have long served as a proxy for political showmanship and the occasional settling of a cultural score. But never before or since in international competition has there been a match of two countries harboring this much ill will.

Before the match, Hungary was faced with a dilemma. They were the defending Olympic champion. Should they play the game straight and get to the final, or use it as a means of vengeance on behalf of their fallen countrymen? They chose to do both. Hungary's star forward, Ervin Zador, was quoted as saying, "We felt we were playing not just for ourselves but for every Hungarian. This game was the only way we could fight back." And fight they did indeed, though the Soviets didn't exactly roll onto their bellies and do the dead man's float. At the first whistle, aqua-boxing became a new Olympic sport. The Hungarians struck the first blow, quite literally: as Dezsö Gyarmati fired the ball past the Soviet keeper for the first goal of the match, he slobber-knocked the nearest defender. The Soviets responded in kind when Vyacheslav Kurennoi delivered a knuckle *borschtwich* of his own and was promptly sent to the penalty box. A full-on naval skirmish ensued.

With Hungary leading 4–0 and only a minute to play, the violence peaked: while the referees were attending to other matters, Valentin Prokopov propellered himself up and out of the water and blindsided Zador, who had scored twice, with a Cold War haymaker. Zador's right eye hemorrhaged; there was blood in the water. The crowd had seen enough. Consisting mostly of Hungarian ex-pats seeking safe haven in Australia, they stormed poolside with the seeming intent of rolling up their trousers and joining the fracas. As the spectators' passions boiled over, they pointed, cursed, and spat at the water-treading Soviets. But a sizeable security force quickly intervened—signs around the venue explicitly stated that

---

* The Melbourne Games was the first occasion the Olympics were held south of the equator. Because the seasons are reversed, the '56 Summer Olympics took place in late November and early December.

there was to be no running by the pool—and officials wisely called the game with Hungary declared the victors 4–0. This concluded one of the bloodiest events in Olympic history.

Afterward, the Hungarians threw a couple of red eyes on their bruises and went on to beat Yugoslavia in the gold medal match, 2–1, for their fourth Olympic water polo gold. Nearly half of the Hungarian Olympic delegation defected after the Melbourne Games. Their countrymen spent another four decades under the Soviet heel, including the time spent waiting for David Hasselhoff to outlast his *Knight Rider* contract and go about his true purpose: ending the Cold War.

THE WORST OF GROTESQUE INJURIES

Like an Amusement Park Warning: Not for the Faint of Heart, or the Weak of Stomach

As if attempting to transcend their own mortality, athletes pursue the impossible, using their bodies as the means of transportation. Sometimes they succeed, but sometimes the brute force, blinding speed, and reckless abandon required by sports at the highest level result in calamitous outcomes for the human frame.

CLINT MALARCHUK

In March 1989, Buffalo Sabres goalie Clint Malarchuk was between the pipes when Steve Tuttle of the St. Louis Blues made a dash toward the crease. Sabres defenseman Uwe Krupp was in hot pursuit, and as he made contact with the Blues' right-winger, Tuttle's leg and skate slashed through the air, catching Malarchuk in the throat, just under his mask. In horror-movie fashion, the blade slashed the goalie's external carotid artery, bringing him to his knees. His throat hemorrhaged and blood pooled on the ice below. Conscious throughout the nightmare, Malarchuk asked the trainer attending to his wound if he was going to live, then requested a priest, assuming his time had come. Meanwhile, those bearing witness to one of the more grisly sights in all of sports history were suffering as well: Malarchuk's teammates vomited on the ice, numerous spectators fainted, and two fans actually suffered heart attacks.

Miraculously, Malarchuk survived, doctors having used more than three hundred stitches to close the wound. He would even return to the ice that season, but never regained form. The NHL now requires all of its goalies to wear neck protection. How proactive of them.

DAVID BUSST

When his team's fateful match against Manchester United on April 8, 1996, commenced, Coventry City defender David Busst happened to be competing for a spot on the English national team. But this would be the last match for the twenty-nine-year-old Premier League star. Just two minutes in, while going for the ball on a corner kick, Busst collided with two Man U players and folded his leg under, snapping both his tibia and fibula with such force that they exploded through the skin. Blood flooded the pitch, and Man U's goalie, Robert Schmeichel, turned away in horror, hurling in the box.

The official injury is listed as a compound fracture of the right tibia and fibula—which is akin to describing a freshly severed arm as "a flesh wound." Over the next two years, Busst endured twenty-two operations and at one point, due to chronic infection and limited blood flow, was nearly forced to have his limb amputated. As for Schmeichel, he was one of a few players from that day who had to undergo counseling in order to cope with the sheer horror they had witnessed.

TOMMY DAVIS

A high school basketball star and teammate of future NBA great Lenny Wilkens, the Brooklyn-born Davis turned his back on hoops when Jackie Robinson helped convince him to sign with the home-town Dodgers in 1956. On May 1, 1965—the Dodgers having since moved to sunny Los Angeles—the Giants were in town for a set. During the game, Davis slid hard into second base in an attempt to break up a double play. But the only thing he broke up was his ankle, dislocating it severely. The injury was so traumatic that more than one Giants infielder saw his lunch for the second time that day. Davis was lost for the remainder of the season.

The injury was a career-changer. Prior to the repulsive contortion, Davis had won two consecutive batting titles in 1962 and '63, leading the league in hits the former year and knocking in 153 runs in the latter. Then in '65 his ankle crumpled. He played ten more seasons with ten different teams (including the 1969 Seattle Pilots, made famous by Jim Bouton in "Ball Four"), producing moments of brilliance, which only served as a reminder of his days of Hall of Fame promise.

NFL'S AXIS OF EVIL

There's no arguing that the traumatic leg injuries suffered by Redskins quarterback Joe Theisman, Bengals lineman Tim Krumrie, and Raiders running back Napoleon McCallum, were some of the most visually disturbing that fans of the game had ever seen. And that two of the grotesque injuries occurred on *Monday Night Football* telecasts and the other in a Super Bowl lifts them from freak-show curiosity to a place in pop culture lore.

- ✗ Following a sack-sandwich, Joe Theisman's lower leg bones played peek-a-boo with Lawrence Taylor during a *Monday Night Football* broadcast in 1985. It may have been one of the few sobering moments for the great Giants linebacker. Unfortunately for Theisman, his playing career ended with that stomach-churning break.
- ✗ When Cincinnati nose tackle Tim Krumrie shattered his leg while trying to stop the 49ers Roger Craig in Super Bowl XXIII, the fluttering limb of rubber became the most widely

viewed trauma in NFL history. Amazingly, Krumrie's leg was repaired and he would go on to play six more seasons in the NFL.

✗ During a season-opening Monday night game in 1994, Raiders running back Napoleon McCallum's knee was dislocated on a tackle by San Francisco linebacker Ken Norton Jr. His right getaway-stick would never be the same. The former Naval Academy star tore three ligaments, and his calf and hamstring muscles were ripped from the bone, causing nerve and artery damage. He nearly lost his leg in the subsequent operation and still cannot run to this day.

SID EUDY ("SID VICIOUS")

Professional wrestling is not a sport, it is orchestrated theater. But that doesn't mean its actors aren't athletes. Far from it. Regardless of whether or not they're juiced to the gills, wrestlers do things with their bodies that have to be acknowledged and respected. In doing so, like athletes in "legitimate sports," they put themselves in great peril.

On January 14, 2001, during the WCW's SIN pay-per-view broadcast, Vicious climbed up onto the middle turnbuckle with the intent of delivering a flying karate kick to his opponent, Scott Steiner. He landed awkwardly on his left leg, mauling his foot and ankle in a manner that would have made Gumby jealous. Vicious howled in the middle of the ring as his limb dangled lifelessly. The ex-heel cohort of Ric Flair and onetime member of the "Four Horsemen" was carried out of the arena on a stretcher, his career effectively over. The WCW closed its doors soon thereafter.

WAYNE SHELFORD

In 1986, during rugby's famed "Battle of Nantes," New Zealand's vaunted All Blacks squared off in a test against a physical and determined French national squad. While *Les Bleus* laid a beating on the All Blacks that evening, 16–3, New Zealand's number 8, Wayne

"Buck" Shelford, showed determination on a level that can be appreciated, but not fathomed, by any member of his sex. During a particularly violent scrum, Shelford took a French cleat to his groin, tearing open his scrotum and leaving a testicle dangling in the breeze. Rather than grabbing the nearest starter's pistol in a crazed attempt to take his own life and end the incomparable misery, Shelford instructed the All Blacks trainer to stitch up his nut satchel—on the sidelines!

To the astonishment of those in the stands and watching on the tube, Shelford played the rest of the contest, suffering his only career loss in international play. He claims not to remember a moment from that night, a clear example of the mind's ability to suppress horrifying memories.

UNIFORM VIOLATIONS

Changes in Dress that Leave Fans
Scratching Their Eyes Out

There are a lot of reasons for changing a uniform, and many of them are reasonable. Like, say, the old uniform is a hideous mess that generated about twenty-eight cents in merchandise revenues last fiscal year. Or, the team wearing the uniform has set the standard for incompetence on the field and lawlessness off of it. The sorry Tampa Bay Buccaneers trading in their ninety-eight-pound-weakling "Cream-sickle" look for butched-up scarlet-and-pewter is the perfect example of a team making a uniform change for all the right reasons.

These teams, however, are another thing altogether.

In one case, the timing of the change is understandable, but too much has been lost aesthetically. In another, the timing was an absolute and utter mystery, and the new look was worse than the old. One team got away from the style it wore when good and famous nationwide, and the results were far worse both on the field *and* hot out of the dryer. Another basically copied a uniform belonging to a last-place team in its own division. In all cases, it can be clearly stated: the wrong choice was made.

NEW ENGLAND DUMPS PATRIOTISM—
NEW ENGLAND PATRIOTS, 1993

During the first three years of the '90s, the Patriots were by far the worst team in football, rolling up a 9–39 record in '90, '91, and '92. What's more, the franchise had taken a PR bath in the wake of the Lisa Olson incident, in which several naked Pats players allegedly waved their junk at, and made suggestive comments toward, a female *Boston Globe* reporter. An image change, *any* kind of image change, was necessary in the wake of such disasters. So they brought in a new coach (Bill Parcells) and a new uniform.

Bringing in Parcells would have been enough. Gone was "Pat Patriot" in his three-point stance on the white helmet. Replacing it was a futuristic, aerodynamic Minuteman on a silver shell. The red-and-white uniform was replaced by dark blue and silver. The new ensemble looked like that of a USFL team—a far, feeble cry from the classic, idiosyncratic uniform that had served the Pats so well through the years. The worst part was the new uniforms weren't even "patriotic," unless the unofficial colors of the United States went from red, white, and blue to navy blue and silver at some point in the early '90s.

Did the new Patriots hate America? Of course not. But their uniforms did.

True, the Patriots have been to four Super Bowls and have won three since the changeover, which sure beats the one Super Bowl appearance and beat-down at the hands of the Bears with the old togs. But New England did dust off the old red, white, and blues for a Thanksgiving Day game against the Lions during their World Championship season of 2003. Not only did Tom Brady and Co. look perfectly at home in the Grogan-esque duds, they were still the same solid Patriots, whipping Detroit 25–10.

BYU GOES FOR GOLD, FAULTS—
BRIGHAM YOUNG FOOTBALL, 1999

Brigham Young won a very mythical National Championship and became synonymous with down-the-field football while wearing crisp royal blue–on-white complete with white helmets emblazoned with the blue Y. In 1999, they dumped the traditional look and came out in navy blue and gold duds with a navy blue helmet. There was no white in sight. They didn't look like Latter Day BYU anymore.

The Cougars actually won eight of their first nine in the new unis, but ended the season with a 21–3 loss to Marshall in the Motor City Bowl. In their only other bowl appearance wearing the new uniforms, the 2001 Liberty Bowl, they were thumped 28–10 by Louisville. They had started the 2001 season 12–0 but gave up one hundred points in back-to-back losses to end the season. When the Cougars sank to 9–15 in '02 and '03, the program got rid of Gary Crowton, and when new coach Bronco Mendenhall arrived in Provo, he got rid of the blue-and-gold and restored royal blue–and-white. In 2006, the traditionally clad Cougars won the Mountain West Conference and thrashed the hell out of weirdly clad Oregon 38–8 in the Las Vegas Bowl. Score one for the old school.

FROM CHAMPION JAYS TO POOR MAN'S RAYS (2004)

Why a franchise with two World Championships would want to emulate the look of a downtrodden expansion team is a mystery that would stump Encyclopedia Brown. But that's what the Toronto Blue Jays did in 2004. After nearly two decades and a great deal of success wearing some variation on the original, light blue–royal blue–white team uniform, the Jays strayed from the concept and adopted stark white home togs, the jersey emblazoned simply with JAYS.

With the lack of standard blue coloration and the lack of the word *blue* on the shirts, Toronto's new uniform bore a striking resemblance to that of the Tampa Bay Devil Rays, who have emitted a strong whiff of suck ever since entering the AL in 1998. The D-Rays also wear white home uniforms and play on artificial turf in a cavernous dome, and they have RAYS on the front of their jerseys. It is all too easy for the casual, beer-drinking sports fan to take a quick glance at a Blue Jays game on TV and ask, "Who's Oakland playing, the Devil Rays?" As if playing in Canada wasn't enough of a struggle against irrelevance.*

ROCKETING INTO HIDEOUSNESS—HOUSTON ROCKETS, 1995

Dumping a uniform right on the heels of back-to-back World Championships seems a little asinine and karmically questionable, but that's what the Houston Rockets did in 1995. Fresh off a Finals in which they humiliated the callow Orlando Magic, the Rockets did away with their venerable red-and-gold-on-white look and replaced it with something a lot messier—a pin-striped ensemble featuring a new Rockets logo and three-dimensional numbers on the upper left breast. There were worse uniforms in the mid-'90s NBA, but there is something singularly off-putting about a franchise changing its basic look immediately after winning it all.

The Rockets had reached the NBA Finals four times, winning twice, wearing their clean, classic old uniform. They haven't been back since. Most uniform changes are brought about by failure and embarrassment. Houston's uniform change merely resulted in such things. Thankfully, in 2003 the Rockets took a baby step back in the right direction, shelving the pinstripes and returning to solid red and white . . . not the classic look, but at least something that didn't make corneas across America howl in agony.

THE BALLSIEST UNIFORM CHANGE EVER—
CLEVELAND INDIANS, 1921

The Tribe and the town of Cleveland were darned pleased with their 1920 World Series triumph over the Brooklyn Dodgers. It was their first-ever Fall Classic Triumph, and they didn't plan on letting themselves forget about it—or letting anyone else, for that matter. So for the following season they removed the block-C from their home jersey, the city name from the road jersey, and replaced both with a simple legend: WORLD'S CHAMPIONS. In what had to be an

* The Rays' and Jays' hats don't look similar, but they're similarly awful.

increasingly annoying sight to the American League in general, the Indians played the entire '21 season, home and road, in their WORLD'S CHAMPIONS uniforms.

If the cheeky choice of uniform was meant as a reminder, fine; if it was intended as a prophecy, it was unsuccessful. The Indians were in first place in mid-September but finished second, four and a half games behind the Yankees. It was the first of a lot of pennants for New York. By failing to cash the checks their jerseys had written, the Tribe had let slip the beast, one that would annually come down from its mountain of money and devour American League villagers for roughly the next eight decades or so. Nice work there.

RYDER CUP NEGLIGENCE

The Ryder Cup began in 1926 as an exhibition match between American and British professionals at the Wentworth Club in the UK. It was about competitive golf between two great poles of influence, and nothing more. Now the biennial cross-Pond match has morphed into the sports world's version of the red carpet. Great emphasis and measures are taken to clothe the opposing squads in the finest respectively matching garments, both on and off the course.

Each side has taken a turn when it comes to questionable sartorial selections. But the U.S. squad has dominated the struggle for worst threads like the Europeans have dominated the real matches since winning at the Belfry in 1985. Red, white, and blue—there is no greater combination of sovereign colors. Yet the U.S. team chooses to de-emphasize their use almost every year. And in 1999, it got insulting.

Sure, after American Justin Leonard holed a forty-five-foot bomb of a putt with his match all square on the seventeenth hole at The Country Club in Brookline, Massachusetts, things became a little hectic. The American squad got carried away, forgetting that they played a gentlemen's game, screaming and hollering like sober mental patients. (The wives were out on the green celebrating, too, of course.) And when the frazzled Jose Maria Olazabal predictably missed the putt to give the Americans the historic comeback victory, they did so again.

But the déclassé actions of the "obnoxious Americans" weren't the only things that irked the Europeans and their fans. The colonial cretins were clad in equally obnoxious, ultrahideous burgundy, photographic-tribute golf shirts. Captain Ben Crenshaw should've saved the motivational photos for the locker room, as opposed to turning his players into walking bulletin boards of tastelessness.

THE NATIVE AMERICAN CONUNDRUM

"We're Calling Our Teams the WHAT?"

The American Indian has long been a cherished part of the sports traditions at many universities. But the 1960s and '70s—that famous era of amplified bitching and moaning—brought what was considered a negligible issue of discontent from the back burner to the forefront of the national discourse. Moralizers began to condemn "the continued racist exploitation of an indigenous culture." There's one thing for sure: when someone starts breaking out the "isms," something's sure to get banned at some point thereafter.

Sure enough, in August 2005, the NCAA barred from hosting postseason events colleges and universities that used "hostile and abusive mascots, nicknames, or imagery" pertaining to native cultures and tribes. While stopping short of an all-out Native American mascot prohibition, the ruling served as a shot across the bow. Many schools were affected by it: the University of Illinois (Illini), Florida State (Seminoles), St. John's (Redmen), Syracuse (Orangemen), Marquette (Warriors), Stanford (Indians), Eastern Michigan (Hurons), William & Mary (Indians—The Tribe), Dartmouth (Indians), and the University of North Dakota (Fighting Sioux) are some of the higher-profile schools that have been caught in the net. But more than fifty academic institutions across the country have nicknames or mascots that incorporate names of or make direct reference to Native American people and/or culture. Somehow the earth continues to spin on its axis despite this grotesque travesty.

Some schools appealed the mandate and won exemptions, citing regional tribe approval (translation: hush $.) The Florida State Seminoles and the University of Utah Utes are two examples. Others lost, conceding the battle over their beloved mascot to either definitive legal judgment or simply in the court of influential opinion.

The war over whether or not the use of such mascots is appropriate has been waged and effectively decided; the fallout is much more interesting. The affected athletic departments, with a thankless task, scrambled for an impromptu solution. Many schools dropped the ball, so to speak, and their mascot improvisations were comical at best.

SYRACUSE UNIVERSITY

Incorporating two characteristics of the upstate New York region's heritage—salt production and the Onondaga and Oneida Indian tribes—the Syracuse University athletic teams were once known as the Saltine Warriors, and nicknamed the Orangemen. Today, however, they are merely the Orange, and the mascot with white-gloved hands protruding from an area normally reserved for ears goes by the name of "Otto the Orange." Like a deleted scene from an old Fruit of the Loom commercial, the school's website describes Otto as a "fuzzy and fruity figure.'"

ST. JOHN'S UNIVERSITY

Another Big East school suffering a similar fate, St. John's changed their nickname from the Redmen to the Red Storm, which sounds like a venereal disease from the Cold War era.

MIAMI UNIVERSITY OF OHIO

This school was also forced to ad-lib when their nickname, the Redskins, was deemed offensive. So, in 1996, they opted for the Red Hawks instead. Next time you run into an ornithologist, ask if they've seen any red hawks soaring around lately.

STANFORD UNIVERSITY

Located in northern California and, thus, well ahead of the politically correct curve, Stanford dropped their old nickname of the Indians and adopted the Cardinal as their official mascot in the early '70s. Whether it was an attempt to honor the school's chosen colors, the passerine songbird, or the esteemed rank within the Catholic Church has yet to be determined. The more relevant issue here is Stanford's unofficial and abomination of a mascot: the Tree. A dancing prankster and arrogant parody of the proud college mascot tradition, the Tree is one of the sadder sights in all of sports.*

DARTMOUTH COLLEGE

The mascot issue is one that has come and gone, over and over again, on this school's New Hampshire campus. Since the '20s. Dartmouth has unofficially been known as the "Big Green." Until the early '70s, when the school officially cut its ties with the nickname, they were known as the Indians. Some students and alumni continue to favor its use. (The same is true at Marquette, once the Warriors, now the Golden Eagles.)

What's most interesting about Dartmouth's mascot perplexity is its inability to come to a consensus on a new one. In 2003, a poll was conducted. The "Moose" came out on top, but most continued to ignore the new moniker despite the outcome. So much for democracy.

* Stanford's football team hasn't won a Rose Bowl since the name change. We're just throwing that out there.

That same year, the college's esteemed comedy magazine, the *Dartmouth Jack-O-Lantern,* took matters into its own hands and invented "Keggy," the "anthropomorphic beer keg." While humorous indeed, Keggy serves more as an embarrassing symbol and reminder of Dartmouth's divided campus than as an uplifting centerpiece of school pride.

THE MINNESOTA MASSACRE

The Gophers–Buckeyes Brawl of '72
and How It Paid to Be Dirty

For years the University of Minnesota basketball team had watched others represent the Big Ten in the Big Dance. But in 1971, led by players like Jim Brewer, Corky Taylor, Clyde Turner, and a brawny forward named Dave Winfield, the Gophers finally became a factor in the conference championship conversation. The mastermind of the turnaround was the coach, a thirty-one-year-old defensive expert named Bill Musselman. The hard-driving Musselman, a proponent of making an opponent pay for every drive to the bucket, found a willing audience for his aggressive theories. The Gophers, with their new rugged style, chewed up the Big Ten standings as conference play opened in 1972.

Bobby Knight was in his first year at Indiana, Ohio State, coached by Knight's mentor, Fred Taylor, was the Big Ten's premier program, a three-time NCAA finalist and the defending conference champion. The Buckeyes had a solid core returning from a squad that had come within an overtime period of the Final Four the previous year, including the centerpiece, all-conference center Luke Witte.

Musselman targeted the Buckeyes as the team through which the upstart Gophers would have to go to win the Big Ten, and he circled on his calendar the two teams' meeting in Minneapolis's

Williams Arena on January 25, 1972, calling it the biggest game in the history of the Minnesota program. The intense young coach, an Ohio native, whipped his team and the campus into a frenzy prior to the game. Although he may not have been directly culpable for what would unfold, Musselman had created the conditions that led to possibly the ugliest scene in the history of college basketball.

Appropriately enough, the Buckeyes and the Gophers were undefeated in conference play when they took the floor that cold January night. As expected, the game was a bruise-inducing tug-of-war. Forced to withstand the physical play of Minnesota and the hostility of the Williams Arena crowd, Ohio State persevered and fought to a 50–44 lead with less than a minute left. With thirty-six seconds to play, Luke Witte drove the lane and was knocked to the deck by a Clyde Turner foul that bordered on mugging. Turner was immediately ejected from the game as Witte sat on the floor attempting to collect his wits.

Gopher Corky Taylor then pulled one of the most low-down dirty tricks ever seen in American sports. In an outwardly friendly gesture, Taylor came over to the dazed Witte and offered his hand as if to help him to his feet. When Witte took it, Taylor yanked him up and hiked his knee into the Buckeye center's groin. As Witte sagged back to the floor in pain, Ohio State guard Dave Merchant shoved Taylor away and was attacked from behind by Minnesota's Jim Brewer. All hell then broke loose.

Witte, still on the floor, was viciously attacked by Minnesota reserve Ron Behagen, who came off the bench and stomped the Buckeye around the head and neck. Dave Winfield found Buckeye guard Mark Wagar, grabbed him from behind, and punched him into unconsciousness. Fans rushed the floor and joined in the assault. According to a 2007 *Columbus Dispatch* article, among them were members of Minnesota's football team, who relished the chance to give Fred Taylor's boys a little of what Woody Hayes's boys gave *them* on a yearly basis.

Witte was carried off on a stretcher, to taunts, flying objects, and loud wishes for his death from the fans. He and Wagar were hospitalized with concussions. Witte also suffered a scratched cornea and required twenty-nine stitches to his face. His vision permanently dulled, he was never the same player after the stomping, which remains one of the more chilling pieces of sports footage ever shot.

Minnesota suspended Taylor and Behagen for the remainder of the season. The Big Ten took no action whatsoever.

Ohio State's Fred Taylor, one of the game's premier coaches and still a relatively young man at forty-seven, was broken a bit by the melee. His Buckeyes would not win the Big Ten in 1972—what happened in Minneapolis saw to that—and they wouldn't win the conference title again under his tutelage. Anguished over what happened to his boys that night, and embittered over the conference's failure to levy any kind of sanction over it, he retired from coaching in 1976. He would later say that his greatest regret was not resigning in protest of the conference's lack of response to the beating. Taylor died in 2002.

Although it didn't salvage the game itself, the Minnesota Massacre paid dividends for the Gophers. With their main stumbling block effectively kneecapped, they indeed won their first-ever Big Ten title in 1972, good for the program's first-ever NCAA Tournament appearance. In their opening game of the tourney, they were promptly whipped by Florida State.

Musselman left the Twin Cities after the 1971–72 season. Almost immediately afterward, the NCAA placed Minnesota's basketball program on probation for more than a hundred rules violations committed during his tenure. Always known for his defensive mind, Musselman meandered through a long career as a head coach and assistant in the NBA, CBA, and at the college level prior to his death in 2000, winning some, losing some, but never quite escaping the shadow of January 25, 1972.

So it didn't end all that well for anyone involved. But the truth, cold and hard as a Minnesota winter, was that the brutality visited upon the Buckeyes that day a generation and change ago helped secure a long-awaited conference championship for the Golden Gophers. That the violence probably wasn't premeditated almost doesn't matter. It worked out as if it had been. For Bill Musselman and the Minnesota Golden Gophers, crime paid.

Texas Rangers outfielder Jeff Burroughs is escorted off the field by bat-wielding teammates during the Ten-Cent Beer Night melee at Cleveland Municipal Stadium—June 4, 1974. *AP Images*

FAN FOIBLES

The Lowest Common Denominator of Behavior

- ★ TEN-CENT BEER NIGHT
- ★ FIVE FAN-FUBARed FORFEITS
- ★ WHEN FANS ATTACK
- ★ THE WORST OF YOUTH SPORTS
- ★ THE MALICE AT THE PALACE

TEN-CENT BEER NIGHT

Cleveland, Ohio, June 4, 1974

In 1974, the Cleveland Indians were a solid, healthy organization, as long as you ignored the fact that the team was on the brink of bankruptcy and working on a practically unbroken, two-decade-long streak of suckitude.

The Indians played their home games in cavernous Cleveland Municipal Stadium, the worst facility in baseball. Built in 1932, the Stadium was the first fully publicly funded facility of its kind, which wasn't surprising: only a government project could produce something so enormous, ugly, and unsuited for its eventual purpose. Cold, dank, with seats for more than seventy thousand—many of which were blocked by steel poles—the Stadium was itself an impediment to the fortunes of a team that had long proven that it didn't need any help screwing things up.

Twenty years had passed since the Indians last won an American League pennant. Five had passed since the team's last winning season. And in 1973, the Tribe had assumed the position to which its fans, ownership, and players had grown accustomed: last place in the American League East. Accordingly, the team also finished last in the league in attendance, and by a wide margin. (An average of slightly more than seventy-five hundred went out to Tribe games in '73.) The team wouldn't have sold out Volunteer Stadium in Williamsport, Pennsylvania, let alone the monstrosity it now called home.

So the consortium that ran the Indians had a problem. The club had lost $1.4 million in 1973. Being as cash-strapped as it got among ownership groups at the time, they needed to get the turnstiles a-spinning, and quickly. The problem was, Cleveland fans weren't terribly keen on shelling out their hard-earned Rust Belt money on an uninspiring team that played in a place equipped with possibly the worst bathroom facilities in the history of American sporting venues.

What was ownership's solution? To opt for the cheapest, most temporary fix possible, of course.

Thus was born Ten-Cent Beer Night. Three of these libation-induced evenings of delight were scheduled for the 1974 season. The first came on Tuesday, June 4, when the Texas Rangers arrived to begin a three-game series. There had been recent trouble between the Tribe and the Rangers: a week earlier, Cleveland first baseman John Ellis and Texas utility man Lenny Randle had come to blows during a game in Arlington. Fueled by their own team's cheap beer promotion, Rangers fans doused Indians players with discounted suds, moving Ranger Toby Harrah to compare them to the rowdy *beisbol* fans of Latin American winter leagues. He hadn't seen nuthin' yet.

A total of 25,134 paying customers were on hand that Tuesday night in Cleveland, the largest attendance for a weeknight game in nearly two years. It didn't take long to figure out that the bulk of the crowd wasn't there for baseball. It was about the fire-brewed Stroh's to be had at just ten cents a cold, frosty cup. You could even carry off six at a time, if you were up to the challenge. And if you spilled, a dime was all it took to make the party foul fair. Fans who *may* already have been lubricated when they got to the Stadium formed long, weaving, sometimes peeing lines to beer trucks that had been parked beyond the center-field fence.

The first breach of the playing field came early, when an overweight woman lifted her shirt upon reaching the Tribe's on-deck circle and planted a kiss on home plate umpire and crew chief Nestor Chylak. Fan incursions onto the field this night were repeated and excessive, even by the relaxed standards of the 1970s. They began early, and although they varied in intent and levels of bonhomie, they never really stopped throughout the course of the game. Smoke bombs and firecrackers went off periodically in the stands, and fights broke out between members of the predominantly male and predominantly intoxicated crowd.

As for the game, right out of the gate it shaped up as a Texas runaway. After a scoreless first inning, the Rangers began chipping away at Tribe starter Fritz Peterson (who somewhat famously traded wives with a teammate while playing for the Yankees). A Tom Grieve home run and back-to-back doubles by Jim Sundberg and Cesar Tovar chased Peterson in the third inning. Grieve's second home run, a fourth-inning solo shot off Dick Bosman, made it 3–0. As Grieve rounded the bases, a naked man dashed out onto the field and slid into second base. The umpires didn't acknowledge it, but he was safe.

A run-scoring single by the Tribe's Oscar Gamble, owner of one of the more renowned 'fros of the period, cut the deficit to 3–1, but the Rangers came back with two in the sixth and led 5–1. By then, fans were pelting denizens of the Texas bull pen with firecrackers, forcing home plate umpire Chylak to order them moved to the dugout for their own protection. Around the seventh inning, boozed-up fans began invading the outfield in squadrons. One ran up to Ranger right fielder Jeff Burroughs and shook his hand, presumably congratulating him on the MVP season he was having. At this point, most of the Tribe's front office personnel began filing out of the Stadium, unwilling to bear witness any longer to the carnage they had wrought. The ballpark had been left to the Indians, to the Rangers . . . and to the drunks. And the drunks outnumbered everyone.

As the fans grew ever drunker, rowdier, and bolder, the Indians began to mount a comeback. Three hits and a walk cut the Texas lead to 5–3 in the bottom of the sixth. It was still 5–3 when the Tribe came to bat in the bottom of the ninth. With one out, a

George Hendrick double and an Ed Crosby single cut the deficit to 5–4. After the Tribe loaded the bases, a sacrifice fly by John Lowenstein tied the score. With two outs in the ninth, the Indians had men on first and second and looked to be on the verge of a comeback victory.

At that point the crowd became unmanageable. A group of drunks climbed over the right-field wall and accosted Burroughs, stealing his cap. From the Rangers dugout, manager Billy Martin saw his best player under attack, and made up his mind. Alcohol-fueled hijinks were all in good fun to the hard-drinking, hard-fighting Martin, but nobody messed with his superstar and got away with it. Martin armed his men with Louisville Sluggers and led them onto the field to save the beleaguered outfielder. From there, as the kids say, it was on.

Drunken fans stole the bases. Someone hurled a full jug of Thunderbird wine of indeterminate vintage at Ranger rookie first baseman Mike Hargrove (who kept a photo from that night on the wall of his office when he managed the Tribe in the '90s). Hargrove, for his part, wrestled to the ground and pummeled a fan who came up behind him with ill intent during the melee. Billy Martin later claimed to have broken his bat over the skull of a rioter. It was good, maybe, that Billy was there; this was one thing he wouldn't have wanted to miss. The drunks were impartial; not only did they go after Texas players, but Cleveland players as well. Indians relief pitcher Tom Hilgendorf was struck in the head by a stadium chair. So was Nestor Chylak, for that matter.

Chylak, for his part, wanted the game to continue. He didn't want to deprive the Indians of a chance to complete their comeback. But when he felt the press of an object on the back of his foot, turned around, and saw a large hunting knife sticking out of the ground, his qualms vanished. He declared the game a forfeit: Rangers, 9–0. Nursing his head injury afterward, Chylak said of the scene: "They were just uncontrollable beasts. I've never seen anything like it except in a zoo."

At any rate, the wayward promotion and the resulting suds-soaked riot was a sociologist's dream come true. Windy theories were expounded about the unfocused rage and antiauthoritarian bent of the day's youth. Ranger Cesar Tovar put it more succinctly, when asked to compare the behavior of Cleveland fans to those in his native Venezuela. "These people are different, very different. Got no respect for the police," Tovar said. "Of course, they'd shoot the people who tried that at home."

The tally for Ten-Cent Beer Night: nine arrests; seven people sent to the hospital for riot-inflicted wounds from chairs, fists, airborne jugs of cheap wine, et al.; and one forfeited baseball game. Even though the promotion had cost them a game in a season in which the team had caught a mild case of contention (the Tribe was only three and a half out in mid-August before fading), the Indians had every intention of going ahead with the remaining scheduled Ten-Cent Beer Nights, and only desisted when forced to do so by American League president Lee McPhail. It was another two decades before the Indians management realized that having *good players* was the best way to put asses in the seats.

FIVE FAN-FUBARed FORFEITS

Ten-Cent Beer Night wasn't the first or last time a baseball team was forced to forfeit because of the actions of its fans. Far from it. Here are five more examples.

BALL DAY, DODGER STADIUM, LOS ANGELES—AUGUST 10, 1995

The first ten thousand attendees at the game against the Cardinals received souvenir baseballs. When Dodger outfielder Raul Mondesi and manager Tommy Lasorda were both ejected in the bottom of the ninth inning for arguing balls and strikes in a game L.A. was losing 2–1, Dodger fans expressed their displeasure by chucking their free baseballs onto the field of play—a Rawlings rainstorm of biblical proportions. After pleas to stop the bombardment were ignored, umpires called the game and awarded it to the Cardinals by forfeit. At the time, the Dodgers were just a game behind Colorado in the NL West standings, making this potentially the costliest forfeit in Major League history.

DISCO DEMOLITION NIGHT, CHICAGO—JULY 12, 1979

Disco Demolition Night was the brainchild of Chicago DJ Steve Dahl and Mike Veeck, son of legendary White Sox owner Bill Veeck. Any fan who came out to that night's doubleheader versus Detroit with a disco record got in for fifty cents. The records were to be destroyed by a remote-controlled bomb on the infield between games. All involved agreed that this would be a real hoot and would boost attendance besides. They were right. Something like sixty-five thousand people were inside and outside Comiskey Park by the time the first game began. The old park already rang with explosions and smelled like the inside of a VW Microbus when Dahl, riding in the back of a Jeep and clad in a military helmet, detonated the records. At this point, fifteen thousand so-called fans poured onto the field, necessitating police action (the Chicago cops responded with gusto, as they were wont to do). Irate at the torn-up condition of the field and believing—with reason—that his players were in danger, Sparky Anderson refused to bring his team back out for the nightcap. The umpires backed him up and the White Sox were forced to forfeit. As a price for his sponsorship of the promotion, Mike Veeck was blackballed from organized baseball for over a decade.

THE LAST GAME, RFK STADIUM, WASHINGTON—SEPTEMBER 30, 1971

It was the final game for the Senators in Washington, and D.C. fans were in the mood to send the team off to Texas in style. With Washington leading New York 7–5 in the top of the ninth inning, spectators poured onto the field. Attempts to clear the field were unsuccessful, and the Yankees were awarded the forfeit, giving them a winning record of 82–80 for the season. Four players—Toby Harrah, Jeff Burroughs, Dick Bosman, and Rusty Torres—played in this game as well as the Ten-Cent Beer Night that would be forfeited three years later.

DAMNED KIDS, POLO GROUNDS, NEW YORK— SEPTEMBER 26, 1942

The New York Giants thought they were doing the good, patriotic thing when they admitted hundreds of children into this late-season doubleheader for free as an inducement to bring scrap iron for the war effort. They weren't, as it turned out. In the eighth inning of the nightcap, with New York leading the Boston Braves 5–2, the little brats got bored and invaded the playing field toting scrap metal, which moved umpire Ziggy Sears to forfeit the ball game to the Braves.

SNOWBALL FIGHT, POLO GROUNDS, NEW YORK—APRIL 11, 1907

Snow has long created havoc with the early-season schedule, but never like this. An Opening Day tilt between the New York Giants and Philadelphia Phillies was first delayed in the bottom of the seventh inning when a mass snowball fight between fans, which had been heretofore confined to the bleachers, spilled out onto the field. Eventually the field was cleared of the warring factions, but in the ninth, with New York behind 3–0, they again invaded, and this time they encountered no resistance. With no hope of getting the game started again, umpire Bill Klem forfeited the game to the Phillies.

WHEN FANS ATTACK

The Worst of Fan Projectiles

Be it a ball, a discus, a javelin, or even an opponent, throwing things is one of the cornerstones of sport—a test of physical strength and technique. It is not, however, considered a cornerstone of spectatorship. But perhaps it should be.

The emotions borne of the success and failure of a loyal fan's favorite team inspire action, all the more so when alcohol is added to the equation. Following success, high fives, hugs, jubilant dancing, and screaming usually suffice. But in the event of failure, many fans feel that a more spirited expression of their emotions is necessary. Apparently taking their cue from the players on the field, these fans reach for the nearest deployable object and hurl it onto the playing surface—a physical manifestation of their disappointment, frustration, and anger.

Fortunately for players, coaches, and referees, most things in a stadium are bolted down. However, angry fans are determined, and would-be projectiles are as varied as they are commonplace. In some cases, they even fall from the sky.

SNOWBALLS

For those interested in testing their throwing arms from the stands, snowballs are generally a good option. Unlike many flying objects, they don't need to be smuggled into the stadium. Plus, they can be manufactured quickly and on the spot. All you need is high humidity and temperatures in the low thirties or lower, and you're good to go. And simply by being thrown, the snowball is fulfilling the one and only purpose it has for existing. The snowball-thrower isn't wasting anything valuable; he's just following the laws of nature. It's also environmentally friendly and does no damage. Unless someone's eye gets put out.

November 11, 1985, Mile High Stadium, Denver, Colorado—
The Snowball Game

There seems to be an unwritten rule stating that *Monday Night Football* cannot go for more than a period of three years without broadcasting from Mile High Stadium during a raging snowstorm. The combination of Rocky Mountain blizzards and the raucous Denver faithful gives the Broncos a massive home-field advantage, never more so than on November 11, 1985, during a Monday Night contest between the Broncos and the San Francisco 49ers. Late in the first half, with San Francisco trailing 14–3, 49er kicker Ray Wersching and holder Matt Cavanaugh lined up for a chip-shot nineteen-yard field goal. Just as the ball was snapped, a snowball shot out of the end zone seats and exploded on the field directly in front of Cavanaugh, causing him to bobble the snap. Wersching never even got the kick off. Denver wound up winning 17–16, making the anonymous snowball thrower, not John Elway or Joe Montana, the critical element to the game's outcome.

The San Francisco *Examiner* later sniffed out the Snowball Man, who admitted under anonymity to being the fateful chucker. He apologized to the 49ers and their fans. With a Denver "W" safely in the books, contrition must have come easy.

Postscript: Fourteen years and twelve days later, on November

23, 1999, opposing players finally came to grips with the snow-wielding Broncomaniacs. Following a wintry Monday Night game between Denver and the Raiders, Oakland cornerback Charles Woodson drilled a female fan with a snowball, drawing an arrest warrant from the Denver PD. The 330-pound tackle Lincoln Kennedy followed suit by climbing over a six-foot chain-link fence—an amazing sight in itself—and decking a Denver-area mechanic who had hit Kennedy in the face with his own snowball. According to the *San Francisco Chronicle*, some of the snowballs thrown by Broncos fans were packed around D-cell batteries. (More on batteries later.)

December 23, 1995, Giants Stadium, East Rutherford, New Jersey—The Snowball Game

As they watched their team finish up a disappointing season against the San Diego Chargers in thirty-five-degree sleet at the Meadowlands, Giants fans grew surly. Being New York fans, they decided the best way to deal with their frustration was to take it out on someone. That someone was the visiting team, and the method was New York–hard; not snowballs, but *ice* balls. Anyone in Charger blue and gold, be they players, coaches, equipment managers, trainers, or whatever contingent of 'Bolts fans dotted the stands was deemed a legitimate target. Ice balls rained down on the San Diego sideline.

It was all fun and games until someone got knocked out. In the third quarter, with New York leading 17–3, Charger equipment manager Sid Brooks had his lights put out by an icy missile that hit him in the back of the head, dropping him face-first to the turf. The fired-up Chargers responded by ripping off twenty-four unanswered points and winning 27–17. San Diego safety Shaun Gayle nailed the Giants' proverbial coffin shut when he returned an interception ninety-nine yards, sprinting through a deluge of ice balls like Union gunboats running past Vicksburg.

By the way, all games involving snowballs are referred to as "the snowball game."

PLASTIC BOTTLES

A plastic bottle is light (as long as it's empty), and isn't exactly a lethal weapon when tossed. So from the thrower's perspective it can serve as a childish, petulant, yet harmless way of offering his two cents on matters of sport. The bottle can also be purchased at the ballpark, making it readily available. You don't need to be "hard-core" to throw a plastic bottle—you only need to be stupid, in all likelihood drunk, and short on common sense. Unfortunately, that's a big percentage of the crowd at any sporting event.

December 16, 2001, Jacobs Field, Cleveland, Ohio—Bottlegate

With less than a minute remaining, the Browns, needing a win to stay in contention for the playoffs, were trailing Jacksonville 15–10 and faced a fourth down on the Jaguars' 15-yard line. Quarterback Tim Couch hit Quincy Morgan, who bobbled a wobbly pass and trapped it as he hit the ground in first-down territory. Quickly the Browns spiked the ball to protect their dubious first down by avoiding the replay system. After a conference, the officials decided to go ahead and review the play anyway. They waved off the catch. Browns fans, angered by the fact that the officials had violated one of the core tenets of the replay system and the fact that their team sucked, produced a shower of plastic bottles, some empty, some not, in the general direction of the playing field. Players, coaches and officials fled for the tunnel, bent over, with arms protecting their heads. The players were lucky: they had helmets. Forty minutes later the teams came out and finished the last few seconds of the game.

Browns management was alarmingly cavalier about the affair, none more so than team president Carmen Policy, who responded with a moral sensibility honed by years of service as a consigliere to the Youngstown mob and years more as a shameless manipulator of the NFL salary cap in San Francisco. "If we had won like this in Jacksonville, I would expect this to happen," said Policy. At any rate, the bottles "didn't carry much of a wallop." Hey, nobody got put in the trunk of a car or anything, so what was the problem?

September 15, 1907, Robinson Field, St. Louis, Missouri—A Bottled Blast from the Past

Back in the old days, concessionaires sold beer and other beverages to fans in glass bottles. Being glass and thus intrinsically fun to break, bottles were a popular projectile for riotous turn-of-the-century baseball fans. On September 15, 1907, a St. Louis fan named Hugo Dusenberg hit American League umpire Billy Evans with a glass soda bottle, fracturing his skull and nearly killing him. Nowadays this kind of thing would cause some kind of Draconian reaction by the authorities, for the safety of everyone and, of course, for the children. Not so then. Ballparks continued to sell drinks in glass bottles for decades after Evans was nailed, because back then people were expected to behave themselves and act like adults. That, and plastic had not yet been invented.

October 17, 1999, Fenway Park, Boston, Massachusetts—Tim Tschida Adulation Night

The 1999 American League pennant race came down to two teams, the Boston Red Sox and the New York Yankees—an obscure rivalry often overlooked by the national media. The Sox came into the ALCS battered and bruised but excited by their instant-classic divisional series win over the Indians. In contrast, the Yankees were rested and cleanly starched coming into the championship series, thanks to a sweep of the Texas Rangers, who rolled over and played dead, as usual.

For the Red Sox, behind 2–1 in the series, Game Four was a must-win. Combine that tension with a chilly and rainy fall evening that signaled the inevitable arrival of another oppressive New England winter and, of course, overserved fans; what you had was a simmering Crock-Pot ready to boil over at any time.

With the Yankees leading 3–2 in the bottom of the eighth and Jose Offerman on first, Joe Torre brought in closer Mariano Rivera to shut the door. He immediately induced a slow roller to second from John Valentin. Yankee second baseman Chuck Knoblauch made the scoop, applied the now-infamous phantom tag to the passing Offerman, and, as both Sox and Yankees fans collectively held their breath, winged an errant knuckler toward first. Tino Martinez happened to catch this one and recorded the inning-ending double play, leaving MVP candidate Nomar Garciaparra waiting in the on-deck circle.

Two errors (a total of four by the Sox committed that evening) and a Rod Beck meatball enabled the Yankees to blow it open in the top of the ninth. When the Sox came up in the bottom of the ninth, facing a 9–2 deficit, fans were slightly perturbed. Garciaparra was ruled out at first in a bang-bang play that the fans disagreed with. So did manager Jimy Williams, whose subsequent on-field tantrum included everything but holding his breath and turning blue. Red Sox fans responded by raining bottles onto the field, resulting in the umpires clearing the field of play and an eight-minute delay to restore order. The Yankees eventually won, and clinched yet another trip to the World Series the following night in Boston.

FRUITS AND VEGETABLES (OLD SCHOOL)

The use of edible flora as airborne weapons is no longer in vogue, but its origins can be traced back to pre-vaudevillian times. It survived for many years as a method of celebration in college football (think Big Eight fans firing oranges around their stadium as their team clinches a bid to that fruit's namesake bowl in Miami). Practiced with a less exuberant tone, the art of fruit-and-veggie throwing in the pros vanished completely decades ago, due to a dearth of produce stands at stadiums.

October 9, 1934, Navin Field, Detroit, Michigan—Ducky Ducks

Like a lot of Depression-era ballplayers, Joe "Ducky" Medwick of the Cardinals (the last man to win a Triple Crown in the National League) was also a man not to be trifled with. He once knocked out his own starting pitcher in the dugout when the man made a disparaging comment about Medwick's fielding in the previous inning. But he couldn't knock out every single fan in the ballpark, and remains the only player to be pulled from a World Series game for his own safety.

It was Game Seven of the hotly contested 1934 World Series in Detroit. St. Louis blew it open early with a seven-run fourth and led 7–0 in the sixth inning when Medwick belted a triple into the alley, barreling over Tiger third baseman Marv Owen on his way into the bag. Owen popped up and the two briefly exchanged shoves and colorful words. By the time Ducky returned to left field in the bottom of the inning, it was 9–0 Cardinals and the Tiger fans had found their scapegoat. They pelted Medwick with whatever they could get their hands on, including fruits and vegetables, much of it rather gamy. Medwick was forced to leave the game. The Cardinals cruised, 11–0.

BATTERIES

Batteries are small and compact, and won't be confiscated at the gate, at least not under normal conditions. A battery is also an object that just about anyone can throw for great distances, making it the ideal projectile for drunks who are trying to skull the plate umpire from Row Z of the upper deck. And a battery means business when it's airborne. Snowballs are for kids; batteries are for adults with grave intent.

July 20, 1980, Three Rivers Stadium, Pittsburgh, Pennsylvania— Target Dave Parker

Big Dave Parker was a two-time MVP for the Pirates, but he was never a favorite of the Pittsburgh fans, who were exasperated by his seemingly constant injury problems, and suspected that baseball's first million-dollar-a-year player wasn't exactly busting his butt to earn his gigantic paycheck. On July 20, 1980, during the opening game of a doubleheader at Three Rivers Stadium, a Pirates fan who probably thought all these things and a whole lot more took a nine-volt battery from a transistor radio and fired it at Parker as he stood in right field, narrowly missing his head. Parker took one look at the battery bouncing on the Three Rivers carpet and made his unhurried way to the Pirates clubhouse. He would not return for the remainder of the game or the nightcap.

Other objects thrown by Pittsburgh fans at "Park 'Em" Parker during the 1980 season included a bag of nuts and bolts and, the week after the battery incident, a 38-caliber bullet.

September 24, 1989, Cleveland Municipal Stadium, Cleveland, Ohio—Dawg Pound Batteries

John Elway was Public Enemy Number One in the city of Cleveland in the late 1980s. So when the Denver Broncos came to town on September 24, 1989, and fans got a shot at getting some payback for Elway's tormenting their favorite team, they took it. A variety of items were sent hurtling toward the Broncos, especially toward their quarterback. Denizens of the Dawg Pound were known to be liberal when it came to throwing dog bones onto the field, but this time the usual biscuits were mixed with batteries, a higher grade of ammunition. The bombardment got so bad late in the third quarter that the referees allowed the Broncos to switch sides of the field. Much to the delight of the ruffians in the Pound, the Browns won on a late field goal. Three and a half months later, the Broncos beat the Browns for the third time in the AFC Championship Game, in a game in which the only things being thrown in quantity were Bronco touchdown passes.

ANIMALS (DEAD OR ALIVE)

Certainly the practice of heaving dead octopi on the ice at Red Wings games comes to mind when talking about animals being thrown, but that's tame in comparison to these examples.

December 6, 2003, Lawson Arena, Kalamazoo, Michigan— Venison on Ice

Notre Dame's men's hockey team took a five-game unbeaten streak into Kalamazoo to face the Western Michigan Broncos for two games leading into the holiday break. The Broncos shocked the

Irish in Friday's game 8–6, and led 5–4 in the closing minutes of Saturday's tilt. After the Irish pulled their goalie, Western Michigan's Brent Walton scored an empty netter to secure the win, and that's when it happened. A severed deer leg cartwheeled through the air and landed on the ice, nearly striking an ND skater.

Of course there is the question of how one would go about smuggling a severed deer leg into an arena, but more interestingly, given five prior opportunities to rid himself of the bloody leg in celebration of WMU goals, why did the fan wait until the end of the game to throw it?

November 23, 2003, Nou Estadi del Futbol Club Barcelona,
Barcelona, Spain—The Pig's Head

It should come as no surprise that some of the worst instances of fan-thrown projectiles come from European soccer matches. It is not uncommon to see bags of urine, road flares, and chunks of the stadium tumbling through the air. After all, these are the same fans who, upon his move from Tottenham to Arsenal, hung Sol Campbell's effigy from a lamppost and burned it.

So in 2003, when Portuguese-born soccer star Luis Figo finally returned to FC Barcelona after defecting to archrival Real Madrid in 2000 (he had missed the 2001 match in Barcelona due to injury), the fans were prepared to let their hatred be known. When Figo ran to take a corner kick during the match, an unprecedented wave of projectiles rained down—coins, bottles, shirts, trash, and *a severed pig's head*.

The head can be seen on display at the Kultort Museum in Essen in an exhibit on soccer fanaticism.

December 28, 2002, the Delta Center, Salt Lake City, Utah—
The Flying Rat

During a game between the Utah Jazz and the Philadelphia 76ers, Karl Malone was in the middle of his ten-second free throw routine when a rat, hurled from the upper deck, landed with a thud just outside the circle. Reports vary as to the state of the rat in flight, but many sources claim the rodent was alive prior to crashing into the floor. Regardless, it was dead on impact, and while the officials looked on in horror, Jazz forward Scott Padgett booted the rat off the court and under the first row next to the Utah bench, sending courtsiders scrambling. The Jazz went on to win. The rat thrower eluded security and fled the arena.

SUNDRY ITEMS

May 2001, Stadio Giuseppe Meazza, Milan, Italy—The Scooter

Inter Milan fans are known for throwing things onto the field. In April 2005, after a goal was disallowed, they halted a game with rival AC Milan by showering the field with lit road flares, one of which struck AC keeper Dida in the shoulder. But their crowning moment came in a match in 2001 against another Italian club, Atalanta BC.

Prior to the match, Inter Milan fans stole a scooter from an Atalanta fan, dragged it into the stands, burned it, and then heaved it over the railing in the upper deck. *Il Belpaese*, indeed.

July 30, 1991, Yankee Stadium, New York, New York— Bleacher Creatures

During his heyday with the A's, no player was a bigger lightning rod than Jose Canseco, and nowhere was he more disliked than in New York City. Early in the '91 season, Canseco had engaged in a colorful exchange with a Yankees fan from Jersey named Kenny Shab. A brawl in Yankee Stadium, even one involving players, isn't really unusual, but it got stranger when Oakland came to New York in late July. During the first game of a three-game series, Canseco was pelted with a number of items including cabbage and an inflatable sex doll. The doll presumably represented Madonna, with whom Canseco was having a much-publicized relationship. The A's won anyway, 10–8.

THE WORST OF YOUTH SPORTS

Parents Try Their Hand at Hooliganism

The National Council of Youth Sports recently reported that there are more than 52 million boys and girls participating in organized youth sports throughout the United States. Participation continues to grow at a robust rate, thanks in part to better safety precautions, well-publicized health benefits in this age of rampant obesity, Title IX legislation rousing little girls from their traditional tea parties, and the hypercompetitive college admissions process increasingly demanding more diverse applicants.

It all makes for a Sarajevo-like powder keg on lawn chairs and bleachers throughout America's parks and fields, as up to 100 million parents with frayed nerves and not enough patience with human failure stalk the sidelines, every ounce of their self-esteem and mental balance tied to the immediate success or failure of their child. Hundreds of incidents that involve parents going berserk at youth sporting events are reported each year, and surely a multiple of that goes unreported, as wild-eyed moms and dads hurl themselves in anger at pretty much everybody except the teenager selling sno-cones.

✗ **The poster boy** for parents run amok is Thomas Junta, the hockey dad from Massachusetts. It was Junta who in 2002 sparked a firestorm of scrutiny after repeatedly driving the head of youth hockey coach Michael Costin into a concrete floor at rink-side until Costin, the father of another team member, was dead. In a grim bit of irony, Junta was apparently enraged over the violent nature of the practice Costin was running.

✗ **In 2002,** following a teen baseball tournament in Florida, a man bit off another man's earlobe, setting off a melee that resulted in, among other things, an infant girl getting knocked to the ground from her mother's arms. This incident occurred five years after the infamous Tyson–Holyfield fight/ear chomp, truly a paradigm-shifting moment in anger-management history.

✗ **In 2006,** a Stockton, California, youth football assistant coach ignited a stands-clearing ruckus when he charged onto the field and blindsided a player from the opposing team who had just finished delivering a hit of his own to the coach's son.

✗ **Disagreeing** over playing time is a time-honored reason for parent-coach disputes at the youth level. In 1999, a forty-year-old New York father was charged with assault for breaking the nose of his son's hockey coach because the coach didn't play the boy in the final minutes of a game.

✗ **In 2001,** a forty-two-year-old South Dakota man literally fought City Hall when he struck a referee, who happened to be the town's mayor, during a soccer match involving eleven-year-old girls.

✗ **In 2000,** City Hall gained the upper hand (as it always does) when a Texas police sergeant and youth coach, angered after being ejected from his son's game, proceeded to go home, change into his police uniform, wait in the parking lot following the game, and issue a traffic violation to the game's umpire as he was leaving the facility.

✗ **In 2005,** an Ohio baseball coach went on trial for manslaughter after punching a forty-year-old parking lot volunteer in the face. The victim fell and struck his head on a concrete parking slab and died the following day. The apparent genesis of the dispute was the $5 parking fee, which infuriated parents who were already being gouged by the organizers of the tournament on their children's participation fee. Several people were injured to the point of hospitalization in the parking lot brawl, in addition to the fatality.

✗ **Youth football,** where little kids are often cut, benched, and screamed at by hard-driving coaches as if they're in the NFL, has long been a scene that has winked at the excesses of coaches, parents, and boosters. In 2004, following a heated youth football game, a New Orleans woman assaulted a fellow woman coaching her son's eight- to nine-year-old team. The attacking party was apparently upset because the coach was blocking her view during the contest. Sheriff's deputies were called to the field and the woman agreed to leave. In the spirit of Marques Johnson's character in *White Men Can't Jump,* the woman returned a few minutes later carrying a Tec-9 semiautomatic pistol. Fortunately, she didn't use it.

THE MALICE AT THE PALACE

In the aftermath of Malice at the Palace, the rumble between the Indiana Pacers and Detroit Pistons fans on the night of November 19, 2004, there was plenty of head shaking and tsk-tsking between members of the media class, who were quick to condemn the fight in the utmost terms and ponder its deeper meanings as they showed it over, and over, and over again.

Frankly, it was all more than a little overwrought.

Because the truth of the matter is, Malice at the Palace wasn't a sign of the Apocalypse. It was not a "stain on the sport," because it didn't reflect the sport of basketball, and since it involved fans, it fell outside the realm of bad sportsmanship. It contained action and entertainment on a historic level, keeping eyes glued to every screen on which it was played for days. Taken for what it was, Malice was, quite simply, superb, memorable theater.

Here's why.

LIKE TNT, MALICE AT THE PALACE KNEW DRAMA

Like a great thriller, the drama of the Malice built in stages. There was no single, shocking event, followed by an aftermath. It began as an eye-catching but somewhat common event. It was rooted in the playing surface and continued to build, each subsequent development only advancing on what the previous event allowed. There was a logical sequence, each moment larger and more jaw-dropping than the one before it.

The Malice took place during an early-season showdown between the two best teams in the Eastern Conference: defending World Champion Detroit and Indiana, winners of sixty-one games the previous year. The debacle was initiated by a hard foul from Indiana's Ron Artest on Detroit center Ben Wallace with 45.9 seconds left to play. The Pistons were losing by fifteen and the normally cool Wallace snapped. He shoved Artest backward with all the power his sinewy 6′10″ could muster. Artest performed an exaggerated, Ric Flair-esque backward stumble, Wallace went after him, and both benches cleared near the scorer's table. Had it ended here, no one would remember it.

But it didn't. Wallace, acting out of character, was still in a fury. He made repetitive lunges at Artest, while teammates and referees attempted to hold him back. The stoppage dragged on. Meanwhile, presumably because he was bored—he had taken no real part in the rhubarb so far, except to commit the initial foul—Artest decided to lie down on the scorer's table while Wallace continued to rage. As he enjoyed his dramatic catnap, a cup pinwheeled down from the stands and bounced off Artest's chest. Mass hysteria ensued.

Artest, easily escaping the feeble clutches of an Indiana assistant trying to restrain him, made a beeline for the man he believed threw the cup and landed a haymaker (as it turned out, he had the wrong guy). His teammate Stephen Jackson soon followed, and a clot of Pacers players in their own turn climbed over the scorer's table and invaded the stands. Artest was eventually dragged back to the playing surface, but his night wasn't over: he coldcocked a pudgy Detroit fan who had made the mistake of posturing in a fighting stance. Jermaine O'Neal went into a forward slide and belted the same guy while he was scrambling to his feet. Detroit coach Larry Brown's attempts to restore order were sabotaged by a faulty microphone, which he slammed down on the scorer's table in frustration. Eventually the players were dragged off the floor. The Pacers had to run through the tunnel with their heads down, like steers to the slaughter pen, as Pistons fans rained missiles down on them.

Now that's drama.

HISTORY WITH A CAPITAL *H*

What is History with a capital H? Simple: it's something you've never seen before, and may never see again, in life or in sports. It's one of those moments so memorable that you know exactly what you were doing when it took place: the JFK assassination; the *Challenger* explosion; the (dreadful) last episode of *Seinfeld;* Northwestern going to the Rose Bowl. These moments are all *History.* And when damn near an entire NBA team invades the stands and engages in an all-out brawl with the season-ticket holders, well, that's History too.

It's the singular nature of Malice that makes it something to remember. Somewhat resembling Halley's Comet: the flying ice ball of cosmic dust doesn't really have any material effect on your life, but you should watch it when it appears anyway. After all, you might be dead by the time it comes around again.

EVERYBODY WANG CHUNGED THAT NIGHT

It was fun for everyone involved. Well, almost everyone. Of course, there were consequences for active participation (see table below).

THE PERPS AND THEIR PUNISHMENT			
PLAYER	GAMES	SEASON SALARY	SALARY LOST
Ron Artest	73	$6,158,000	$4,995,000
Stephen Jackson	30	$5,100,000	$1,700,000
Jermaine O'Neal	25	$14,800,000	$4,111,000

PLAYER	GAMES	SEASON SALARY	SALARY LOST
Ben Wallace	6	$6,000,000	$400,000
Anthony Johnson	5	$2,200,000	$122,222
Reggie Miller	1	$5,500,000	$61,111
Chauncey Billups	1	$5,455,000	$60,611
Derrick Coleman	1	$4,500,000	$50,000
Elden Campbell	1	$4,400,000	$48,888

And John Green, the Pistons fan who chucked the now infamous cup, got his season tickets revoked and was permanently barred from ever attending any event at the Palace at Auburn Hills.

But forget that Ron Artest, Stephen Jackson, and Jermaine O'Neal lost almost $11 million combined in wages from the suspensions. For the willing participants, it was all about behaving like the world was going to end the next day. Nobody was thinking about consequences.

✗ **Ron Artest,** quite simply, was reacting to events in the way his hardwiring demands. Once that cup bounced off of him, everything that followed was instinctual. It's said that people feel best when they're just being themselves. If that's true, Ron Artest probably felt pretty wonderful while he was serving knuckle sandwiches to Detroit fans.

✗ **Jermaine O'Neal** was clearly a more reluctant participant than Artest or Stephen Jackson, but in the act that earned him his suspension—landing a sliding sucker punch to the woozy fan who had just been flattened by Artest—he revealed himself as *that* guy. The one who'll watch his friends brawl, contemplate hailing a cab, then dash in for the dirty-pool punch when he sees that his boys are kicking ass.

He wasn't willing to go into the stands, but he *was* willing to hit someone who was already down. He was also *that* guy who holds fire until he's been restrained, then really wants to mix it up, making a couple of halfhearted attempts to go back onto the floor after he'd been dragged into the tunnel.

At any rate, J.O. had his fun too.

✗ **Stephen Jackson** was one of the biggest instigators of the on-floor confrontation. He was the first Indiana pacer into the stands after Artest, and once he got there, he blasted a drink-throwing fan without hesitation. He was Sonny Corleone, Bunny from *Platoon,* O-Dog from *Menace II Society,* and Mr. Blonde from *Reservoir Dogs* all rolled into one. It was clear that he was having the most fun of any of the fight's participants. Even when he was in the stands throwing haymakers on punchy, defenseless middle-aged men, he was thinking what everyone watching at home was thinking: "This is *AWESOME!*"

When he'd finally been subdued and led off the battlefield, he raised his arms in triumph amid the storm of projectiles as the Pacers were hurried through the gauntlet of a tunnel to the locker room. Then he took off his jersey and stomped bare-chested through the walkway with his arms out in front of him, as if he was walking toward a mosh pit. Oh yeah, Stephen Jackson had a blast.*

✗ **And the fans** can't be forgotten. To be sure, there were a lot of Pistons backers who didn't do much besides get into a fetal position and try to protect their important parts (not that there's anything wrong with that). But enough civilians came running through the aisles and hurdled over seats with

---

* In October 2006, less than two years after the riot, Jackson was involved in a 3 a.m. altercation outside an Indianapolis strip club. He was reportedly punched in the mouth and hit by a car, and retaliated by firing five shots from a 9-millimeter pistol into the air. For some guys, the bar of acceptable behavior is a little lower than it is for the balance of humanity. He is to be commended for not actually firing at a live human being. It was a nice display of self-control for the volatile swingman.

their fists cocked to do proud the town that produced Thomas "the Hit Man" Hearns. And nobody runs pell-mell a hundred feet over uncertain terrain to get into something they're not going to have fun doing, right?

BEST OF ALL

We can write about the brawl with a smile on our faces because somehow nobody was really hurt all that badly in Malice at the Palace. The whole thing was like the climactic fight scene in every episode of *The A-Team*: guys are getting tossed onto tables, flipped over bars, thrown through windows, punched in the face by two fists at a time . . . and yet? And yet everybody just gets up, brushes themselves off, and runs away without a drop of blood to show for it. There's devastating action—chairs flying, giant men throwing wild punches, objects fired at people from close range. Yet there were no serious injuries. Sure, some people got banged up, but no old woman got caught in the crossfire and broke her hip. It was an enjoyable show for the viewing audience. It was unique, exciting, and pleasingly violent to the eye. And everyone involved was left alive, sentient, and more than capable of telling the tale . . . which they will do ad nauseum.

Could someone have been seriously hurt? Absolutely. But no one was.

LEST WE FORGET . . .

It was ESPN analyst Bill Walton who added the perfect touch of mawkishness to the whole tawdry affair. Normally given to absurdly overblown declarations during games, the Big Redhead finally found himself calling a game situation worthy of his bombast, and his grave condemnations lent the perfect melodramatic touch. During the on-floor fracas, immediately preceding the fateful toss of the cup, Walton urgently declared, "They need to somehow find a way to get this game *over* with as quickly as possible." He was strangely silent during the first moments of the riot (perhaps he was sorting out what year it was: 2004 or 1974), then simply remarked, "This is a disgrace." Bill Walton can be out there, but the man smelled trouble in the wind that night. Perhaps one of his few memories of the '70s was of playing in the mayhem-filled NBA of the time.

Walton also had the ultimate "Famous Last Words" of Malice at the Palace when, just before the foul by Artest that launched the riot, he intoned: "The Pacers are playing a very intelligent game tonight."

OH YEAH

The final score of the game, or at least the score when play was suspended with less than a minute left:

Indiana 97, Detroit 82

So, Malice didn't affect the outcome of the game, which had long since been decided. That's a good thing, too.

ON THE OTHER HAND

It pretty much demolished the Indiana Pacers. Indiana was the winningest team in the East the year before, losing in the Conference Finals to Detroit, and was out to a strong 7–2 start in the young 2004–05 campaign after kicking the tails of the Pistons and their fans on November 19, 2004. But it never recovered from the personnel disruptions resulting from the brawl. O'Neal, Indiana's best player and maybe the best big man in the Eastern Conference, was lost for twenty-five games. Jackson, the team's newly acquired scorer, was out until the end of the regular season. And the suspension wiped out the season of Ron Artest, the best man-on-man defender in the game and the player who gave the Pacers their muscular identity as a team.

The Pacers, with their top three players out of the lineup, were decimated. They had to play with eight bodies for several nights immediately following the brawl, because backup point guard Anthony Johnson was also suspended, for five games. Somehow, with a skeleton crew, they won their first three after Malice. But then reality caught up. The team sank quickly in the playoff chase.

O'Neal's return in January helped, but it wasn't enough. The Pacers squeezed out a 43–39 record and made the playoffs as a seventh seed, whereupon they were quietly dispatched in the first round by Miami. It was a far different ending to the season than had been anticipated back in November.

Artest appeared on morning television a few days after Malice and used the public forum to pitch the latest CD from Allure, an En Vogue-esque girl group he was producing. That may not have been what viewers were expecting, but Artest assured the public that the record was "hot." The subject of persistent trade rumors, Artest started the 2005–06 season in his Pacers uniform, but soon got hurt, badmouthed the Pacer organization for not supporting him with enough fervor during the suspension, and got himself traded to Sacramento, a place where the forgiving Arco Arena denizens will cheer Jack the Ripper if he puts up 20–10 a night.

So it wasn't all to the good. But just because there were consequences doesn't mean the Malice at the Palace wasn't a theater for History.

A sullen Chris Webber shortly after he calls a timeout his team did not have in the 1993 NCAA Tournament Championship game against North Carolina. The Tar Heels won, 77–71. *AP Images/Susan Ragan*

WHAT WERE THEY THINKING?

The sad sagas of very public sports figures who ultimately proved to be all too fallible.

- ★ "FIFTH DOWN"
- ★ AFTER THE GLORY
- ★ THE WORST OF CRIMINAL ACTS BY AN ATHLETE
- ★ THE WORST MISTAKES LEADING TO A LIFETIME OF RIDICULE

"FIFTH DOWN"

Columbia, Missouri, October 6, 1990—
The Worst Officiating Gaffe in Sports
History. Maybe. Probably.

October 6, 1990. Columbia, Missouri. The powerful Colorado Buffaloes were in town to take on their Big Eight Conference rival, the Missouri Tigers. Coming off an undefeated regular season and an Orange Bowl berth, the Buffs had high hopes going into the 1990 season. But they struggled early, tying Tennessee in the Pigskin Classic and losing a one-point heartbreaker to underdog Illinois two weeks prior to their visit to the Show-Me State. Colorado coach Bill McCartney couldn't afford another such slipup if he wanted to keep his team's flagging National Championship hopes alive.

The Tigers, on the other hand, had no such aspirations, but at an even 2–2 for the season, they still had a shot at their first bowl appearance since 1983. With a road matchup at mighty Nebraska looming, Mizzou desperately needed an upset over the Buffaloes to keep its season from going in the usual direction—sideways.

For three quarters and roughly thirteen minutes, everything went according to plan for Missouri. Containing the Buffalo athletes to a reasonable extent, the Tigers led Colorado 31–27 late in the fourth quarter. With two minutes remaining, the Buffaloes mounted one final drive behind the arm and legs of substitute quarterback Charles Johnson (the future Pittsburgh Steelers receiver), who had started for the injured Darien Hagen. With thirty-one seconds to play, Colorado, needing a touchdown to win, had a first-and-goal on the Missouri three-yard line.

On first down from the three, Johnson spiked the ball to stop the clock. The down markers were never switched over to "2." Neither the folks on the sideline nor on the field seemed to notice. On the *second* first down, running back Eric Bieniemy was stuffed at the one. Colorado took a time-out with eighteen seconds remaining.

On what should have been third down, but was second, Mizzou's defense again stacked Bieniemy up short of the goal line. With two seconds left and the marker showing third down, Johnson spiked the ball again, to stop the clock for the second time. It should have been the last play of the game, but the marker now showed fourth down, giving Colorado one last chance. And on "fourth" down, Johnson kept it himself and just barely broke the plane. Touchdown! The Buffs had come back to foil Missouri's upset bid, 33–31.

It wasn't until the gun sounded that what should have been obvious began to dawn on all parties involved: Colorado had been given an extra down. Charles Johnson later claimed that he thought the sequence of downs was correct at the time. The TV announcers seemed to have caught the oversight after second down, but quickly reverted into oblivion as play continued, and not one player or coach for the Missouri Tigers, who stood to lose the most, walked up to an official as it unfolded and said, "Yo, stripes, it should be third down now, not second." It was as if everyone involved in the game became so engulfed in the goings-on that they forgot the existence of the four-down rule. It was a tad bizarre, and it only got weirder: after Johnson scored, *Missouri* students charged the field and began to tear down the goalposts in jubilant error.

Coach McCartney had little interest in giving back his team's victory. For his part, he pointed out that the slickness of the artificial turf at Mizzou's Memorial Stadium had hindered his superior skill players to a degree commensurate with cheating (to be sure, CU had two or three potential scoring plays on its game-winning drive wiped out by the turf, which played like concrete coated in Clark W. Griswold's polymer-based, friction-free applicator). Journos with a case of self-righteousness hurled thunderbolts at McCartney, but warm gestures of magnanimity and the favors of self-elected moralists didn't win games or import the legions of athletes who kept his program afloat. Besides, the Buffs really, *really* needed this game— they had a National Championship to think about.

And sure enough, Colorado got its National Championship. The Buffs swept their remaining regular-season games and edged Notre Dame 10–9 in the Orange Bowl (here the zebras stepped up for UC again, flagging the Irish for a questionable clipping penalty with less than a minute left, wiping out an electrifying Raghib Ismail punt return touchdown that would have given Notre Dame the lead). The Associated Press voted Colorado number one in its final poll, giving the Buffs a piece of the first and only National Championship in program history.

Missouri tanked, as could be expected. The week after the fifth down, Nebraska abused the demoralized Tigers, 69–21. Mizzou went on to a lowly 4–7 record, its seventh consecutive losing season in a streak that would reach thirteen. How the 1990 season would have turned out had the fifth down never happened is a matter of conjecture. Suffice it to say that losing what would have been a monumental upset thanks to an extra down given to an opponent must have taken some wind out of the sails of the Tigers.

Commentators at the time readily contrasted Colorado's response with Cornell's response to its own fifth-down controversy half a century before. Back in November 1940, going into their meeting with Dartmouth, the Big Red was riding an eighteen-game unbeaten streak, while the Indians, usually a powerhouse in their own right, had a lackluster 3–4 record. But Dartmouth came ready to play, and late in the game took a 3–0 lead. Cornell drove downfield in the waning minutes, had a first-and-goal, ran four plays, and failed to score. Despite the fact that the markers had been counted off correctly (unlike the Colorado case), referee Red Friesell believed it was still just fourth down and gave Cornell another play. The Big Red scored with no time left and won, 7–3.

Within a day or two, observers dissecting the sequence on film had unearthed Friesell's error. The crestfallen referee wrote an impassioned letter to the Dartmouth team, pleading forgiveness for the gaffe. Cornell generously offered to give the victory back to Dartmouth, which the latter accepted. The final score became, and is, Dartmouth University 3, Cornell University 0. Cornell lost its winning streak and a chance at the National Championship, but, unlike the Colorado Buffaloes of a half century later, the Big Red won the long-term PR battle called history.

AFTER THE GLORY

Athletes: Some Hopelessly Misguided. Others Regrettably Persistent

Many athletes describe retirement from the game as being akin to attending their own funeral. They had basked in the limelight, become addicted to the rush of adrenaline, and lived solely for the thrill of competition. Hell, strange women were all too willing to bed down with them simply because of who they were—often more than one at a time. It's understandable that some athletes just can't let it go, retire young, and energetically pursue terminal relaxation. But that doesn't mean we, as fans, can't ridicule them for what they choose to do instead.

ED "TOO TALL" JONES

Several ex-football players have gone into the fight game, Mark Gastineau and Lyle Alzado among them. The case of Ed "Too Tall" Jones is interesting because, unlike those of Gastineau and Alzado, his football career wasn't over when he donned the gloves. As a matter of fact, he was just entering his prime.

Too Tall's skyscraper height (he was 6'9") helped make him one of the most disruptive ends in the NFL and the freakish element in

Dallas's quarterback-terrorizing "Doomsday Machine" defense. But the former Tennessee State star's heart was always in the ring. In 1979, after just five seasons in the league, he traded in his helmet for a pair of Everlasts and embarked on a new career as a heavyweight fighter.

The Cowboys fumed impotently over Too Tall's decision to channel Clint Eastwood's Philo Beddoe character who was then punching it up in theaters with his orangutan buddy Clyde. Shorn of their giant defensive end, they managed to win the NFC East in '79 but were sent to the canvas by an L.A. Rams comeback in the playoffs.

As it turned out, Too Tall missed just one season of football thanks to his new gig. And he didn't do too badly as a fighter—he won all six of his professional bouts—but he possessed weaknesses that were exposed early. He discovered, for instance, that he was very vulnerable to more mobile opponents. The speed that had devastated offensive tackles in the NFL wasn't adequate to maneuver Jones around a squared circle in the company of faster men who were looking to chop him down, body first. Plus, unlike quarterbacks, fighters slug back.

After a year of pounding it out with ham 'n eggers in places like Las Cruces, New Mexico, Too Tall felt his head brushing up against the rather low ceiling of his boxing abilities. Being an intelligent man, he made the prudent decision to return to football. As deeply displeased as they were with his initial defection, Tom Landry and the Cowboys were more than happy to welcome Too Tall back into the fold.

He loved boxing, he tried it; he gave it up and went back to the gridiron. But in doing so, he may have cost his team a Super Bowl.

BO JACKSON

Bo's baseball career was a little bit of a shame only because it took precedence over his football career. He was certainly a specimen— he had great power (his mammoth blast to straightaway center off Rick Reuschel in the '89 All-Star Game is awesome testimony), great speed, and a cannon of an arm—but he had a yawning hole in his game. Namely, he struck out. A lot. Even in his best season, 1990, when he hit a career-high .272, he still whiffed in 31 percent of his plate appearances. Bo was a potential 30–30 guy, maybe even 40–40, but he was also a potential strikeout record-breaker. Small wonder that one of the most famous televised images from Bo's career is that of him breaking a bat over his knee after being rung up.

Now, Football Bo was something else altogether. Once he put on a helmet, pads, and cleats, he had no discernible weaknesses. At 6'1" and 227 pounds, Bo was a perfect storm of power and speed who could blast over linebackers and dash away from safeties with equal aplomb. In his rookie career, playing in just seven games, Bo rushed for 554 yards and an almost-otherworldly 6.8 yards per carry, including his famed 221-yard Monday Night masterpiece in Seattle (the night he established permanent ownership of Brian Bosworth's soul). In 515 career carries, he averaged 5.4 YPC.

Simply put, Bo Jackson was—potentially—an all-time-great caliber running back.

Averaged out over sixteen games, below are Bo's first, and only, four seasons in the NFL.

Bo averaged fewer than fourteen carries per game during his thirty-eight-game NFL career. Coming on in midseason, he didn't go through training camp or preseason, and had to be weaned into the Raider offense gradually, which accounts for the lack of carries.

Year	Attempts	Yards	Touchdowns	Yards per carry
1987	185	1,266	9	6.8
1988	218	928	5	4.3
1989	252	1,381	6	5.5
1990	200	1,117	8	5.6
TOTAL	855	4,692	28	5.6

It can be assumed that his touches per game would have trended upward with the benefit of a full NFL season, and while his yards per carry would have likely trended downward correspondingly, the critical numbers—yards and touchdowns—would have done just the opposite.

Had Bo consistently come into training camp on time, he would have been the focal point of the Raider offense right from the get-go. He would have had ample time to hit, to be hit, and to get himself adjusted to football speed. God only knows the kind of ridiculous numbers he would have put up under those optimum conditions. He had a shot at Canton, but Cooperstown was undoubtedly out of range.

Bo knew baseball. But Bo knew football a whole lot better.

MARCUS GASTINEAU

In his nearly ten seasons as a linebacker for the New York Jets, Mark Gastineau was a five-time Pro Bowler, proprietor of the single season sack record with twenty-two (a record that stood for seventeen years until Brett Favre decided it should change hands and laid down like a frightened puppy dog for the Giants' Michael Strahan), and wreaker of havoc every gridiron Sunday. When Gastineau abruptly announced his retirement from professional football seven weeks into the 1988 season, he stated that it was to spend more time with his lady friend, actress Brigitte Nielsen, who was reported to be suffering from cancer. But there was a darker truth behind his retirement: Gastineau would later admit that he left the league to avoid testing positive for steroids. With the exception of four games in the Canadian Football League in 1990, Gastineau's gorgeous mullet and porn-star 'stache were done terrorizing professional quarterbacks forever.

Instead of kicking back and cashing royalty checks earned from his Brut underwear ads, Gastineau continued to crave the spotlight. In 1991, while holding hands with Nielsen, Gastineau announced that he desired to become a professional boxer. This was not the first time Nielsen found herself standing beside a steroid-using pugilist, but this go-around she wouldn't be forced to cheer in Russian at ringside. Unfortunately for Gastineau, he was not like a piece of iron.

Gastineau's first fight was against Derrick Dukes, a professional wrestler, whom he knocked out in the first round. He would go on to win his first nine fights before a pug named Tim Anderson beat him senseless. Apparently, unlike Dukes and others after him, Anderson wasn't the diving type. CBS's 60 Minutes would eventually expose that many, if not all, of Gastineau's less-than-formidable opponents were handpicked by his promoter for their willingness to hug the mat for a ten count after a glancing Gastineau blow. His boxing career produced a record of fifteen wins, two losses, and one no contest, and ended in 1996 when he was knocked out by another former football player, Alonzo Highsmith.

Aside from his shameful exit from football (a sport he dominated) and his own personal contribution to the corrupt history of boxing (a sport long synonymous with scandal), Gastineau would spend eleven months in prison on Rikers Island for repeated parole violations stemming from drug possession and his history of violence toward women. He's another example of an athlete struggling to find his way "after the glory."*

THE WORST OF ATHLETES WHO PLAYED TOO LONG

Willie Mays

It would have been graceful for the Say Hey Kid to retire after the 1972 season, when at the age of forty-one he returned to his ances-

---

* What, no Michael Jordan in this spot? Nope. Conspiracy theories about being kicked out of the league by Commissioner Stern for gambling aside, M.J. has always insisted that, despite his sub–Mendoza Line numbers at Double-A Birmingham, his short-lived baseball career was just the tonic he required. He needed a break from the hardwood after the murder of his father, and being around the hustling, low-paid men of the minors who played for the love of the game refueled his own competitive fires. Upon his return, Jordan dominated the NBA with a renewed and unmatched ferocity.

tral baseball home of New York and hit .267 with eight home runs in 195 at-bats for the Mets. But he decided to play another year. In his final go-around, Willie hit a meager .211, coming perilously close to dropping his career batting average under .300. (It came to rest at .302.)

The Mets, as it turned out, won the National League pennant in 1973. And if Mays failed to distinguish himself in the regular season, he did so in a negative manner in the postseason. In the ninth inning of Game Two of the World Series, while in center field as a late-inning defensive substitute, the forty-two-year-old legend fell down going after a routine fly ball, opening the door to a game-tying rally by the Oakland A's.

Steve Carlton

A notorious physical fitness freak, Lefty should have known better than anyone that his arm was no longer up to the task of consistently getting outs in the Majors, but his heart overruled his head. In his last four seasons, all coming after his fortieth birthday, Carlton went 16–37 with a dismal 5.21 ERA. Formerly as identifiable with the Phillies as the Phanatic, he played with four teams in his last three seasons—San Francisco, Cleveland, Minnesota, and the Chicago White Sox—and ended his career not with the bang of a speech and a tear-filled press conference (not that Lefty would have shed tears, but you get the point), but with the whimper of an outright release from the Twins, on April 24, 1988. All Lefty did by hanging on so long was add losses to his record and basis points to his career ERA. Oh, and delay his Hall of Fame induction a few years.

Jerry Rice

Despite his production dropping in 2003 to sixty-three catches (his lowest total in a noninjury season since 1988) and two touchdowns, despite the Oakland Raiders being clearly in a rebuilding mode following their disastrous '03 campaign, and despite having accomplished everything he could possibly accomplish in pro football, Rice was determined to keep playing in 2004. The Raiders didn't really want him back but didn't want to cut him, so he rode the pine, catching just five passes before being traded to Seattle, which thought it needed a wise hand to mentor its callow receiver corps.

Once in the Emerald City, he promptly asked Seahawk legend Steve Largent for permission to wear his retired #80. Put in an awkward position, Largent assented. Rice caught twenty-five passes, and the Seahawks wound up losing in the first round of the playoffs. Jerry's contributions, including his hideously gauche "borrowing" of Largent's number, amounted to exactly not much for Seattle. Rice attempted to hang on with the Broncos in 2005, but Mike Shanahan, no sentimentalist, asked for his playbook in training camp. Rice did *not* ask to wear #7 during his brief stay in Denver.

Muhammad Ali

A lot of fighters hang on entirely too long, becoming punch-drunk and losing to spry youngsters they would've clobbered in years past. But Ali's decline was more visible than most, because Ali himself was more visible than most. By the late 1970s, it was becoming more and more apparent that the once-peerless heavyweight was losing it, and there was loud talk that, if he continued fighting, he was putting himself in real danger of permanent consequences to his health. Ali continued to fight. He probably should have given it up after barely surviving a bout with Ken Norton in 1976; he definitely should have given it up after losing to Leon Spinks in early 1978; but he didn't actually give it up until 1980, after suffering a one-sided loss to the pride of Easton, Pennsylvania, Larry Holmes.

Actually, even that wasn't enough. On December 10, 1981, the Greatest of All Time came out of retirement to fight Jamaican Trevor Berbick in the Bahamas (Berbick was eight years old when Cassius Clay knocked out Sonny Liston in Miami in 1964). The lack of an American venue and the general skepticism about Ali's physical state made the fight into a sad sideshow. Berbick beat up on Ali for ten rounds and won by decision. "The Drama in Bahama" offered no such thing, but it did result in a unique fact: the late Trevor Berbick is the only man to have fought Muhammad Ali *and* Mike Tyson. Ali, who was already showing symptoms of Parkinson's disease when he took the ring against Berbick, clearly sacrificed way too much for boxing.

THE WORST OF ATHLETES WHO TRIED THEIR HAND AT ACTING

Bruce Jenner

Long before he set out in dogged pursuit of Burt Reynolds's staggering record for most plastic surgery procedures in a lifetime—a yeoman's task indeed—Bruce Jenner was "The World's Greatest Athlete." And long prior to becoming the poster boy of shameless self-promotion (one brief visit to Jenner's website will get you on board with this school of thought—he was voted Father of the Year!), he was America's golden boy—and for good reason. In 1976, he became an Olympic decathlon champion with an inspiring performance at the Montreal Summer Games, setting both an Olympic *and* a world record of 8,634 points. Soon thereafter he was in every grocery store's cereal aisle across the country, famously emblazoned on the coveted Wheaties box.

It's more difficult to identify Jenner's second career because he's managed to transform himself into a modern-day Renaissance man, dabbling in just about everything from book writing (and you hold in your hands evidence that proves that *anyone* can do that) to motivational speaking, corporate cheerleading, producing television shows, broadcasting, hosting a talk show, and acting.

In 1980, Jenner made his acting debut in the film *Can't Stop the Music*, a disco-era musical comedy about the Village People, starring Valerie Perrine of *Superman* ("Miss Teschmacher!") fame. The star-studded cast also included Steve Gutenberg (before his own career took off like Sputnik) and the movie, billed as the musical comedy smash of the '80s, was a megastinker and ginormous flop.

But *Can't Stop the Music* also proved to be an inauspicious beginning for Jenner's acting career. He would never again appear in a feature film. According to imdb.com, he later appeared on *CHiPs* (five episodes with Ponch and John!) and an episode of *Murder, She Wrote* and was a celebrity host of *Double Dare*. No Anthony Hopkins, that Bruce Jenner.

Shaquille O'Neal

To steal a phrase from Officer Shaq's other profession, Mr. O'Neal is a repeat offender. He has appeared in eight movies, but his most forgettable performances came as Neon in *Blue Chips*, Kazaam in, ah, *Kazaam*, and Steel in, ahem, *Steel*.

Brian Bosworth

Aside from allegations of steroid use at Oklahoma, and his grievous underachievement in the NFL, the Boz's transgressions have been more cinematic as opposed to cocaine related. Boz has made appearances in *Three Kings* and the insulting remake of *The Longest Yard*—which, by the way, set the record for most appearances by cocaine-abusing ex-athletes. Bosworth's most memorable performance was his first, when he starred in *Stone Cold* as a maverick cop who enforces his own brand of justice.

Michael Jordan

M.J. generally gets a pass when he screws up, but we can't give him one when it comes to his acting in *Space Jam*. His performances on *Saturday Night Live*, however, were high comedy, even if he never managed to get through a skit without breaking down and laughing.

Brett Favre

The Southern Miss and Packers QB played a janitor in the 1996 movie *Reggie's Prayer*. Yet another movie afflicted with the mass athlete agglomeration disease, the cast included Pat Morita, M. C. Hammer, Mike Holmgren, Bryce Paup, Willie Roaf, Gale Sayers, Reggie White, Rosie Grier, and Keith Jackson. However, Favre's most widely viewed movie performance was as himself ("Brett Fav-ruh") in *There's Something About Mary*. Steve Young was apparently originally slated for the role, but he's a staunch Book of Mormon–beater and objected to the movie's content.

Bart Conner

Most everyone associates Barthold with the gold medal–winning U.S.A. men's Olympic gymnastics team in 1984. During those same Summer Games he also won individual gold in the weirdest and most senseless of all gymnastics events: the parallel bars. More recently he has served as the high-pitched color commentator who repeatedly yells, "She stuck it!" during the 5,486 hours of network Olympic gymnastic coverage every four years. But did you also know that Conner appeared in two episodes of *Highway to Heaven* and also starred as Bart Taylor, the top BMX factory rider, in the kiddie racing movie *Rad*? Now you do.

Dennis Rodman

Entire books could be written on the curious nature of Dennis Rodman's decision-making process. In fact, they have been. But his acting in the movie *Double Team* as weapons dealer Yaz caused many moviegoers to choke on their buttery kernels. When Jean-Claude Van Damme and the ultimate C-lister, Mickey Rourke, noticeably outclass you, you can kiss your Oscar fantasy good-bye.

Howie Long

His persistent flattop look is memorable. His starring role as firefighter Jesse Graves in *Firestorm* was not. But he landed this part due to his stellar work in John Travolta's *Broken Arrow* two years prior.

Bob Uecker

He won the World Series with the St. Louis Cardinals in 1964, but his six-year Major League baseball career yielded only a .200 life-time batting average. His acting career was similarly up-and-down. Uecker's work as a play-by-play man in the movie *Major League* ("Juuuuust a bit outside") was stellar. But he also starred as George Owens on the hit series *Mr. Belvedere*—the whimsical adventures of an English housekeeper who was also a large and unlikable man. Not exactly the summit of comedic television.

THE WORST OF CRIMINAL ACTS BY AN ATHLETE

When the Genetically Gifted Reveal Themselves to Be Judgmentally Impaired

BYRON MORRIS

In August 2000, when Byron Morris pled guilty to charges that he and two accomplices conspired to distribute at least 220 pounds of marijuana in Missouri and elsewhere, it might've been lost in the white noise that is the media's daily reporting of the *bad* news. But Byron was *Bam,* as in "Bam" Morris, former star running back for Texas Tech and winner of the prestigious Doak Walker Award.

Despite suiting up for Super Bowl XXX, Bam's pro career as a ballcarrier for the Pittsburgh Steelers, Baltimore Ravens, and Kansas City Chiefs was of marginal proportions. So when he retired unexpectedly after the 1999 season, already on probation for a prior felony-possession-of-marijuana charge, it was to no one's surprise that Bam pursued and was convinced that he'd found greener pastures. (Pun absolutely intended.) But Bam's shelf life as a distributor of Mother Earth's finest herb was as brief as that of an NFL lineman's knees. He was sentenced in 2000 for the aforementioned distribution charges, and a character rehabilitation clinic by the name of Leavenworth anxiously awaited his arrival.

NATE NEWTON

Nate Newton was a cute and cuddly teddy bear of a man you may better know as the three-hundred-pound-plus, six-time Pro Bowl offensive lineman for the great Troy Aikman–led Dallas Cowboys teams of the '90s. He's one of a few immovable objects from those fantastic offensive lines that enabled first ballot Hall of Fame running back Emmitt Smith to run straight downfield to the all-time yardage record.

But on November 4, 2001, in St. Martin Parish, Louisiana, police discovered more than two hundred pounds of marijuana stowed away in Nate Newton's van. Following the passing of approximately two fortnights, Big Nate was caught with an additional 175 pounds of marijuana on Interstate 45, making nearly a quarter ton of cannabis found in Nate's possession in about one month's time.

ORLANDO CEPEDA

Expectations were high for Orlando Cepeda in his hometown of Ponce, Puerto Rico. To begin with, his father was Pedro Perucho "The Bull" Cepeda, the legendary Puerto Rican baseball star. So when he arrived as a twenty-year-old to the Major Leagues in 1958, the Baby Bull had some big hooves to fill. And he filled them from Day One. In his first Major League game, Orlando homered off of Don Drysdale and helped his San Francisco Giants defeat the Dodgers. Cepeda won 1958 Rookie of the Year honors and went on to a career in which he became a seven-time All Star, appeared in three World Series, won an MVP award, and—in his best season, 1961—hit .311, slugged forty-six home runs, and batted in 142 runs.

He retired in 1975, beloved by all—until he was arrested at the San Juan airport on charges of trying to pick up 160 pounds of marijuana. His star fell. He was sentenced to five years in prison but only served ten months. Eventually the island of Puerto Rico forgave and forgot and reembraced its native son—it was only 'bammer, after all—and so did the Hall of Fame Committee, which elected him to Cooperstown in 1999.

But athletes have never limited themselves to blue-collar crimes of the recreational drug-trafficking type. Their unlawful behavior throughout history has run the gamut, from serial killings to pedophilia, showing a level of diversification that would make a large-cap portfolio manager green with envy.

THE KILLERS

Rather than enjoy an opportunity for which millions would kill, these athletes went straight to the killing.

Rae Carruth

In the 1997 NFL Draft, the Carolina Panthers selected Rae Carruth, All-American receiver from the University of Colorado, in the first round with the twenty-seventh overall selection. Carruth's rookie season proved to be a promising one, as he led all league newcomers in receptions and receiving yardage. That year would be his best as a professional. In the opening contest of the 1998 season, Carruth broke his foot and didn't catch a pass all season. As for the following year, well, that was abruptly halted by events a bit more tragic.

On November 16, 1999, in Carruth's Charlotte, North Carolina, neighborhood, a woman was severely wounded in a drive-by shooting. The victim, Cherica Adams, survived the attack, but soon fell into a coma. Before doing so, she identified Carruth, her boyfriend at the time, as driving one of the vehicles involved in the shooting. Adams died a month later. Soon after the shooting in Tennessee, Carruth was found hiding in the trunk of a car like a container of antifreeze.

At his trial, Rae Carruth was found guilty of conspiracy to commit murder, shooting into an occupied vehicle, and using an instrument to destroy an unborn child. Yes, Cherica Adams was pregnant, and Carruth was the father. He was sentenced to at least eighteen years and eleven months at Nash Correctional Institution near Raleigh, North Carolina. As for the unborn baby boy whom Carruth had attempted to destroy, Chancellor was saved by doctors in an emergency C-section procedure, but was born with cerebral palsy due to complications related to his premature entry into the world.

Vere Thomas St. Leger Goold

Goold was an Irishman from County Cork, son of a baron, and in 1879, the first Irish lawn tennis champion. The logical next step for him and his strung racquet? Wimbledon, of course. Even in this prestigious event's infancy, the place to be was the All England Croquet and Lawn Tennis Club, where tennis greats and socialites alike would convene to impress one another. And Goold, with his aggressive style of play, was an instant hit with the grass-court set. Predictable baseline exchanges, tea, and parasols characterized the typical tennis match at the time, but Goold and his repeated attacks to the net aroused the sedated crowds. He made it all the way into the championship match but was defeated in the All-Comers Final by Reverend John Hartley, 6–2, 6–4, 6–2. His tennis career didn't last much longer, but he was apparently determined to make a name for himself anyway.

In 1907, Goold and his wife arrived in England from a "business holiday" in Monte Carlo. They had spent much of their time gambling in an attempt to alleviate their overwhelming debt, which is generally a sound strategy. They were carrying two bags, neither of which was filled of cash. When a baggage handler at the train station noticed a strange odor emanating from the luggage's interior, he notified the police. Upon inspection, the remains of a dismembered woman were discovered. The Goolds were arrested and, during the investigation, the victim was discovered to be Emma Liven, a Danish woman who had foolishly lent the desperate couple 1,000 francs and jewelry worth many times that. When she demanded repayment, an argument ensued and poor Emma became the victim of a coed stabbing. Both were sentenced to life imprisonment. Goold died only two years later, in 1909, at the infamous prison on Devil's Island.

O.J. Simpson

Just in case you've been hiding out in a cave like a Japanese Army deserter from World War II and missed the fall from grace of this Hall of Fame running back, his first-person account, *If I Did It*, is currently on shelves. To make a long story short, while the law says he didn't kill his ex-wife, Nicole, and her friend Ron Goldman, the world at large feels strongly that he did.

Randall Woodfield

Everyone knows O.J.'s story, but not many are familiar with Randy Woodfield's. Born in 1950, in Salem, Oregon, Woodfield resembled the consummate all-American boy. He did well in the classroom and was the star of his high school football team. But Randy liked to take "it" out. When he was first arrested for indecent exposure in high school, his coaches had the charges buried. After all, Randy had a future on the field as bright as the Pacific was wide.

In 1970, while attending Portland State University, Woodfield was arrested for vandalizing an ex-girlfriend's apartment. He was arrested for indecent exposure in 1972 and then again for good measure the following year. Despite his obvious tendency toward perversion, the Green Bay Packers thought Randy exhibited something special, so they drafted him in the seventeenth round in 1974.* However, after Randy was involved in a (dirty) dozen more flashing incidents, the Packers decided he wasn't bringing the right type of attention and skill set to their storied franchise, so they sent him home to Oregon.

---

* The Pittsburgh Steelers got five future Hall of Famers in the 1974 Draft. The Packers got a future serial killer. The Draft is an inexact science.

Arriving back in the Northwest not as a conquering hero but rather as a disgraced young man, Woodfield's criminal behavior intensified. The following year, he robbed and sexually assaulted several women at knifepoint and eventually served four years for second-degree robbery. Randy was just getting warmed up. In 1979, he went on a two-year crime spree, holding up various businesses and robbing homes up and down Interstate 5 in western Oregon and northern California. Many of his female victims were sexually assaulted and/or murdered. In 1981, Woodfield was arrested for a murder that took place in Beaverton, Oregon, and for the double murder of a mother and daughter in Redding, California. He's currently serving a 157-year sentence in an Oregon State prison. While he was found guilty of four murders, he was connected to more than eighteen premature deaths and more than sixty sexual assaults. Today, Randy Woodfield is known as the I-5 Killer.

Charles Smith

Charles Smith is hardly in the same category as the prior discussed cold-bloods, but death by one's hand is no more arbitrary than it is definitive. Smith was a star guard for Big Papa John Thompson at Georgetown University and was also a member of Coach Thompson's 1988 U.S. Olympic bronze-medal basketball team—the last U.S. Olympic hoops team, by the way, comprised entirely of amateur players, notable for giving the Soviets one of their last Cold War victories. Smith found his way onto the Boston Celtics roster and played sixty games for them during the 1989–90 season.

On the night of March 22, 1991, Charles Smith was behind the wheel of a van crossing Commonwealth Avenue in Boston. Unfortunately, Boston University students Michelle Dartley and An Trinh were also crossing Comm Ave. Smith hit and killed them both, fled, and was arrested a mile from the scene. He was convicted in March 1992 of negligent driving, leaving the scene of an accident, and causing the deaths of both Dartley and Trinh. He served twenty-eight months at the Suffolk County House of Correction.

Norman Selby

Kid McCoy, as he was better known, was born in October 1872 and was a professional boxing champion. The Real McCoy (the boxer is rumored to have been the origination of the phrase) was slight of build, but threw a vicious, corkscrew knockout punch. He was elected into the International Boxing Hall of Fame in 1991 for a boxing career in which he won eighty-six bouts—sixty-four by knockout—and lost only six. Three of those losses came to heavyweight greats Tom Sharkey and "Gentleman" Jim Corbett, and the other to light heavyweight champion Jack Root.

McCoy's career after leaving the ring was equally dynamic, but less of a success. He became addicted to alcohol, tried his hand at acting, then settled on home-wrecking. He dated Theresa Mors, a wealthy and betrothed antique dealer. In August 1924, Mors—during her divorce proceedings—was killed by a gunshot to the head in the forbidden love nest she shared with McCoy. The following morning, McCoy held twelve hostages at gunpoint, robbed a few of them, and shot one in the leg as the insolent man tried to escape. The champion boxer was charged with his lover's murder, found guilty of manslaughter, and sentenced to ten years in the famed San Quentin prison.

McCoy was married ten times in his life—four times to the same lass—and in 1940, three years after he was released from jail, gave himself a permanent knockout with an overdose of sleeping pills.

Leonard Little

On the night of October 19, 1998, St. Louis Rams rookie defensive end Leonard Little celebrated his twenty-fourth birthday in the style befitting a rich young athlete. He got piss-wasted, jumped behind the wheel of a brand-new Lincoln Navigator, and attempted to drive home. While weaving his way through the streets of St. Louis, Little ran a red light and broadsided a car being driven by Susan Gutweiler, a forty-seven-year-old wife and mother. Gutweiler suffered a broken neck and died the following day. In June 1999, Little pleaded guilty to involuntary manslaughter. His punishment for taking a human life was ninety days in jail and four years' probation, as well as the continuation of his lucrative NFL career. It wasn't exactly a commensurate sentence, and it didn't stick—in April 2004, Little was again arrested for driving under the influence, much to the outrage of Gutweiler's family, for whom it was bad enough to be constantly subjected to the celebrity status of the man who had killed their matriarch.

Jayson Williams

Ebullient and gregarious as well as one of the game's top rebounders, Jayson Williams was considered an antidote to the rock-bottom Q-rating of most of the NBA's stars. But the popular ex-St. John's Redman had a darker side—a fondness for alcohol and guns, and a corresponding inability to handle either like an adult. Williams once winged New York Jet receiver Wayne Chrebet, and another time killed one of his own rottweilers with a shotgun blast, aimed the weapon at Nets teammate Dwayne Schintzius, and ordered him to remove the dead animal, unless he wanted to be next.

On the night of February 14, 2002, Williams and several friends and family members had attended a Harlem Globetrotters game, gone to dinner (where they spent nearly $2,000 on food and booze), and returned to Jay-Will's New Jersey estate. It was late at night, the liquor was flowing, and Williams, feeling quite the lord of the manor, was in a mood to show off. He opened the gun cabinet in his bedroom, hauled out a Browning shotgun, and began twirling it to entertain his guests.

The gun went off. The driver of the group's limousine, fifty-five-year-old Costas Christofi, lay sprawled on the floor, dead from a blast to the chest. Jayson Williams was in trouble.

Having dug a hole for himself, he then decided in his drunken panic to keep digging. Although an honest explanation to the police of what had happened would have been the wise course, Williams decided to stage the scene to make it look as if Christofi had shot himself. He wiped down the shotgun, placed it in the dead limo driver's hands, and got rid of his own bloody clothing. Then he persuaded several of his guests to go along with the charade. (Not surprisingly, they weren't inclined to contradict Jay-Will at the moment.) The evidence didn't support the cock-and-bull suicide story. Williams was charged with aggravated manslaughter. Although he was acquitted of this charge, in 2006 he was ordered to stand trial on a lesser charge of reckless manslaughter.

ASSAULT

The broadest category of criminal act, "assault" is of course inclusive of the ignominious *sexual* assault and battery charges. And athletes, both professional and amateur alike, unfortunately have long proven to possess a tendency toward engaging in this unfortunate behavior. While there are a few legitimate contenders vying for the predator crown, on this topic there's no more obvious person to start with than . . .

Lawrence Phillips

Lawrence Lamond Phillips is a former Nebraska Cornhusker, St. Louis Ram, Miami Dolphin, San Francisco 49er, Barcelona Dragon, Florida Bobcat, Montreal Alouette, Calgary Stampeder, and, more recently, a Southern California pickup-football participant. "Loose Larry" was arrested in August 2005 on suspicion of attempted murder after he allegedly drove a stolen car into a throng of boys with whom he had just played pickup football at Exposition Park in Los Angeles. And they say people in L.A. are apathetic about their sports!

Phillips's body of work—his rap sheet, so to speak—is so lengthy that it can only be properly presented in bulleted format:

- ✗ 2005, arrested on suspicion of attempted murder after allegedly driving a stolen car into a throng of boys with whom he had just played pickup football

✗ 2005, charged with assault by San Diego police for allegedly choking his girlfriend into unconsciousness

✗ 2003, charged with sexual assault, assault, and uttering threats, apparently against another girlfriend

✗ 2000, charged with attacking a girlfriend in Beverly Hills and sentenced to six months in jail after pleading no contest to felony charges of beating the woman and making a terrorist threat

✗ 1997, released after pleading no contest to hitting a woman after she refused to dance in a nightclub. Pleaded guilty to battery and was placed on six months' probation

✗ 1996, arrested three times and spent twenty-three days in jail for violating probation after a drunk-driving incident in California

✗ 1993, while attending Nebraska, pleaded no contest to domestic violence in a confrontation with a girlfriend. (Read: dragged a woman downstairs by her hair and bashed her head against a mailbox.)

Monster.com takes on a whole new meaning upon reviewing this résumé. It's worth noting that Phillips hawked his Big Twelve conference championship ring for $20 at a Las Vegas pawnshop. *Hello, Rock Bottom!*

Mike Tyson

Coming of age in a tough Brooklyn neighborhood, Mike Tyson's ills, missteps, and personal demons are well known and well publicized. He's a pop culture icon and one of the most controversial acts in sports history, although the act has long grown weary. His bipolar leanings are no better represented than by the divergent tattoos on his right and left deltoids: busts of Mao Zedong and Arthur Ashe. But on fight night, when he first appeared from the tunnel and approached the ring, there was no man in the history of boxing who elicited such pangs of anticipation, whether they were from the terrified fighter facing him, the spectator at ringside, or the viewer at home inching toward the edge of the couch.

In 1986, Iron Mike became the youngest man ever to win the heavyweight championship by TKO'ing Trevor Berbick in the second round. Less than a year later he unified the three title belts by defeating Tony Tucker in a twelve-round decision. Tyson proceeded to clobber challengers in a fashion so dominant that no one quite knew what to make of the phenomenon. His glittery ascent was as short-lived as many of his mismatched bouts. His decline, however, has been a protracted affair.

It officially began on February 11, 1990, when Tyson lost his title to James "Buster" Douglas in Tokyo. It would get much worse. In 1992, he went on trial for his alleged 1991 rape of Miss Black Rhode Island, Desiree Washington, in an Indianapolis hotel room. He was found guilty and served three years in jail. Events since his release and formal name change to Abdul Aziz have included biting off a portion of Evander Holyfield's ear during a match between the two, serving an additional two years in the clink for assaulting motorists, declaring bankruptcy, and undergoing an arrest for drunk driving and drug possession. This story will almost certainly not have a happy ending.

Bill Tilden

Born in Philadelphia in 1893, Bill Tilden picked up tennis at the age of five and immediately found success with it. His professional career commenced in 1915 when he began competing for titles at the state and national levels. As he played tennis throughout World War I, his talent grew, and so did he. In 1920, Big Bill made it onto the American Davis Cup Team. While a member, he led the U.S. squad to seven consecutive victories from 1920 to 1926. He won Wimbledon three times in his career and was U.S. national champion on five occasions. Standing 6'4" and brandishing a rocket serve clocked at more than 150 mph, Bill Tilden was the best tennis player in the world. He was elevated to rock-star status on par with the likes of Babe Ruth. But the two legends' respective flamboyance had different reasons for existence.

Tilden played tennis into the 1940s and was fortunate to enjoy limited success in literature and film as well. In 1946, he was living in L.A. when he was arrested on Sunset Boulevard for placing his hand in a teenage boy's pants. The victim wasn't a ball boy, and Tilden wasn't in search of a bouncier Wilson. Rather, the lad was a prostitute whose services Tilden had solicited. Likely because of his celebrity status, Tilden was charged only with a misdemeanor (contributing to the delinquency of a minor) and was sentenced to a year in prison. Big Bill was arrested again in January 1949 after he picked up a sixteen-year-old hitchhiker and made lewd advances toward him. Once again Tilden was shown leniency and served only ten months for the new molestation charge despite the fact that he was already on probation.

Alas, Bill's downfall had begun, and his star power dwindled as the tennis world increasingly distanced itself from the convicted pee-pee toucher. He eventually went broke—his flamboyant proclivities also included the procurement of many luxury items now referred to as "bling"—and died of a stroke in 1953.

Luis Polonia

Luis Polonia was not a great athlete. And he certainly was not a great public figure, before, during, or after his playing days. Luis was just a good old-fashioned idiot pervert who was arrested in August 1989, in his Milwaukee hotel room, for having sexual relations with a fifteen-year-old girl. He pleaded no contest and served sixty days in the big house. (And not the one in Ann Arbor, either.)

Sly Williams

Sylvester Williams was a University of Rhode Island graduate, class of '79. He remains seventh all-time in Ram scoring with 1,777 points, and ranks in the top ten of thirteen other statistical categories. He was drafted in the first round after his junior year at URI, and in slightly more than six seasons in the NBA he played with the New York Knicks, the Atlanta Hawks, and the Boston Celtics.

In 2002, Sly—a nickname not befitting of his actions—then forty-four, was charged with first-degree rape, sodomy, and first-degree kidnapping for allegedly tying up and holding a woman captive in a closet for approximately twenty-four hours and threatening her with a knife in September 2001. He was also accused of raping a second woman in January 2002. The two cases were consolidated. Prior to jury selection for his trial, Sly pleaded to the lesser kidnapping charges and received a sentence of five years in a Broome County, New York, jail.

Eddie Griffin

Eddie Griffin was a McDonald's All-American and was selected as the seventh pick of the 2001 NBA Draft out of Seton Hall by the New Jersey Nets, who immediately swapped his draft rights to the Houston Rockets. His first two years with Houston were productive on the court, but off the hardwood Eddie's love for the drink began to plague him. He was released by the Rockets in 2003 and spent the following season at a rehab clinic named after a nice old First Lady. Upon release, he was signed by the Minnesota Timberwolves and once again put up solid numbers on the court.

Griffin is no stranger to violence: he was kicked out of Philadelphia's Roman Catholic High School for fighting with a teammate in a cafeteria brawl, was reputed to be involved in numerous altercations with players and coaches while at Seton Hall, and in February 2004 was accused of hitting his girlfriend and shooting at her, eventually pleading guilty to deadly conduct. The judge threw the book at him, and Griffin was sentenced to eighteen months' probation and ordered to take anger-management classes.

But in March 2006, he turned the tables . . . and assaulted himself. The Minnesota Timberwolves center was allegedly drunk and watching porn in his luxury SUV when, while trying to do a little "one-handed driving," he crashed into a parked Suburban. Griffin reportedly received special treatment from the police officers who arrived on the scene, as they drove him home and neglected to test for alcohol consumption.

Thomas Henderson

After quitting the air force before he was even sworn in, Thomas "Hollywood" Henderson enrolled at Langston University, where he had much success on the NAIA school's defensive line. He was selected eighteenth overall by the Dallas Cowboys in the 1975 NFL Draft and would go on to be an All-Pro outside linebacker for America's Team from 1975 to 1979. A gifted athlete—he occasionally returned kicks and, as a rookie, took one ninety-seven yards for a touchdown—the explosive Henderson was the prototype for the speed-rushing, big-play linebackers who revolutionized NFL defenses in the 1980s.

Hollywood liked to have fun, too—a lot of fun. No matter the situation, he was determined to enjoy himself in a manner he saw fit. For example, Hollywood made a habit of blowing lines of cocaine on the sidelines during games—including Super Bowl XIII in 1979. Following his firing by Tom Landry, Hollywood briefly spent time with the Houston Oilers and the San Francisco 49ers, but his hard-partying lifestyle put him into a downward spiral that touched bottom in November 1983, when Henderson was arrested for smoking crack cocaine with two teenage girls in California. He was accused of threatening them with a gun and sexually assaulting them.

Despite his claims of innocence, Hollywood pleaded no contest to the charges and served eight months in court-ordered drug rehabilitation and two years in prison. Unlike so many others before and after him who made similar mistakes and suffered similar consequences, the rest of Thomas Henderson's story is an uplifting one. He's maintained a clean lifestyle since his arrest in 1983, and in 2000 he won $28 million in the Texas Lottery. He used the money to start a youth charity and donated much of it to the community in East

Austin where he was once a wee lad. He's now a motivational speaker.

WHITE-COLLAR VARIETY

Billy Cannon

In 1959, Billy Cannon was an All-American halfback and Heisman Trophy winner for the LSU Tigers. Out of college, Cannon signed with the AFL's Houston Oilers, a coup for a struggling league locked in a struggle with the established NFL. In 1961, Cannon led the league in rushing with 948 yards for Houston's last-ever championship team. He went on to a successful eleven-season professional career as a running back and tight end with the Oakland Raiders, the Kansas City Chiefs, and the Oilers.

After retirement, Cannon became an orthodontist, but he eventually ran into serious financial problems. (A dearth of teeth in the Baton Rouge area may have been a factor.) His one attempt at balancing his checkbook was to counterfeit legal U.S. tender. But the U.S. Treasury rose up and stonewalled him like an SEC defense. In 1983, Billy Cannon was sentenced to five years in prison for counterfeiting.

Since his release, Cannon, in order to protect his Heisman trophy from creditors, and to obtain unlimited free lunches at T.J. Ribs restaurant, sold the prized award to the owner of Baton Rouge's proud purveyor of trans-fats.

Denny McLain

In 1968 Dennis Dale McLain became the last thirty-game winner in baseball history. At just twenty-five years of age, the big-boned Detroit right-hander looked as if he was in the budding stages of a Hall of Fame career. As it turned out, McLain opted for a lifetime spent in another "Hall"—that of Justice.

Even before his problems became a matter of public record, McLain's choices of friends and nocturnal habits were the subject of whispering campaigns around baseball. McLain had missed time near the end of the 1967 season with an injured foot—a boo-boo he claimed he had incurred getting off the couch while watching an episode of *The Untouchables*. Word in clubhouses and back rooms was that McLain's foot had actually been "stomped" by members of the Detroit underworld as punishment for failing to pay off gambling debts. The rumors have never been substantiated, but considering McLain's suspension by the American League in 1970 for consorting with gamblers, it doesn't seem all that much of a stretch.

The suspension was the signal for McLain's downfall. In his last three seasons in the majors, he went 17–34, dogged all the while by suspensions, arm and weight problems, and all-around bizarre behavior (including carrying a gun onto a team flight and, predating the Deion Sanders–Tim McCarver flap by a couple of decades, dumping ice water on a pair of Detroit sportswriters). By the age of thirty he was out of baseball and on his way to a life of travail, almost all of it self-imposed.

In 1977 McLain, who had made over $100,000 annually playing baseball (a lot in those days, when it wasn't uncommon for ballplayers to make $25,000 per year), filed for bankruptcy. In 1984 he was handed a twenty-three-year prison sentence for extortion and cocaine trafficking. The sentence was thrown out two years later. McLain's way of "paying forward" for his turn of good fortune was to steal nearly $3 million from the pension fund of a company he had bought in 1993. In 1996 he went back to the clink on charges of embezzlement and money laundering. This is Denny McLain, the only man to win thirty games since 1934.

THE WORST MISTAKES LEADING TO A LIFETIME OF RIDICULE

In the Blink of an Eye, a Notable Gaffe Can Redefine an Athlete's Entire Body of Work

To err is human. To err in a manner that results in the shame produced by your action following you around for years is reserved for the elites—celebrities, politicians, and, of course, athletes. Yet even among the countless goofs, gaffes, and blunders of sport, only a few can be counted as the Worst. These are acts that, whether for their circumstances, consequences, or sheer numskullery, stand out from the middling crowd.

YOU'RE GOING THE WRONG WAY!

It's a warning to live by, as Neal Page and Del Griffith found out in *Planes, Trains and Automobiles*. And on a couple occasions, it's a warning that would've proved very handy on the playing fields.

Jim Marshall's Wrong-Way Run

The funny thing about this snafu is that Jim Marshall should have been the last player on earth involved in it. Still the record-holder for consecutive starts by a nonkicker (270), Marshall was durable, reliable, and, above all, intelligent—the kind of guy they call a "pro's pro."

So there is no logical explanation at all for why, on October 25, 1964, in a game at San Francisco's Kezar Stadium, Marshall scooped up a fumble by the 49ers' Bill Kilmer and raced with it sixty yards to the wrong end zone. Marshall simply said he lost his sense of direction, which is obvious enough. It didn't occur to him that he'd done something out-of-school until 49er center Bruce Bosley, the first man on the scene, congratulated him on a job well done.

To his credit, the Vikings defensive end possessed enough gentlemanly restraint to minimize the damage his blunder caused. Instead of spiking the ball in the end zone, where it would have remained live and possibly led to a 49er touchdown, he flipped it casually out of play, resulting in a safety. The Vikings hung on to win the game, 27–22. Other than attaching a boo-boo to an otherwise faultless career résumé (aside from those, ahem, four Super Bowl losses) and landing him a bundle on the dinner-speaker circuit, it was no harm, no foul for Jim Marshall.*

The Wrong-Way Bucket: Cavaliers versus Trail Blazers, 1970

The Cleveland Cavaliers and the Portland Trail Blazers, twin first-year expansion teams, were a combined 11–49 when they met at the dingy old Cleveland Arena on the night of December 9, 1970. As is often the case with matchups between more or less equally horrible teams, it was nip-and-tuck all the way. Early in the fourth quarter it was 84–81 Portland, with the teams in a jump-ball situa-

---

* The same can't be said for Roy Riegels, who secured infamy in the 1929 Rose Bowl. In the first half of a scoreless game, the University of California center recovered a Georgia Tech fumble, became dazed and confused, and sprinted sixty-five yards the wrong way with his teammates in hot pursuit. Tailback Benny Lom finally got to Riegels at the Cal one-yard line and turned him around, but he was immediately swarmed by Tech defenders. Cal elected to punt out of its end zone on first down (it wasn't uncommon in those days for teams to punt without running three downs). Georgia Tech blocked the punt out of the end zone for a safety, and Cal wound up losing 8–7.

tion. The Cavaliers controlled the tip, and the ball came out to Bobby Lewis, who fired an outlet pass to the first man he saw in Cleveland wine-and-gold: guard John Warren, who was streaking to the wrong basket. Warren's nifty drive and layup made it 86–81, Portland. The Blazers used the bucket to kick-start a run that put the game away, dropping the Cavaliers to a record of two wins and twenty-eight losses on the 1970–71 campaign.*

OWN-GOALS

When you get right down to it, when you break it down, where the rubber meets the road (pick your preferred cliché), can there be a bigger mistake in athletic competition than to score for your opponent? Certain *futbol* "fans" in Colombia didn't think so; witness the unfortunate case of Andres Escobar, who handed the United States a gift win in the '94 World Cup with an own-goal and was murdered ten days later. An added dollop of senseless tragedy to this senseless act: Escobar's own-goal came against a country that collectively didn't (and still doesn't) give a rat's patootie about *futbol*.

Steve Smith Polarizes Alberta

It was Game Seven of the 1986 Smythe Division Finals between the two-time defending Stanley Cup Champion Edmonton Oilers and the Calgary Flames, a rivalry as bitter as the winter weather in their shared province. Early in the third period, with the score tied 2–2 and overtime looming, Steve Smith retrieved the puck behind his own net and attempted to clear it. Staring intently at the puck, he didn't appreciate the fact that Oilers goaltender Grant Fuhr was directly in his line of fire. Smith's clearing pass hit the back of Fuhr's leg and, to the horror of more than seventeen thousand fans at Edmonton's Northlands Coliseum, ricocheted right back into the Oiler net. Calgary

---

* John Warren knocked down the gift shot despite the efforts of Portland's Leroy Ellis, who actually tried to play defense on the play.

took the lead 3–2 and hung on to win by the same score, depriving Gretzky, Messier, and Co. of a shot at a Stanley Cup hat trick.

The blunder happened to occur on Smith's twenty-third birthday. One would imagine that he drank rather heavily that night.

The self-induced short circuit in Edmonton's dynasty wasn't long in being repaired. The Oilers reeled off two more Stanley Cups in a row in 1987 and '88, giving them four in five years. Following the Cup-clinching win in 1987, the season after the gaffe, the conscientious Gretzky handed Smith the Cup to make the first lap around the ice. But fans in the continent's northernmost, one million–plus metropolis weren't quite so forgiving. Missing out on a record-tying five straight Cups stuck in their Canadian craws. The fact that Smith's contributions were critical to three Cup Championships didn't trump the fact that his contribution was essential to the one that got away. Own-goal-related taunts at home in Edmonton were Smith's lot in life until he left for Chicago in 1991.

Staf Stuffs His Own Net

Playing for the Belgian *futbol* squad Germinal Ekeren against Anderlecht in 1995, Staf Van den Buys pulled off the most dubious of all hat tricks, sending all three goals into his own side's net. Ekeren lost to its own player 3–2. Van den Buys's reverse hat trick stands up as the international *futbol* record for most own-goals in a single match. In some parts of the world, he wouldn't have lived long enough to score that third goal.*

IT AIN'T MY FAULT

There are times when athletes are more victims of the surrounding situation, of politics, and of someone else's incompetence than of their own mistakes.

---

* Even the world's only self-inflicted hat trick isn't as bizarre as what English footballer Chris Nicholl pulled off in 1976. Playing for Aston Villa against Leicester City, Nicholl proved himself the ultimate "man of the match," scoring all four goals for both sides in a 2–2 draw.

1972 Olympic Sprinters—You're Late!

Americans Eddie Hart and Rey Robinson, co-record holders in the 100-meter dash, were considered locks for medals in the '72 Olympics in Munich. It was joked that the only way the two weren't going to be holding gold and silver medals and humming the "Star-Spangled Banner" on the stand was if they were to not show up for the 100-meter race at all. And in the quarterfinal, that's exactly what happened. Told mistakenly that they were to race in the evening and not the afternoon, the pair showed up late for their heat and both were disqualified without setting foot on the track. Robinson's discovery of his own DQ was particularly gruesome: while waiting for a bus to the event, he looked up at an ABC TV monitor and watched as it started, his own name on the screen, with "N/A" next to it. Ouch.

Another athlete, sprinter Eddie Taylor (father of NFL defensive back Bobby Taylor), was also given the incorrect time for his heat, but managed to make it on time.

The culpability for the error lay in the murky buck-passing that existed within the bowels of USA Track & Field. The International Track & Field Committee had changed the start time forty-eight hours earlier, and nobody on Team USA bothered to tell the athletes this very important piece of new information. Whether it was the direct fault of sprint coach Stan Wright for not telling the pair the correct time, team coach Bill Bowerman for not telling Wright, or team manager George Wilson for not telling Bowerman didn't really matter. What mattered is that it cost two men a chance at an Olympic medal, through no fault of their own.

Well . . . maybe a little fault of their own. They were the fellows competing—they should have known the proper time, even if no one else did, and made sure of it. After all, it kind of was the Olympics.

Fred Merkle's "Bonehead" Baggage

There is a special hell reserved for those who are known for one stupid thing they did in their youth, and Fred Merkle lived in it. On September 23, 1908, at the Polo Grounds, with two outs in the ninth inning of a tie game between the Giants and the Cubs—who were competing ferociously for a pennant—the nineteen-year-old rookie for the New York Giants, who had just kept the inning alive with a vital hit, pulled up short of second base on a game-winning single by Al Bridwell. Normally this was accepted practice, but the rule stated that Merkle's force-out at second was still in effect, and, after a protracted search for the game ball, Cubs second baseman Johnny Evers was given either it or another one altogether and stepped on the bag. Umpire Hank O'Day ruled Merkle out, ending the inning with the score still even. By then fans had flooded the field, and the game was declared a tie.

New York appealed O'Day's decision, but National League president Harry Pulliam detested Giants manager John McGraw, a notorious bully and umpire-baiter. The rule had long been ignored in the breach, this was true, but Pulliam decided to enforce it just this once. He backed his umpire.

Naturally, the Giants and Cubs finished the season tied for first in the National League. So on October 8, 1908, in front of an over-flow crowd at the Polo Grounds, the two clubs met to decide the pennant. Chicago overcame an early deficit to defeat Christy Matthewson and the Giants 4–2. The Cubs went on to their last World Series victory to date.

That was about the only positive to come out of the Merkle affair. Pulliam shot himself to death the following summer, a consequence of stress, much of it induced by McGraw's loud, constant bitching about the league president's handling of the situation the previous fall. Fred Merkle, on the other hand, never did live down the blunder he committed at the age of nineteen. For the rest of his career and for the rest of his life, he was saddled with one of the least complimen-tary nicknames in the history of sports: "Bonehead."

In the last several years before his death in 1956, Merkle, by then an old man, refused to give interviews. He simply didn't want to talk about September 23, 1908, anymore. And who could blame him? Sure, his blunder was of Little Big Horn proportions, but we all do stupid things when we're nineteen. Most of us get a chance to live on and forget them. Merkle never did.

268 ★ THE WORST OF SPORTS

THE SCARLET LETTER

All it takes is one action, thought-out or thoughtless, undertaken in a split second, to undo a man's place in the eyes of his fellows—even if that place is thought to be all but secured.

Roberto Duran—"No Mas"

Roberto Duran was fearsome, intimidating, menacing—the Man with the Hands of Stone. It took many grueling years for Duran to build that reputation. And it took only two words to destroy it permanently.

It was the night of November 25, 1980, in New Orleans. Duran and Sugar Ray Leonard were battling for the WBC welterweight title. Five months earlier in Montreal, Duran had taken the belt from Leonard in a fifteen-round donnybrook, but the rematch in the Big Easy was taking a very different shape. Sugar Ray, at his absolute showboating best, was having his way with the slower Duran, repeatedly beating him to the punch and escaping the Panamanian's heavy counters. Duran wasn't really being physically hurt, but his pride was being plenty wounded by Sugar Ray's added arsenal of taunts, funny faces, and trick punches that looked straight out of *The Three Stooges*. Roberto Duran was a proud man, but not proud enough to withstand Leonard's antics. Near the end of the eighth round, he had had enough. He turned to the referee and, although he may not have used the exact phrase *"No mas,"* that's the way history chose to record it.

And that's the way history remembers Roberto Duran. The Man with the Hands of Stone has become That Guy Who Quit against Sugar Ray Leonard. Bummer, history is sometimes.

Worse is what transpired in the Lennox Lewis–Oliver McCall bout on February 7, 1997. Like Roberto Duran, McCall had already beaten his opponent; he knocked Lewis out in London in 1994 to win the BCS heavyweight belt. The rematch in Las Vegas was highly anticipated, and for the first couple of rounds or so it played out relatively evenly. But in the third, McCall, who had a history of drug and mental issues, just lost it. He began to drop his arms in the ring, refusing to defend himself against Lewis (who seemed more confused than anything by McCall's actions). By the fourth round McCall was openly weeping, much to the horror of his handlers, the packed house at the MGM, and the many thousands of pay-per-viewers who had dropped fifty bucks or so to watch the damned thing, not to mention the sunken costs of the beer and sheet pizzas. When McCall told his corner he wanted to continue, then came out for the fifth and still refused to defend himself, referee Mills Lane stopped the fight.

Chris Webber—"Time-out!"

Nineteen seconds remained in the 1993 NCAA Tournament Championship game. Dean Smith's North Carolina Tar Heels led Michigan 73–71, and UNC's Pat Sullivan was at the free-throw line, looking to extend the advantage. The hourglass was draining fast for Michigan's Fab Five in its quest for a title and, more important, a justification of its wild hype.

Sullivan's free throw rimmed out, and caromed to Michigan's Chris Webber. Never mind his standing as the leader of the so-called Fab Five, his reputation as an elite player on a national level, or his impending lottery pick-status—at that moment, no one on the floor, in the stands at the vast Louisiana Superdome, or among the millions watching CBS, wanted the basketball in his hands less than Mayce Edward Christopher Webber.

Faced with a choice of fight or flight, Webber called for a time-out. Michigan had no time-outs left, which would have meant a technical foul had any of the referees bothered to grant him his request. None did. He then moved his pivot foot and took a giant hop-step, a move that is illegal in any basketball rulebook but was strangely not called by the referees, despite the Carolina bench erupting into frantic gestures to suggest such a call.

Webber then dribbled more or less aimlessly to the right of the UNC basket, where he allowed himself to be trapped by two Tar Heel defenders. Out of options, with his team in total disarray and just wanting to be rid of the ball, Webber again touched hands in the "time-out" motion. Deciding he was out of mulligans, the referees awarded him the "TO," *and* with it a plain old "T"—a technical foul, which meant two free throws and the subsequent possession for North Carolina. The Tar Heels swished their free throws and pulled away to win, 77–71. Michigan had had a chance to tie the game in the final ten seconds, but never even got off a shot.

That epic brain-freeze in 1993 followed Webber throughout his NBA career, which has also been marred by frustration and failure. Seen as a franchise player, C-Webb has never played in an NBA Finals, and was a part of the Sacramento Kings team that pulled one of the all-time *el-foldos* in the 2002 West Finals against the Lakers. Winning cures all, but there hasn't been enough winning to erase the stain of the time-out from Chris Webber's résumé.

Leon Lett—The Dynamic Duo of Colossal Humiliation

This Emporia State football alumnus was a two-time Pro Bowler and three-time Super Bowl Champion. But he'll be forever remembered for two very distinctly memorable synapse failures, both occurring in the calendar year 1993.

Lett's first public display of moronitude took place on one of the world's biggest stages: Super Bowl Sunday. Late in the fourth quarter of his team's demolition of the Bills, Lett recovered a fumble and rushed down the field. As he went rumblin' and stumblin' toward the end zone, his premature exuberance got the best of him. Extending the ball out and down with one arm in celebration as he slowed to a jog, Lett allowed hustling Buffalo receiver Don Beebe to come up from behind and jar the ball loose, resulting in a touchback. Luckily for Lett but unfortunately for fans of the B-Lo, that was one of the few highlights for the Bills as the Cowboys won in a rout, 52–17.

Leon's second mental implosion came on Thanksgiving Day 1993. It was a frigid day in Dallas, once again prompting uncomfortable Texans to question why their stadium had a big hole in the roof. The sleet and snow made their way through the missing hatch in Texas Stadium and glazed the playing surface until it resembled an unwanted fruitcake. The Cowboys were ahead 14–13 with fifteen seconds remaining when Dolphins kicker Pete Stoyanovich lined up for a forty-one-yard field goal. The kick was blocked and squirted to the Cowboys one-yard line. Dallas players and fans alike rejoiced, as time was about to expire on another Turkey Day victory. But Leon Lett wasn't done playing. He dove on the previously about-to-be-declared-dead ball, but it escaped his clutches like a frightened butterball. The Dolphins recovered and Stoyanovich booted the nineteen-yard game winner through the uprights.

Lett and Dallas ultimately recovered, going 12–4 and winning their second consecutive Super Bowl.

Kermit Washington—The Mandible Rearranger

On December 9, 1977, yet another brawl had broken out on an NBA court, this one between the Los Angeles Lakers and the Houston Rockets. As he charged into the fray in an apparent attempt to untangle his teammates, Rudy Tomjanovich was formally introduced to Kermit Washington. It was an introduction Tomjanovich will always forget.

Washington slugged Tomjanovich in the mug so forcefully that his face literally separated from his jaw. As the Rockets' Tomjanovich lay unconscious on the floor, in a pool of his own blood, spinal fluid seeping, time seemed to stop at The Forum in Inglewood, California. And as he stood over Tomjanovich's limp and hemorrhaging frame, bewildered and fast becoming aware of what he'd just done, the Lakers' Washington still had no idea how drastically his life was going to change. His name would become synonymous with violence in sport.

Ironically, before his fist made putty of Tomjanovich's face, Washington was considered one of the kindest men in basketball, a blue-collar, lunch-pail forward who played a little more than nine seasons in the league, was named to the Western Conference All-Star team in 1980, and averaged a double-double for two seasons. Yet Kermit Washington will forever be remembered, almost exclusively, for nearly killing a fellow player during an NBA game. All it took was one punch.

The 1998 *Sports Illustrated* cover proclaiming sluggers Mark McGwire and Sammy Sosa Sportsmen of the Year. They looked, well, enhanced.
Walter Iooss Jr./Sports Illustrated

By Any Means Necessary

Everyone wants to win. But not everyone is fast enough, strong enough, or skilled enough to do so honestly. So cheating was invented to fill the void. Since they've been laying down chalk lines, inflating balls, putting up hoops, and keeping score, fast and loose has been a viable option for those devoid of moral fabric.

★ THE 1890s BALTIMORE ORIOLES
★ OLYMPIC FRAUDULENCE
★ CHEATING AS A WAY OF LIFE
★ THE 1998 HOME RUN CHASE

THE 1890s BALTIMORE ORIOLES

A Legacy Defined by Their "Artful Chicanery"

The lack of discipline on the ballfield, the sometimes-riotous crowds, and the hard, pissed-off set that played the game made the National League of the 1890s a wild, unchained place. Players rode horse-drawn trolley cars from the hotel to the ballpark, and along the way they were often verbally harassed and pelted with gamy objects. Once inside, the players harassed the umpires, spiked and fought with their opponents, and even squared off against fans. More than one game ended with brawling "cranks" (as fans were known then) and players alike getting clapped in irons and hauled off in paddy wagons by mustachioed law-enforcement types. And the teams, taking advantage of the laissez-faire conditions and the fact that games were officiated by only one umpire, did whatever it took to win, oftentimes crossing the very blurry line between fair and foul.

The symbols of this rough and rowdy period were the original Baltimore Orioles, National League Champions in 1894, '95, and '96. The Orioles' hell-for-leather style wasn't unique—everybody played that way. Baltimore just did it best.

The Orioles couldn't have picked a more fitting host city for their rowdy exploits. Baltimore was a dockworker's and longshore-man's town; a place of hard-fisted sensibilities; the home of street gangs with names like the Blood Tubs and the Pug Uglies. In fact, Charm City's *charmless* reputation long preceded the National League itself. En route to Washington for his first inaugural in 1861, Abraham Lincoln was compelled to sneak through Baltimore at five in the morning in a disguise to avoid the predations of gangs who *may* have favored the Confederacy but *definitely* despised "Black Republican" lawyers from Illinois. The first Union soldiers to die in the Civil War did so in the streets of Baltimore, the bloody result of a pitched battle between armed citizens and a Massachu-setts regiment that was simply passing through on the way to the capital. Baltimore was what you'd call a tough town.

But the Orioles weren't a tough team—not at the beginning of the so-called Gay '90s. A refugee from the defunct American Asso-ciation, Baltimore played like a team on the run in 1892. In their first year of National League play, they lost 101 games and finished dead last in a twelve-team league. Fortunes changed for the better, however, following the arrival late that season of a new manager, Ned Hanlon.

Temperamentally, Hanlon didn't seem like the type who'd as-semble what was perhaps the most ornery team in baseball history. A former center fielder, Hanlon was mild-mannered and somewhat colorless, directing his club benignly from the bench in street clothes (a relatively common practice in those days). He looked more like a lawyer than the manager of the brawling Orioles.

Appearances can be deceiving. As a player, Hanlon compen-sated for his marginal talent with speed, hustle, and smarts. He wanted his team to play in the same manner, and baiting the um-pires and bending the rules like taffy were considered good, heads-up baseball at the time. Hanlon had no problem utilizing such hooliganism for the sake of victories, even if he wasn't inclined to get his *own* hands dirty.

After buying a share of the Baltimore club to give him a free hand, Hanlon went out and got the players to play the type of game he wanted. He turned the O's around in a hurry: in 1894, just two years after losing 101 games, Baltimore won the National League pennant. The Orioles would go on to win three consecutive NL flags, dominating the league with a style the serene Hanlon airily described as "baseball as she is played." His prize pupil, a small, pugnacious Irish-American third baseman named John McGraw, had another, more honest term for it: "artful kicking." Whatever worked.

THE HIDDEN BALL TRICK

Left fielder Joe Kelley (a rakish sort who enjoyed carrying a mirror to his position so he could check himself out from time to time) would hide an extra ball in the outfield grass, which was left tall as a meadow's heather by the ballpark's groundskeepers. When a gap shot got by Kelley, he wouldn't bother to chase it down—he would simply produce the hidden ball and hurl it into the infield. This trick worked until the inevitable day when the game ball and the hidden ball were both fired back to the infield on the same play.

RUNNER'S INTERFERENCE

In the event of a sacrifice fly, third baseman McGraw would position himself behind the runner and slip a finger into his belt before he tagged up. The split second or two it took for the runner to break loose of McGraw's finger hook often enabled the Orioles to prevent the run from scoring. Legend has it that McGraw was finally foiled by Louisville power-hitter Pete Browning (the man after whom the original Louisville Slugger bat is named). Quietly unbuckling his belt while standing on third, Browning simply ran away from McGraw's grasp, leaving the feisty infielder with *two* handfuls of cowhide and nothing more.

Even if his own dirty tricks fell flat sometimes, McGraw still had plenty of help. Runners circling the sacks against the Orioles encountered a gauntlet of elbow jabs, hip checks, and tripping attempts as they made their way from base to base.

RUNNER'S INTERFERENCE (CONT'D.)

Catcher Wilbert Robinson's method of slowing down would-be run-scorers was to remove his equipment—shin guards, chest pad, mask—and chuck it at runners as they came down the third base line. As blatant as this tactic was, Robinson generally got away with it, as the lone umpire* was either distracted by some other happening or, even if he saw Robinson's tricks, felt more like going along to get along than enforcing the rules of the game.

The rotund, garrulous Robinson, a brilliant handler of pitchers, had other tricks, too, which included dropping pebbles and dirt into the shoes of batters to slow them down on the bases. He may be best known for catching a grapefruit dropped out of a biplane while managing the Dodgers in 1917. Robbie was anticipating a baseball, and when the piece of citrus exploded in his glove, the manager, mistaking the flying juice for his own blood, fell to the ground screaming that he had been killed.

BASERUNNING TRICKERY

Acting as if they were baffled first-year Little Leaguers, Baltimore base runners often took advantage of a distracted or out-of-position umpire, cutting directly across the infield from first to third or, even more boldly, from second to home, not even stopping at the mound to exchange pleasantries.

---

* The lone umpire of the nineteenth-century baseball game was a long way from the imperious Joe-West-and-Ken-Kaiser type that ruled the action in a later era. In fact, umpires weren't Gay at all in the '90s—they were men alone, harassed and vilified by fans, and on at least a few occasions physically assaulted by irate players. If they ignored the rules, they did so because they were looking out for their own hides. It's difficult to argue with that line of thinking.

GROUNDSKEEPING TRICKERY

Messing with the field of play to improve the home team's advantage is an honorable tradition in baseball,* but the Orioles were among the first clubs to turn the groundskeepers into full-fledged agents of victory. The small and fleet-footed Willie Keeler became one of the game's batting legends by striking the ball high off the ground in front of the plate and racing to first as fielders waited for it to come down. The grounds crew kept the area around home plate rock-hard, enabling Wee Willie to get more air under his famed "Baltimore Chop." The Orioles also had proficient bunters up and down the lineup, so the foul line chalk was raised and angled in a manner to keep their little taps from rolling foul.

To be sure, the 1890s Orioles were a lot more than just thugs and cheats. They had plenty of skill, too. Baltimore was almost revolutionary in its strategic use of the hit-and-run play and in the legal, lawful aspects of what is called "small ball" today or "inside baseball" back then—bunts, double steals, sacrifices. Three members of Hanlon's Orioles—John McGraw, Wilbert Robinson, and shortstop Hughey Jennings—later became Hall of Fame managers themselves, thanks in part to the tutelage of their old skipper. They were somewhat like the Oakland Raiders of the '70s—they played dirty and flouted the rules, but they were also good.

The O's were also an example to others. From the Comiskey Park concrete crew to the Candlestick Park infield being watered into a swamp whenever the Giants hosted Maury Wills and the Dodgers to Bill Veeck's rolling his portable outfield fence back when the Yankees came to town, Baltimore's Gay '90s groundskeeping spawned imitators and duplicators throughout the years. Their play inspired as well: Kent Hrbek's meaty, out-inducing hip check of skinny Ron Gant in the '91 World Series, for example, was Orioles-esque in its

---

* Decades later, Comiskey Park's grounds crew—in an assist to the light-hitting, speedy Go-Go Sox—followed Baltimore's example, then took it to a new level; not only did they angle the foul lines, they buried concrete a few inches in front of and below home plate, giving a bionic bounce to chop hits.

intent and execution. And every time a batter charges the mound and triggers a bench-clearing melee, Ned Hanlon smiles somewhere.

Eventually, the battling Orioles of yore aged and faded and broke up. The franchise itself was contracted out of existence by the National League in 1900. But while they could take the game out of Baltimore, they could never quite take the Baltimore out of the game.

OLYMPIC FRAUDULENCE

The Noble Games of Piety and Purity that Never Really Were

Citius, altius, fortius: *swifter, higher, stronger.*

When Pierre de Frédy, Baron de Coubertin helped found the modern Olympics in 1896, *les crapauds* appropriated this phrase and endorsed it as the Games' official motto. It conveys courage, determination, and the earnest pursuit of something worthy through the marriage of mind and body. But what it doesn't readily divulge is the less-inspiring history of Olympic cheatery, a scourge that traces its roots to the ancient Olympic Games about twenty-five hundred years ago.

In the Games of Olympia, cheating was punished severely, often with a good flogging and a hefty fine. These fines financed the construction of tributes to Zeus: bronze monuments depicting the ruler of Mount Olympus. At the base of each, the cheating athlete's name and birthplace and a description of the offense were inscribed. Like bounced checks hung prominently in a butcher shop, these statues lined the entryway into Olympic stadium, through which the athletes of subsequent Olympiads would pass prior to competition. The fallible athlete, his family, and the entire province from which he hailed were shamed for generations.

Over the centuries, acts of cheating have ranged from bribery to deception to the now-most-prevalent means: performance enhancement. The first recorded incident of cheating occurred in 388 BC, when the boxer Eupolus of Thessaly bribed three of his opponents to hit the dirt. Eupolus's fines alone are said to have paid for six statues of Zeus.

The skullduggery continued from wrestlers greasing themselves with oil prior to grappling—making their bare asses, we imagine, more difficult to get a hold of—to marathoners hitching rides while on some of the more remote portions of the course. One such moment involved the much-maligned Roman emperor Nero. The man reputed to have fiddled while Rome smoldered fancied himself an artist and a performer. So in AD 67, as a means to improve relations with the Greeks, Nero decided that he himself should compete in the Games. The fact that they weren't scheduled to be held that year was not a concern, and for a princely sum they were arranged out of sequence.

The primary dilemma with such a grand public relations scheme was that Nero wasn't athletically inclined—in other words, he stank like Rome before the "great sewer." Yet it's reported that he went on to win every event in which he participated—the modern equivalent of six gold medals. Nero was no Mark Spitz, so how did he manage to accomplish such a feat? He created *new* events, of course—poetry reading, for one. But Nero's greatest transgression occurred in the prestigious ten-horse chariot competition, during which he was thrown to the earth like a drunken bar patron from a mechanical bull. He did not finish the race yet was proclaimed the winner by terrified judges. Style points, perhaps?

Upon Nero's demise by his own hand just one year later—it's always a shame to see athletes robbed of their prime performing years—his "victories" were expunged from the official record.

SKATEGATE

Bribery has never gone out of style. As recently as the 2002 Winter Games, it was once again made clear that the straight and narrow is not always the path chosen by Olympic judges. Obviously, figure skaters cry about as readily as most humans blink, but in Salt Lake City, salty discharge from the ducts was excusable when the Canadian pair, Jamie Salé and David Pelletier, was robbed of a deserved gold medal, and Russians Yelena Berezhnaya and Anton Sikharulidze were showered with stuffed animals, flowers, and, of course, the gold medal in a controversial 5–4 decision. "Skategate" was born.

The melodrama that ensued was fit for daytime television. The French judge, Marie-Reine Le Gougne, broke down in her own fit of tears and confessed that she'd been pressured by the head of the French skating organization, Didier Gailhaguet, to vote for the Russian pair. Apparently, the scheme was the result of a preconceived vote swap meant to benefit a French ice-dancing pair scheduled to compete a few days later. Upon review, the International Olympic Committee later awarded a second gold medal to Salé and Pelletier ("Congrats, you tied!"). The case, which included an investigation and resulting charges filed against a reputed Russian mob boss, is still pending.

Prior to the Games, tradition maintains that Olympic judges and officials take an oath of their own while holding the Olympic flag. But in so many cases throughout history, it's evident that "impartiality" and the "true spirit of sportsmanship" were forgotten the instant the judges set it down.

ROB(BED) ROY

In the 1988 Seoul Games, American boxer Roy Jones Jr. faced South Korean opponent Park Si-Hun in the middleweight final. Jones Jr. was so superb, so dominant in the fight, that when announcers Marv Albert and the Fight Doctor Ferdie Pacheco compared him to Sugar Ray Leonard, Willie Pepp, and Muhammad Ali, it bore no markings of Costas-esque melodrama.

The nineteen-year-old Jones Jr. landed thud after thud upon Park's headgear. In the second round, the referee jumped in to give the Korean a standing eight count. Right jab, left hook—over and over Jones Jr. used this combination and his superior speed to abuse

Park at will. Roaring with each of Park's errant flails, the home crowd did its part to spur their fighter on, despite the odds—and to dissuade the judges from reality. When the final tone sounded, with the Korean fighter staggering, the three-round punch tally was lopsided to say the least: Jones—86, Park—32.

So when the judges, in a 3–2 decision, awarded the gold medal to the wobbly Korean, something was obviously "up." An IOC investigation would eventually conclude that overly patriotic South Korean officials had coerced the judges. Thank you, Holmes and Watson. This controversy led to a new scoring system for Olympic boxing. We're sure Jones is much happier with that righteous progression, as opposed to a gold medal.

Track and field, more than any Olympic sport, has seen its improprieties receive serious coverage. It started simply enough with intentional false starts in foot races being employed to gain an edge over one's opponent. In 1904, such an infraction resulted in a two-yard penalty. *(Note: Would Linford Christie have abided by such a ruling? Or would he have just stood in place, refusing to budge like the sculpted British sprinter stubbornly did in the 1996 Atlanta Games?)*

The first track and field participant to be disqualified for taking drugs was Polish discus thrower Danuta Rosani in 1976, but that was just the first chip in the Eastern bloc. The East Germans raised eyebrows in the '70s and '80s, not only with the gender-indeterminate nature of some of their "female" athletes, but also with the fact that their gold medal bounty doubled in a four-year span. It was later discovered that the East German Stasi, in an effort to show dominance over their Western counterparts, had implemented a systematic doping program until the fall of the Berlin Wall in 1989. It would be one of many scars to mark the face of Olympic history at the hands of the cold war.

But the *Worst of Sports* is not a slave to cold war propaganda: the United States and its free-market, free-will loving allies have also committed crimes against sporting morality.

BIG BEN

The most famous drug-related incident in Olympic history occurred during the Seoul Games of 1988. By the time Canadian resident Ben Johnson and American Carl Lewis dug into their blocks for the much-anticipated 100m final, Big Ben had established an edge over his rival since the 1984 Games, at which Lewis's four gold medals established him as a track and field icon. Akin to boxers engaging in prefight hype, the two exchanged jabs in the press. But it went deeper than sensationalism; there was sincere disdain between the two, the result of drug use allegations raised by Lewis. Johnson attributed them to sour grapes, but Lewis urged the public to focus on Johnson's curiously rapid progression in the event determining the world's fastest man.

A year prior, at the World Championships in Rome, Johnson beat Lewis for the 100m title, setting a new world record of 9.83 seconds. Lewis declared that Johnson would never beat him again.

The showdown in Seoul was over as soon as Johnson exploded from the blocks. When the two sprinters reached their respective top-end speeds, the gazellelike Lewis made up a bit of the difference on the fast-starting Johnson, but it wasn't nearly enough. It was a whitewashing. Johnson took the gold with one arm and one finger extended into the air, glaring back at the trailing Lewis. He had lowered his world record to 9.79 seconds.

The debate over who was the fastest man on the planet had been decided. But shortly thereafter, many more questions were asked and answered, and a new debate ensued. At the peak of his career, Johnson had taken an astonishing half second off his time in four years. How had he managed to do so? Well, three days following the race, Johnson's urine samples tested positive for the steroid stanozolol, and he forfeited his world record and gold medal to Lewis in the biggest performance-enhancement scandal in Olympic history. That's how.

Not that American athletes have always passed on the syringe. Aside from those *suspected* to be drug cheats—Carl Lewis* one of

---

* Carl Lewis was ultimately cleared of drug charges, although cover-up rumors continue to float about like Carl over the long-jump pit.

the more famous among them—many prominent competitors have been busted in violation of the Olympic oath's guiding principles, which were updated in 2000 to reflect the cheating of the times:

> *In the name of all the competitors I promise that we shall take part in these Olympic Games, respecting and abiding by the rules which govern them, committing ourselves to a sport <u>without doping and without drugs,</u> in the true spirit of sportsmanship, for the glory of sport and the honour of our teams.*

ALL IN THE FAMILY

Marion Jones, the three-time gold and two-time bronze medal winner in the 2000 Sydney Games, is a prime example. Her first husband, shot-putter C. J. Hunter, is a convicted steroid user. Her second husband and the father of her child, sprinter Tim Montgomery, is an admitted steroid user. Her former coach, Charlie Francis, was Ben Johnson's coach at the time he was busted in 1988. Another instructor, Trevor Graham, has spent a good majority of his time entangled in federal grand jury investigations. She was a client of Victor Conte's now-infamous BALCO organization. Be wary of the company you keep. In 2006, it was reported that Jones tested positive for EPO, a banned performance enhancer, but was then cleared. Her once-astounding career has since fizzled.

Continuing that "birds of a feather" line of thinking, Irish swimmer Michelle Smith exchanged vows with Erik de Bruin, a Dutch shot-putter who had served a four-year ban after testing positive for illegal levels of testosterone. Smith won three gold medals and a bronze at the 1996 Summer Games in Atlanta, while skeptics loudly cast doubt on the integrity of her performance. Her marriage to de Bruin, rapid improvement, and substantial muscle gain were more than enough evidence for a conviction in the court of public opinion.

Two years after the Atlanta Games, the International Swimming Federation banned Smith for four years. She never tested positive for a banned substance, nor was she ever stripped of her medals. Her ban took effect after a urine sample was found to be contaminated with alcohol at levels so toxic they would have killed her had that much alcohol actually been in her system. It was concluded that Smith was attempting to cover up traces of the performance-enhancing drugs she was taking.

DOPES

A favored method of cheating in the endurance athlete community has been blood doping. Developed in Sweden in 1972, the method includes withdrawing blood from the athlete, separating out the red blood cells, putting them in cold storage, and reinjecting the higher-concentrated RBCs months later. The result is an increased oxygen-carrying capacity, enabling the athlete to endure intense activity for longer periods of time and warding off the inevitable lactic acid drowning. In 1984, U.S. Olympic cycling coach Eddie Borysewicz set up an ad hoc blood-doping clinic—laboratory hanky-panky that was legal at the time—in a Los Angeles motel room to service a team that hadn't medaled in Olympic cycling since 1912. Coincidentally, the 1912 Games were in Stockholm. Not coincidentally, four of the seven U.S. cyclists who doped went on to win medals in Los Angeles. The practice of blood doping was banned by the International Olympic Committee less than two years after the Los Angeles Games of the XXIII Olympiad.

FAUX DOPES

Cheating in the Olympics need not involve cash, political heavy-handedness, or advanced scientific trickery. Sometimes all that's required is a little Broadway-inspired acting. In the 2000 Sydney Paralympics, controversy erupted over one of the Games' more subjective classifications of entrants: the intellectually disabled. The Spanish basketball team captured the gold, dominating on the court with a suspiciously high level of sophistication. After capturing the gold, it was later determined that ten of the twelve members of the team had no mental deficiency whatsoever—rather, they were just playing dumb. The team was forced to return its medals and the

International Paralympic Committee decided to dispose of the intellectually disabled category, declaring that eligibility was too difficult to determine.

JUST ONE OF THE GUYS

Misrepresentation is nothing new to the Olympic Games either. Stella Walsh was a Polish-American sprinter who represented the United States at the 1932 and 1936 Olympics, taking gold in the 100m during the '32 Games in L.A. and silver in '36 in Berlin. Over her entire career she set twenty world records and dominated the once-relevant Amateur Athletic Union in the sprints, long jump, and discus. She was a pioneer for her gender in the sport of track and field.

In 1982, Walsh was shot and killed outside a Cleveland shopping mall. A subsequent autopsy revealed that she had male genitalia and a rare combination of male and female chromosomes. Stella was never fond of showering with the other girls after practice; now we know why.

HOMETOWN LETDOWN

In 2004, the Olympics returned to Athens for the first time since the birth of the modern Games in 1896 (the Athens "Intercalated Games" in 1906 were a failure and are not recognized). The lighting of the torch during the opening ceremonies was a feverishly anticipated moment, one in which Greek sprinting hero and pop culture god Kostas Kenteris was widely expected to do the honors. So when Kenteris, the Sydney 200m champion, and his Greek training partner Ekaterini Thanou, the Sydney 100m silver medalist, were hospitalized following a motorcycle crash less than twenty-four hours before the Games would commence, the Greeks were a bit on edge.

The injuries were not serious, but it was revealed that Kenteris and Thanou had both skipped out on their drug testing, which automatically results in a failed test. Kenteris withdrew from the

200m. On the night the 200m was contested—sans Kenteris—large sections of the seventy-five-thousand-strong crowd postponed the start of the race for more than five minutes because the starter's pistol could not be heard over the raucous boos and jeers. It was a bedrock-low moment for Greek athletics and the Olympic Games as a whole.

But as long as the spoils await the victor, Olympic cheaters will hatch and attempt to slither their way to the medal stand. The noble and worthy global gathering that takes place every Olympiad should be embraced for its inherent good, but the cheaters will always try to win, and some of the winners will have cheated.

CHEATING AS A WAY OF LIFE

Southwest Conference Football, the 1980s

Only being #1 counts for anything . . . getting there is all that counts as long as you don't land in jail.

—SWC booster

The Southwest Conference was an odd duck among the big conferences. Eight of its nine members resided in the state of Texas, with the ninth being the University of Arkansas. It had the stature and glamour of a nationally respected league, but the regional feel of a Division III conference. It was big-time college football in every sense, but it was also Texas Football, writ large, right down to its big reward for the champion: the Cotton Bowl in Dallas.

Being Texas Football, the SWC employed eyebrow-raising methods of procuring talent. Everyone, from the lords of the league (UT, Texas A&M, and Arkansas) to its serfs (SMU, TCU, Texas Tech) wanted to win just as badly as everyone else. And the vast majority of the battle took place within the borders of a state known for its preponderance of Quonset hut high schools with fifteen-thousand-seat sunken-field stadiums—Texas, where they take their football rather seriously.

It was the 1980s, the golden autumn of the state's oil boom. *Dallas* was on the air and on the cover of *TV Guide*. It was an era of appetite and the ruthless pursuit of satiation, and not just at 10 p.m. on Friday night right after *The Dukes of Hazzard*. Rules were for suckers, not those on the make—and those on the make definitely included the Southwest Conference's football programs.

Six of the nine SWC members—Texas, Texas A&M, Texas Tech, TCU, Houston, and SMU—were hit with NCAA sanctions of varying levels of severity during the '80s. Only Arkansas, Baylor, and Rice, the scrawny nerd of the conference, escaped the Two-Ay's wrath. One school received the ultimate (and in Texas, apropos) punishment: the "death penalty" to its football program. The notable offenders were the conference's longtime also-rans, especially the smaller private religious schools that didn't have the facilities or the official budget of the big boys, but did have heavy-hitting "friends of the program" with a keen interest in success and a disdain for the rules.

TEXAS CHRISTIAN UNIVERSITY

The league's perennial weak sister, TCU hadn't had a winning season since 1971, but in '84 the Horned Frogs got it together under second-year coach Jim Wacker, starting out 8–1 and making a run at the SWC title before fading and settling for a trip to the Bluebonnet Bowl in Houston. Just like almost everyone else's, Texas Christian's success was store-bought.

On May 10, 1986, the NCAA laid down the law on TCU for a variety of infractions that included cash handouts by boosters to as many as seven players (many of which took place at a near-campus pizza parlor), among them the focal point of the palm-greasing campaign, star running back Kenneth Davis (Thurman Thomas's future backup in Buffalo). The Frogs were banned from a bowl appearance in '86, ordered to hand over the program's TV revenues from 1983 and '84, and stripped of thirty-five scholarships over the next two years. By then, TCU had slipped back down into the conference's basement anyway.

THE UNIVERSITY OF HOUSTON

In terms of sheer volume, Houston's malfeasance might be the most widespread of all the unsavory SWC members. In 1988, some 250 violations of one level of severity or another, including direct cash payments to players, were uncovered within the football program, leading to five years of probation and a two-year ban on postseason play and national television appearances. The Cougars stormed to a 19–3 record in that two-year period and boasted the 1989 Heisman Trophy winner in Andre Ware, but were unable to showcase the program nationwide thanks to their rampant cheating and the punishment they sustained for it. Of course, the cheating was the primary reason Houston had a program worth showcasing in the first place.

The chicanery at Houston went beyond simple payouts, and it went on during probation. Head coach John Jenkins, who took over the job in 1990, conducted practices that exceeded the twenty-hour-per-week limit mandated by the NCAA, and held mandatory summer practices, also in violation of the rules. (Jenkins would also roam the practice field in the passenger seat of a car with tinted windows, armed with a pair of binoculars so he could watch his players.) Jenkins even ordered his assistants to doctor newspapers, cutting out statistics that were nonbeneficial to the program before photocopying the edited results and sending them to recruits.

THE UNIVERSITY OF TEXAS

Even mighty UT, which should have been above such slimy doings, got nailed. On June 17, 1987, the NCAA put the probation whammy on the Longhorns for as many as sixty-three violations, among them the ubiquitous handouts from boosters. Unlike its fellow conference offenders, Texas's monkeyshines took place at a time when the Longhorns were playing their worst football in years. In 1986, playing with compensated talent, UT had its first losing season since the '50s. Obviously, the burnt-orange boosters weren't getting enough bang for their buck.

The Longhorns didn't exactly provide the stoutest flagship in those days. They spent much of the period in the middle ranks of the SWC, and maybe they should have stayed there—in their one Cotton Bowl appearance of the period, 1991, they were embarrassed 46–3 by a Miami team that outright intimidated them and sent their partisan crowd scurrying for the exits long before it was over. The enfeebled SWC lost the last seven games of the Cotton Bowl's tenure as the league's championship bowl by an average score of 30–10.

TEXAS A&M UNIVERSITY

The second-most-penalized athletic department in NCAA history is Texas A&M, and a big part of that doleful accomplishment was the football team's head coach in the 1980s, the oily Jackie Sherrill. The coach had a slick reputation going back to his days at Pitt (Joe Paterno, when asked why he didn't pursue NFL openings, said he "didn't want to leave college football to the Switzers and the Sherrills of the world"), and he continued to earn it at College Station as his Aggies played at a suspiciously high level, going 29–7 and reaching three straight Cotton Bowls in '86, '87, and '88. It was suspicious since, prior to the '80s trifecta, A&M had not once been to a Cotton Bowl since 1968.

Sure enough, the Aggies hadn't been on the level. Early in the 1988 season, the NCAA meted out a penalty of two years' probation and a ban on postseason play for a typical laundry list: phony summer jobs, suspiciously obtained goods and services, and good old-fashioned hundred-dollar handshakes.

Sherrill left College Station after that season. He soon landed at Mississippi State, where he brought success and, as usual, trouble in the form of NCAA investigators. Even after his departure, the shadiness quotient in College Station was plenty high—in 1994, the football program was again hit with probation. The Aggies went undefeated that year but were prohibited from playing in a bowl— the second time that has happened in the program's history.

SOUTHERN METHODIST UNIVERSITY (RIP)

From 1980 through the end of the '84 season, the Southern Methodist University Mustangs, famed for their "Pony Express Backfield" of Craig James and Eric Dickerson, went 49–9–1, won two SWC titles, and on January 1, 1983, won a 7–3 snoozer over Dan Marino and Pitt to take their first Cotton Bowl championship since 1949.

There was no need to wonder how on earth the small private school and a longtime conference doormat became one of the top teams in the land almost overnight. It was an open record in the form of the longest list of violations in the history of NCAA football. The Pony program was placed on probation four times in eleven years in the '70s and '80s.* SMU won the Southwest Conference in 1981, but couldn't play in the Cotton Bowl because they were banned from postseason play. In '82, the Ponies went undefeated (playing every game in the state of Texas), but finished second in the polls to one-loss Penn State because everyone felt better about giving a national title to JoePa and his squeaky-clean Nittany Lions than to a bunch of known cheaters.

SMU was on probation again in 1986 when yet more violations were uncovered. Twenty-one football players had received or were receiving heavy-duty cash payments totaling some $61,000, and were living rent-free in apartments provided by already-proscribed boosters, and all while the program was already in dutch with the NCAA. The program's backsliding had opened the door to its dissolution.

With the haste of a condemned man who suddenly realizes he's out of appeals, SMU assiduously cooperated with the investigators and even brought forth its own recommendation of "severe sanctions." But the Two-Ay had had enough of the cock and bull coming out of University Park. On February 25, 1987, the NCAA

---

* SMU's coach for much of this period was the fast-talking Ron Meyer. He's best known for ordering, while coaching the Patriots in 1982, a work-release inmate to drive a snow-sweeper onto the field to clear a spot for a game-winning field goal against the Dolphins. It was a little Texas-style tomfoolery in the snowy fastness of New England.

handed the death penalty to the SMU football program. All squad members were released from their scholarships. The '87 season was canceled. SMU would be allowed to play a shrunken, seven-game road schedule in 1988 before being restored to a full eleven-game slate in '89. Southern Methodist would also be limited to giving out fifteen scholarships in 1988 (not nearly enough to field a competitive team) and had its coaching staff slashed to half of the NCAA maximum.

As if all of this wasn't enough, the NCAA, much like a seasoned button man putting a coup de grace bullet in the head of a mortally wounded target, prohibited SMU from appearing on national TV or in a bowl game during the 1988 season.

The university couldn't field a team and didn't play the shriveled '88 schedule. When the Ponies reemerged in 1989, with seventy-four freshmen on the roster, they were wobbly-kneed, spavined shadows of their former selves; they were the closest Division I college football has ever seen to a pro-style expansion team. The program has galloped to just one winning season since coming back from the death penalty. The sanction quite possibly killed SMU football and, mindful of its shattering effects, the NCAA has skittered away from invoking it ever since.

Said John Lombardi, a former University of Florida president and member of the committee that handed down the sentence: "SMU taught the committee that the death penalty is too much like the nuclear bomb. It's like what happened after we dropped the (atom) bomb in World War II. The results were so catastrophic that now we'll do anything to avoid dropping another one." Some schools (Alabama) have a lot to thank SMU for.

Not coincidentally, the 1980s were the last full decade of Southwest Conference athletic competition. The millions in lost TV and bowl revenues and the attendant loss of national TV exposure, the teams weakened by scholarship forfeitures, and the growing power of college sports condemned the conference. When Arkansas decamped for the SEC in 1992, the doomsday clock began to tick toward midnight. Four years later, the SWC put itself out of its own misery and broke up entirely. Texas, Texas A&M, Texas Tech, and Baylor joined the Big Eight, which became the Big Twelve. TCU, SMU, and Rice went to the Western Athletic Conference. Houston found refuge in Conference USA. The Cotton Bowl has remained a New Year's Day affair, but was knocked down to the status of a second-tier bowl. No longer would national championships be decided in the old dump at the Texas State Fairgrounds.

The non–Big Twelve and SEC refugees seem to have been knocked out of big-time college football for all eternity. There was a time when Houston and SMU were national championship contenders and played on national TV in big-time games (when they weren't on probation); today they're middle-of-the-road scufflers in the backwater leagues of the sport. Rice is still Rice.

Only TCU has benefited—given a chance to punch its weight for once, the Frogs have prospered and have become a small-scale power in the WAC and Mountain West Conference. But even they've lost a little bit. In the star-crossed 1984 season, the battle cry in Frog-dom was *"TCU to the Cotton Bowl!"* And although they never made it to Dallas, and they're much better on the whole these days, *"TCU to the Vegas Bowl!"* just doesn't have the same ring to it.

THE 1998 HOME RUN CHASE

Baseball's Summer of Love, Which Eventually Was Rechristened Its Winter of Discontent

The 1998 home run chase was like a Major League Baseball New Year's Eve rager: party favors were a-plenty, and everyone involved was drinking more than their fair share of the punch. Like Babe Ruth after the Black Sox scandal, Mark McGwire, Sammy Sosa, and, for a while, Ken Griffey Jr. were finalizing baseball's resurgence from the strike-induced doldrums of 1994 and reconstructing the bridge of trust between America's pastime and the consuming public. The game was down, but not out. And the torrid pace of moon shots was bringing it back from the dead. Not even Cal Ripken's consecutive-games-played streak and its accompanying extravaganza in '95 had done for the game what the '98 home run chase did. As the drama unfolded throughout the season, as Big Mac and Slammin' Sammy separated themselves from the pack and spent each at-bat trying to one-up the other, the nation was held spellbound with the sluggers' singular pursuit: to eclipse Roger Maris's thirty-seven-year-old home run record.

But whenever excessive consumption is involved, a hangover is sure to follow. And in the case of the 1998 home run chase—and, really, Major League Baseball as a whole—it's been one of those cheap-beer hangovers, the type that you just can't lick. The first in-dication that everyone was having way too much fun was the reve-lation that Mark McGwire was popping androstenedione, which is a growth hormone considered a legal performance enhancer at the time. Associated Press contributor Steve Wilstein broke the story after observing the bottled hormone lurking in McGwire's locker. The sportswriter was crucified for it. McGwire called Wilstein a snoop; Tony LaRussa, the Cardinals manager, attempted to have him barred from the team locker room; and the media went about ring-fencing and excommunicating one of their own.

At the time it was all going down, the great home run chase was universally praised and glorified. It was a win-win-win-win-win sit-uation for the players, the owners, the media, the fans, and the game itself. McGwire and Sosa were hitting balls into the strato-sphere, all the while saying and doing the right things as part of a public relations campaign that even the savviest politician would envy. And the public was lapping it all up like thirsty Labradors after a vigorous summer jaunt. "They're saving baseball!" one and all proclaimed. Because the game is a cherished piece of Americana and a national treasure that has endured our nation's most difficult struggles for more than one hundred years, no questions were en-tertained. It was peer pressure on the grandest of sporting scales.

But baseball, more so than any sport, is about the numbers. The game's statistics are recorded, manipulated, and analyzed with glee by everyone from the casual fan to the die-hard sabermetrician. Anyone who took a brief glance at the measurables or who knew an iota about the history of the game could have and should have seen the Great Home Run Chase of '98 for the ginormous anomaly that it was.

Prior to 1998, Sammy Sosa averaged one home run per every 19.9 at-bats over nine seasons in the big leagues. In '98, Slammin' Sammy more than doubled his round-tripper output, hitting one home run per every 9.7 at-bats. As sure as any man grows sleepy after a good roll in the hay, something was amiss. Say it ain't So . . . sa. Someone should have, but no one wanted to spoil the do-ings on the North Side, where the happy Dominican was kissing his fingers, leaping out of the box on moon shots, sprinting to his out-field position, leading the Cubs to a wild-card berth, and forcing the sun-splashed and boozy Wrigley denizens to drop their hacky-sacks and—for once—pay attention to the action.

Throughout his eleven-year career prior to the 1998 season, Mark McGwire was a much more prolific home run hitter than Sosa, averaging one blast per every 11.9 at-bats—second in history at the time only to Babe Ruth in that category. Big Mac's numbers were already incredible, but in 1998 he went yard once every 7.27 at-bats. What made McGwire's gigantic leap in productivity even more jarring was that he was thirty-four years old, an age when his career should have been on a sharp downward trajectory. Athletes aren't wine; they aren't supposed to get better with age, but Mc-Gwire did.

Roger Maris's record had stood for thirty-seven years—longer than Ruth's had. Going into the '98 season, he was the only man in Major League history to top the sixty–home run mark. Then, in one year, two men not only beat Maris's record, they obliterated it. One man setting a new record would have been one thing. But anyone, from the MIT professor in the lab to the sports buff on the couch, could have driven a Mack truck through this yawning regression from the mean.

Rationalization is the favored response to an unspeakable but undeniable truth. In the case of the 1998 baseball season, the dilu-tion of pitching talent, smaller ballparks, more sophisticated work-out regimens, and baseball's answer to the magic bullet—the "juiced" ball—were alternately offered up to the gods of reason as an explanation for the surge in home run tallies. It was the second stage of the Kübler-Ross grief cycle: blind denial. The third stage is anger, but it took a while to get there—nearly three years, in fact, after McGwire picked up his son, exchanged mock body blows with Sosa, and hugged members of the Maris family upon eclipsing the record.

Reportedly, steroid use has been prevalent in baseball to varying degrees since the '80s, some even say the '70s (when they began ap-pearing on NFL training tables). There were numerous neon signs posted prior to 1998 that indicated as much: Lenny Dykstra bulking up to secure one hell of a four-year deal from the Phillies in what should've been his twilight years; the roller-blading Brady Anderson, who averaged only nine home runs per year over his first eight seasons in the Bigs prior to miraculously slugging *fifty* for the Orioles in 1996. Still, the public looked away, until three men blew the powder keg to high heaven: Barry Bonds, Ken Caminiti, and Jose Canseco.

When the abrasive Barry Bonds* began his own assault on McGwire's home run record in 2001, eyebrows began to rise. His hulking physique and expanding cranium were hard to miss, and his record-breaking seventy-three home runs that year (one per every 6.5 at-bats!), just a short three seasons after McGwire's, was a bit too much, especially for a thirty-seven-year-old. The nation, post-9/11, was in a reflective state and was attempting to locate purpose and justification for our brief time on earth. The novelty value had worn off. The home run chase was *so* '90s! At least some of the journalists who had danced happily to the tune of McGwire and Sosa's cracking bats were more than eager to ask tough questions of the ornery man who had held a long and open contempt for their profession and the outside world in general.

In May 2002 the now-famous *Sports Illustrated* cover story, "Steroids in Baseball: Confessions of an MVP," hit newsstands. In it, Ken Caminiti admitted using steroids during his award-winning 1996 season and estimated that at least half the league was also using. Caminiti was a sympathetic figure, a seeming tower of strength, admired by his teammates and friends, but haunted by the substance problems that would eventually kill him. With his story, nerds who hoped to protect the integrity of baseball's records were joined by those who wanted something done for the health of the game and its players—as well, of course, as the children.

Tragedy became farce with the appearance on the scene of Jose Canseco, who stopped being a serious figure about the time he let a

---

* Despite perpetual protestations from his ever-growing cranium that he's never taken steroids, Bonds has been convicted in the courts of both logic and reason.

ball go off his head for a home run. In a book released in 2005, Canseco, who won the 1988 AL MVP award and became the game's first 40–40 man while sporting a physique more suited to a bouncer than a ballplayer, admitted to using steroids during his seventeen-year career. He fingered his former Bash Brother Mark McGwire and Ranger teammate Rafael Palmeiro as fellow culprits, and estimated that approximately 85 percent of all Major Leaguers took performance enhancers. Whether or not his estimate was intentionally inflammatory, it confirmed what many already suspected: Canseco was a cheat, and he was not lonely in that regard.

The rest of the low opera—the congressional hearings, Slammin' Sammy's sudden inability to speak English, McGwire's squirming through the testimony, the tawdry unraveling of Palmeiro's once-sterling reputation, and Major League Baseball's first halting acknowledgment of the issue—would follow. Not only were the legacies of McGwire, Sosa, and Palmeiro tarnished, so were those of their colleagues in the long-bombing days of the 1990s. Discussions of who was the greatest this or that will always be derailed by the question: "Was he using?"

The 1998 home run chase spectacle and the ensuing steroid hysteria were the height of hypocrisy. But who were the hypocrites? That's easy: most everyone. *Sports Illustrated* named McGwire and Sosa their Sportsmen of the Year; TV ratings and attendance spiked; Sosa was even present at the 1999 State of the Union address. Sure, McGwire and Sosa were guilty, but the owners, the media, and the league also turned their other cheeks. From those who profited from the chase to those who covered it in blissful ignorance to those who put too weighty a premium on individual records in a team sport to the players themselves—it was a party. Like most parties, it was a group effort. Unlike most parties, *everyone's* stuck with the cleanup.

Part NINE

WRONG NUMBERS

The Worst of Statistics of the Games

Biggest Blown Fourth-Quarter Lead, Pro: November 8, 1987, 25 points, Tampa Bay vs. St. Louis (Buccaneers led 28–3; lost 31–28)

Biggest Blown Lead, College: 35 points (tie)—November 2, 1991, Weber State vs. Nevada (Weber State led 49–14; lost 55–49); October 21, 2006, Northwestern vs. Michigan State (Northwestern led 38–3; lost 41–38)

Biggest Blown Lead, Pro: January 4, 1993, 32 points, Houston vs. Buffalo (Oilers led 35–3; lost 41–38)

Fewest Passing Yards in a Game, Pro: September 10, 1967, –53 yards, Denver Broncos vs. Oakland Raiders (Denver lost, 51–0)

Fewest Passing Yards in a Game, College: September 25, 1948, –19 yards, Heidelberg vs. Ashland

Fewest Rushing Yards in a Game, Pro: October 17, 1943, –53 yards, Detroit vs. Chicago Cardinals (Detroit won, 7–0)

Fewest Rushing Yards in a Game, College: October 7, 1989, –112 yards, Wesleyan vs. Coast Guard

Fewest Total Yards in a Game, College: October 16, 1993, –69 yards, Miles vs. Fort Valley State

Fewest Total Yards in a Game, Pro: November 5, 1979, –7, Seattle vs. Los Angeles Rams (Seattle lost, 24–0)

Longest Home Losing Streak, Pro: 14, Dallas Cowboys, 1988–89

Longest Road Losing Streak, Pro: 24, Detroit Lions, 2001–03

Most Consecutive Postseason Losses: 6, Cleveland Browns, 1969, 1971–72, 1980, 1982, 1985

Most Consecutive Seasons Without a Playoff Appearance, Pro: 39 seasons, Pittsburgh Steelers, 1933–71.

Most Fumbles, Career: 161, Warren Moon

Most Fumbles, Game: November 15, 1964, 7, Len Dawson, Kansas City vs. San Diego (Kansas City lost, 28–14)

Most Fumbles, Season: 23 (tie)—Kerry Collins, New York Giants, 2001; Daunte Culpepper, Minnesota, 2002

Most Interceptions Thrown, Career, College: 117, Steve Hendry, Wisconsin-Superior, 1980–83

Most Interceptions Thrown, Career, Pro: 277, George Blanda, 1949–75*

Most Interceptions Thrown, Game, College: 9 (tie)—October 16, 1965, Henry Schafer, Johns Hopkins vs. Haverford; November 1, 1969, John Reaves, Florida vs. Auburn (Florida lost, 38–12); September 24, 1983, Pat Brennan, Franklin vs. Saginaw Valley

Most Interceptions Thrown, Game, Pro: September 24, 1950, 8, Jim Hardy, Chicago Cardinals vs. Philadelphia (Chicago lost, 45–7)

Most Interceptions Thrown, Season, College: 43, Steve Hendry, Wisconsin-Superior, 1982

Most Interceptions Thrown, Season, Pro: 42, George Blanda, Houston, 1962**

Most Losses for a College Program: 605, Northwestern University (1889–2006)***

Most Losses, Season, College: 13, Army, 2003 (0–13)

Most Penalties in a Game, Pro: 22 (tie)—September 17, 1944, Brooklyn Dodgers vs. Green Bay (Brooklyn lost, 14–7); November 26, 1944,

---

* Blanda led the Oilers to the '62 AFL Championship Game, where he threw five more interceptions in a double-overtime loss to the Dallas Texans.

** Brett Favre has 273 as of the end of the 2006 season.

***The "Mild-Cats" also hold the Division I-A record for consecutive losses with 34 from 1978 to 1981.

Chicago Bears vs. Philadelphia (Chicago won, 28–7); October 4, 1998, San Francisco vs. Buffalo (Buffalo won, 26–21)

Most Penalties in a Game, College: October 11, 1958, 28, Northern Arizona vs. University of LaVerne (California)

Most Penalties in a Season, College: 152, Alabama State, 2001 (12.6 per game)

Most Penalties in a Season, Pro: 158, Kansas City, 1998 (9.9 per game)

Most Points Given Up Per Game, College: 59.1, Macalester College, 1977

Most Points Given Up Per Game, Pro: 38.5, Baltimore Colts, 1950

Most Postseason Losses: 21, New York Giants, 1933–2005 (16–21).

Most Punts Blocked, Career: 14 (tie)—Herman Weaver, 1970–80; Harry Newsome, 1985–93

Most Punts Blocked, Season: 6, Harry Newsome, Pittsburgh, 1988

Most Times Sacked, Career: 516, John Elway, 1983–98

Most Times Sacked, Game: 12 (tie)—October 26, 1980, Bert Jones, Baltimore Colts vs. St. Louis Cardinals (Baltimore lost, 17–10); September 29, 1985, Warren Moon, Houston vs. Dallas (Houston lost, 17–10)

Most Turnovers in a Game, College: 13 (tie)—December 1, 1951, Georgia vs. Georgia Tech (Georgia lost, 48–6); October 1, 1977, Albany vs. Rochester Institute; October 12, 1985, St. Olaf vs. St. Thomas

Most Turnovers in a Game, Pro: 12 (tie)—November 22, 1942, Detroit vs. Chicago Bears (Detroit lost, 42–0); September 24, 1950, Chicago Cardinals vs. Philadelphia (Chicago lost, 45–7); December 12, 1965, Pittsburgh vs. Philadelphia (Pittsburgh lost, 47–13)

Most Turnovers in a Season, College: 61 (tie)—North Texas State, 1971; Tulsa, 1977

Most Turnovers in a Season, Pro: 63, San Francisco 49ers, 1978

Most Yards Penalized in a Game, College: November 4, 1978, 260, Southern vs. Howard

Most Yards Penalized in a Game, Pro: October 10, 1999, 212, Tennessee vs. Baltimore (Tennessee won, 14–11)

Shortest Field-Goal Miss, Super Bowl: 19 yards, Mike Cofer, San Francisco, Super Bowl XXIII

Worst Field-Goal Kicking Season, Pro: 1-of-15, Bob Timberlake, New York Giants, 1965

Worst Margin of Defeat, College: October 7, 1916, 222 points—Georgia Tech 222, Cumberland 0*

Worst Margin of Defeat, College (Modern Era): November 23, 1968, 94 points—Houston 100, Tulsa 6**

Worst Margin of Defeat, College Bowl Game: 55 points—Alabama 61, Syracuse 6, 1953 Orange Bowl

Worst Margin of Defeat, NCAA Division I-A/II/III Championship: 63 points—Dayton 63, Ithaca 0, 1979 Division III

Worst Margin of Defeat, Pro: December 8, 1940, 73 points—Chicago 73, Washington 0

Worst Margin of Defeat, Super Bowl: 45 points—San Francisco 55, Denver 10, Super Bowl XXIV

---

* Cumberland had actually discontinued its program prior to the 1916 season, but Tech coach John Heisman insisted on holding the game, and ran up the score on a scratch squad of students that made up Cumberland's team. Heisman, who was also Tech's baseball coach, wanted revenge on Cumberland for employing professional players in a 22–0 rout of Heisman's baseball team that spring. He got it.

** Houston scored 49 points in the fourth quarter and 76 in the second half. The Cougars' last touchdown was scored by reserve wide receiver and future country music star Larry Gatlin.

BASKETBALL

Biggest Blown Second-Half Lead, College: 31 (tie)—December 30, 1950, Tulane vs. Duke (Tulane led 58–27; lost 74–72); February 15, 1994, Louisiana State vs. Kentucky (LSU led 68–37; lost 99–95)

Biggest Margin of Defeat, College: December 2, 2006, 123 points—Lincoln (Pa.) 201, Ohio State–Marion 78

Biggest Margin of Defeat in Division II/III Championship Game: 25 points—Virginia Union 100, Bridgeport 75, 1992

Biggest Margin of Defeat in an NCAA Championship Game: 30 points—UNLV 103, Duke 73, 1990

Biggest Margin of Defeat in an NCAA Tournament Game: 69 points—Loyola of Chicago 111, Tennessee Tech 42, 1963*

Biggest Margin of Defeat, Pro: December 17, 1991, 68 points—Cleveland 148, Miami 80

Consecutive Home Losses, College: 32, New Hampshire, 1988–91

Consecutive Losses, College: 117, Rutgers–Camden, 1992–97

Consecutive Road Losses, College: 64, Texas–Pan American, 1995–2000

Consecutive Road Losses, Pro: 43, Sacramento Kings, 1991–92

Fewest Points Scored in a Game, College: 4 (tie)—December 12, 1938,

---

* Loyola coach George Ireland had three black starters and liked to run up the score on segregated opponents, such as Tennessee Tech.

Adrian vs. Albion (lost 76–4); February 16, 1971, Oglethorpe vs. Tennessee State (lost 7–4)

Fewest Points Scored in a Game, College, Since the Shot Clock: 21 (tie)— January 2, 1997, Georgia Southern vs. Coastal Carolina (lost 61–21); December 14, 2005, Monmouth vs. Princeton (lost 41–21)

Fewest Points Scored in a Game, Pro: April 10, 1999, 49, Chicago vs. Miami (lost 82–49)

Lowest Team Field Goal Percentage in a Game, Pro: November 6, 1954, 22.9%, Milwaukee Hawks vs. Minneapolis Lakers

Most Consecutive First-Game Losses as #1 Seed, NCAA Tournament: 3, DePaul 1980–82

Most Consecutive Minutes Played Without an Assist, NBA: 770, Yinke Dare, New Jersey Nets, 1994–97

Most Fouls Committed, Career: 4,657, Kareem Abdul-Jabbar, 1969–89

Most Fouls Committed, Season: 386, Darryl Dawkins, New Jersey Nets, 1983–84

Most Losses, Season, College: 30, Grambling, 1999–2000 (1–30)

Most Losses, Season, Pro: 73, Philadelphia 76ers, 1972–73 (9–73)

Most Team Fouls in a Game, College: November 15, 1997, 51, Northern State (South Dakota) vs. Southern Indiana

Most Turnovers Committed, Career: 4,211, Karl Malone, 1986–2004

Most Turnovers Committed, Game: 14 (tie)—March 1, 1978, John Drew, Atlanta Hawks vs. New Jersey Nets; November 17, 2000, Jason Kidd, Phoenix Suns vs. New York Knicks

Most Turnovers Committed, Season: 366, Artis Gilmore, Chicago Bulls, 1977–78

Only School to Lose Consecutive NCAA Championship Games to the Same Opponent: Ohio State, 1961–62 (Cincinnati)

Primary Defender on Wilt Chamberlain the Night He Scored 100 Points: Darrall Imhoff, New York Knicks*

Quickest to Foul Out, College: January 24, 2004, 1:11, Ben Wardrop, San Diego State vs. Colorado State

Worst Free Throw–Shooting Night, Player, Pro: December 8, 2000, 0-for-11, Shaquille O'Neal, Los Angeles Lakers

Worst Three-Point Shooting Night, Team, College: January 21, 1995, 0-for-22, Canisius vs. St. Bonaventure

* Imhoff played twenty minutes and scored seven points before fouling out.

Consecutive Postseason Losses, Team: 13, Boston Red Sox 1986, 1988, 1990, 1995

Fewest Base Hits in a Full Season, AL: 82, Ed Brinkman, Shortstop, Washington Senators, 1965 (444 at-bats)

Fewest RBI in a Full Season, Player: 12, Enzo Hernandez, Shortstop, San Diego Padres, 1971 (549 at-bats)

Fewest Total Bases in a Full Season, AL: 114, Ed Brinkman, Washington Senators, 1965 (444 at-bats)*

Longest Hitless Streak, Season: 70 at-bats, Bob Buhl, Pitcher, Chicago Cubs, 1962

Longest Postseason Hitless Streak: 42 at-bats, Dan Wilson, Catcher, Seattle Mariners, 1995–2000

Lowest Batting Average in a Full Season, AL: .182, Monte Cross, Shortstop, Philadelphia A's, 1904

Lowest Batting Average in a Full Season, NL: .201, Dal Maxvill, Shortstop, St. Louis Cardinals, 1970

Lowest Batting Average While Hitting 25 or More Home Runs in a Season: .179, Rob Deer, Detroit Tigers, 1991

---

* Brinkman, a superb fielder, also hit .185 in 1965. He had a tough year at the plate all around.

Lowest Career Batting Average, 3,000+ at-bats: .170, William Aloysius "Bill" Bergen, Catcher, Cincinnati Reds and Brooklyn Dodgers, 1901–11

Most Balks, Game: May 4, 1963, 5, Bob Shaw, Milwaukee Braves

Most Balks, Season: 16, Dave Stewart, Oakland Athletics, 1988

Most Career At-bats Without a Hit: 42, Randy Tate, Pitcher, New York Mets, 1975

Most Career Losses, Pitcher: 316, Cy Young

Most Consecutive Hit Batsmen, Pitcher: 3, Dock Ellis, Pittsburgh Pirates* vs. Cincinnati Reds, 1974

Most Consecutive Losses, Pitcher: 27, Anthony Young, New York Mets, 1992–93

Most Consecutive Losses in a Season, Pitcher: 19, Jack Nabors, Philadelphia A's, 1916

Most Consecutive Strikeouts, Batter: 12, Sandy Koufax, Pitcher, Brooklyn Dodgers, 1955

Most Consecutive Walks, Pitcher: 7, Bill Gray, Washington Senators, August 28, 1909

Most Double Plays Hit Into, Game, Both Leagues: 4 (tie)—April 28, 1934, Goose Goslin, Detroit Lions; July 21, 1975, Joe Torre, New York Mets

Most Double Plays Hit Into, Season, AL: 36, Jim Rice, Outfielder, Boston Red Sox, 1984

Most Double Plays Hit Into, Season, NL: 30 (tie)—Ernie Lombardi, Catcher, Cincinnati Reds, 1938**; Brad Ausmus, Catcher, Houston Astros, 2002

Most Errors, Career: 975, "Bad" Bill Dahlen, Shortstop, 1891–1911

Most Errors in a Game: 5 (tie)—September 29, 1905, Charlie Hickman, Second Base, Washington Senators; June 11, 1906, Dave Brain, Third Base, Boston Braves; April 22, 1915, Nap Lajoie, Second Base, Cleveland Indians

Most Errors in an Inning: 4 (tie)—June 20, 1914, Ray Chapman, Short-

---

* Best known, of course, for pitching a no-hitter while tripping on LSD.

** Lombardi, legendary for his slowness (he was occasionally thrown out at first from right field) also won the National League batting title in 1938, hitting .342.

stop, Cleveland Indians*; September 13, 1942, Lennie Merullo, Shortstop, Chicago Cubs

Most Errors in a Season: 98, John Gochnauer, Shortstop, Cleveland Naps, 1903**

Most Home Runs Given Up, Career: 505, Robin Roberts, 1948–66

Most Home Runs Given Up, Game: June 12, 1886, 7, Charlie Sweeney, St. Louis Browns***

Most Home Runs Given Up, Season: 50, Bert Blyleven, Minnesota Twins, 1986

Most Losses, Franchise: 9,956, Philadelphia Phillies, 1883–2006

Most Losses in a Season, Pitcher: 48, John Coleman, Philadelphia Phillies, 1883

Most Losses in a Season Since 1901, Pitcher: 26 (tie)—Bob Groom, Washington Senators, 1909; Happy Townsend, Washington Senators, 1904

Most Losses in a Season Since 1901, Team, AL: 119, Detroit Tigers, 2003 (43–119)

Most Losses in a Season Since 1901, Team, NL: 120, New York Mets, 1962 (40–120)

Most Losses in a Season, Team: 134, Cleveland Spiders, 1899 (20–134)****

Most Strikeouts, Season, Player, AL: 186, Rob Deer, Outfielder, Milwaukee Brewers, 1987

Most Strikeouts, Season, Player, NL: 195, Adam Dunn, Outfielder, Cincinnati Reds, 2004

* Chapman is the only man in Major League history to die as the result of an onfield injury. In August 1920, he was fatally struck in the head by a fastball thrown by Carl Mays of the Yankees.

** Gochnauer hit .185 in 1903; shockingly, he was no longer with the club the following year.

*** Four pitchers have given up six home runs in a game, the most recent being R. A. Dickey of the Texas Rangers on April 6, 2006.

**** The Spiders and the St. Louis Cardinals were owned by the same men—the Robison brothers of St. Louis. During the 1899 season, the Robisons transferred every decent player on the Spiders' roster to the Cardinals, leaving Cleveland with nothing but scrap-heap players or worse. The Spiders played their final eighty-one games on the road; the Robisons traded home for away games because they could collect more in gate receipts at other ballparks. It is now forbidden for one party to own multiple teams in any top-level professional sports league.

Most Strikeouts, Season, Team, AL: 1,268, Detroit Tigers, 1999

Most Strikeouts, Season, Team, NL: 1,399, Milwaukee Brewers, 2001

Most Times Caught Stealing, Career: 335, Rickey Henderson, 1979–2003

Most Times Caught Stealing, Season: 42, Rickey Henderson, 1982*

Worst Career Win-Loss Record, Pitcher: 0–16, Terry Felton, Minnesota Twins, 1979–82

Worst Margin of Defeat, Minor Leagues: June 15, 1902, 48 runs—Corsicana Oil Citys 51, Texarkana Casketmakers 3

Worst Margin of Defeat in a Postseason Game: 16 runs—Boston 23, Cleveland 7, 1999 AL Division Series vs. Boston Red Sox

Worst Margin of Defeat, Regular Season: June 8, 1950, 25 runs—Boston 29, St. Louis Browns 4

* Also set the Major-League record for steals in the same season, with 130.

Fewest Goals in a Season, Team: 133, Chicago Blackhawks, 1953–54 (1.9 goals per game)

Longest Winless Streak, Pro: 30 games, Winnipeg Jets, 1980 (23 losses, 7 ties)

Most Consecutive Games Shut Out: 8, Chicago Blackhawks, 1929

Most Lopsided Loss, Junior International Hockey: 1998, 92 goals—South Korea 92, Thailand 0

Most Lopsided Loss, NHL: January 23, 1944, 15 goals—Detroit 15, New York Rangers 0

Most Lopsided Loss, Olympic Hockey: 1924, 33 goals—Canada 33, Switzerland 0

Most Losses, Goalie, Career: 352, Gump Worsley, 1952–74 (335–352–150)

Most Losses, Goalie, Season: 48, Gary Smith, California Golden Seals, 1970–71 (19–48–4)

Most Losses, Team, Season, Pro: 71, San Jose Sharks, 1992–93 (11–71–2)

Most Penalty Minutes, Game: March 11, 1979, 67, Randy Holt, Los Angeles Kings vs. Philadelphia Flyers

Most Penalty Minutes, Career: 3,966, Dave "Tiger" Williams, 1974–88

Most Penalty Minutes, Season: 472, Dave "The Animal" Schultz, Philadelphia Flyers, 1974–75

Most Ties, Season, Pro: 24, Philadelphia Flyers, 1969–70 (17–35–24)

SOCCER

Most Consecutive Losses, World Cup: 9, Mexico, 1930–1958

Most Lopsided Defeat, International Soccer: April 11, 2001, 31 goals—Australia 31, American Samoa 0

Most Lopsided Defeat, World Cup: 1982, 9 goals—Hungary 10, El Salvador 1

Most Losses All Time, World Cup: 22, Mexico, 1930–2006

Worst All-Time Record, World Cup: 0–6, El Salvador, 1970, 1982 (outscored 22–1)

OLYMPICS

Lowest All-Time Medal Count, Countries with Populations of 1 million and more: 1 bronze (tie)—Barbados, Kuwait, Kyrgystan

About the Authors

PHOTO: ALMA OROS

JESSE LAMOVSKY works and writes from his home in Cuyahoga Falls, Ohio. A long-suffering fan of Cleveland teams, Jesse works out his sports angst for humor site ThePhat-Phree.com and for the online daily TheClevelandFan.com. *The Worst of Sports* is his first book.

PHOTO: HAYLEY SPARKS

MATTHEW ROSETTI is a first-time author who, when not writing, masquerades as a banker. He resides in New York City, but hails from Scranton, Pennsylvania, where he once played an entire Little League season, swinging only once. *The Worst of Sports* is his first book.

PHOTO: MIKE POLK

CHARLIE DEMARCO is the editor of The Phat Phree, a comedy writer, and a die-hard Cleveland sports fan. As a child he dabbled in rooting for winning teams, but quickly came to his senses, realizing that cheering for teams from other cities doesn't make you a winner. It makes you a jackass.